PREFACE

1. Scope

This publication provides doctrine for the planning, execution, and assessment of joint distribution operations.

2. Purpose

This publication has been prepared under the direction of the Chairman of the Joint Chiefs of Staff (CJCS). It sets forth joint doctrine to govern the activities and performance of the Armed Forces of the United States in joint operations and provides the doctrinal basis for interagency coordination and for US military involvement in multinational operations. It provides military guidance for the exercise of authority by combatant commanders and other joint force commanders (JFCs) and prescribes joint doctrine for operations, education, and training. It provides military guidance for use by the Armed Forces in preparing their appropriate plans. It is not the intent of this publication to restrict the authority of the JFC from organizing the force and executing the mission in a manner the JFC deems most appropriate to ensure unity of effort in the accomplishment of the overall objective.

3. Application

a. Joint doctrine established in this publication applies to the Joint Staff, commanders of combatant commands, subunified commands, joint task forces, subordinate components of these commands, the Services, combat support agencies, and other support agencies and organizations.

b. The guidance in this publication is authoritative; as such, this doctrine will be followed except when, in the judgment of the commander, exceptional circumstances dictate otherwise. If conflicts arise between the contents of this publication and the contents of Service publications, this publication will take precedence for the activities of joint forces unless the CJCS, normally in coordination with the other members of the Joint Chiefs of Staff, has provided more current and specific guidance. Commanders of forces operating as part of a multinational (alliance or coalition) military command should follow multinational doctrine and procedures ratified by the United States. For doctrine and procedures not ratified by the United States, commanders should evaluate and follow the multinational command's doctrine and procedures, where applicable and consistent with US law, regulations, and doctrine.

For the Chairman of the Joint Chiefs of Staff:

DAVID L. GOLDFEIN, Lt Gen, USAF
Director, Joint Staff

Intentionally Blank

SUMMARY OF CHANGES
REVISION OF JOINT PUBLICATION 4-09
DATED 05 FEBRUARY 2010

- **Discusses use of the term automatic identification technology.**

- **Replaces US Army Rail Operating Battalions and Rail Operating Companies with the expeditionary railway center.**

- **Discusses distribution and retrograde planning requirements for Class IX (Repair Parts) items.**

- **Discusses planning considerations for container management and clarifies responsibilities.**

- **Replaces discussion of specific classes of supply with description of organizations comprising the distribution framework and their relationships in executing end-to-end distribution operations.**

- **Discusses triple container planning factors, employment operations, and configurations.**

Intentionally Blank

TABLE OF CONTENTS

CHAPTER V
 CONTROLLING DISTRIBUTION

APPENDIX

GLOSSARY

FIGURE

Intentionally Blank

EXECUTIVE SUMMARY
COMMANDER'S OVERVIEW

- **Provides an Overview of Distribution Operations**

- **Describes Distribution Capabilities**

- **Explains Distribution Planning**

- **Discusses Execution and Assessment of Distribution Operations**

- **Addresses Controlling Distribution**

Distribution Operations Overview

Joint distribution is the operational process of synchronizing all elements of the joint logistic system using the joint deployment and distribution enterprise.

Distribution includes the ability to plan and execute the movement of forces for deployment and redeployment as well as sustainment and retrograde. It is the operational process of synchronizing all elements of the logistic system to deliver the right things to the right place at the right time to support the joint force commander. The Secretary of Defense directed joint deployment and distribution enterprise (JDDE) community of interest (COI) connects Service, Department of Defense (DOD), and other government agency movements under the end-to-end distribution coordinating authority exercised by Commander, United States Transportation Command (CDRUSTRANSCOM) as the distribution process owner (DPO).

Distribution Operations in the Joint Logistics Environment

The joint logistics enterprise (JLEnt) is a multitiered matrix of key global logistics providers cooperatively engaged or structured to achieve a common purpose without jeopardizing the integrity of their own organizational missions and goals. The JLEnt describes an approach to working across organizational boundaries to generate improved levels of logistics support and core logistics functions, such as supply, maintenance operations, deployment and distribution, health services, engineering, logistic services, and operational contract support.

Joint Deployment and Distribution Enterprise

The JDDE includes equipment, procedures, doctrine, leaders, technical connectivity, information, organizations, facilities, training, and materiel necessary to conduct joint distribution operations. The JDDE COI is the collaborative

---

network of JDDE partner organizations, to include DOD components, sharing common distribution-related goals, interests, missions, and business processes, which comprise end-to-end distribution, in support of combatant commanders (CCDRs). United States Transportation Command (USTRANSCOM) serves as the single coordination and synchronization element on behalf of and in coordination with the JDDE COI to establish processes to plan, apportion, allocate, route, schedule, validate priorities, track movements, and redirect forces and materiel per the supported commander's intent.

Fundamental Considerations for Movement Control

The most basic element of movement control is the movement requirement—a stated movement mode and time-phased need for the transport of units, personnel, and/or materiel from a specified origin to a specified destination. Movement considerations include: centralized control and decentralized execution, regulated movement, optimum use of carrying capacity, forward support, and fluid and flexible movement.

Supply Chain

The DOD supply chain is a global network of DOD and commercial supply, maintenance, and distribution activities that acquires and delivers materiel and logistic services to the joint force. Its fundamental goal is to maximize force readiness while optimizing the allocation of limited resources.

Global Distribution

Global distribution is the process that coordinates and synchronizes fulfillment of joint force requirements from point of origin to point of employment. The ultimate objective of this process is the effective and efficient support of the joint force mission.

USTRANSCOM, as the DPO, must coordinate and synchronize a joint distribution tempo that is responsive to the requirements, capabilities, and military limitations in the operational area (OA). The JDDE leaders and organizations respond to requirements and priorities established by the supported geographic combatant commander (GCC). The GCC determines the point of need, which can be a major aerial port of debarkation or seaport of debarkation (SPOD), an austere airfield, a sea base, or any forward location within the OA (e.g., open fields, parking lots, highways). The joint deployment and distribution operations center is the GCC's staff element that coordinates, synchronizes, and optimizes strategic and theater deployment and distribution operations within the GCC's area of responsibility.

Distribution Operations Capabilities

Joint Deployment and Distribution Enterprise Networks

The four networks of the JDDE are the physical, financial, information, and communications networks. The **physical network** of the distribution system consists of the quantity, capacity, and capability of fixed structures and established facilities supporting distribution and redistribution operations. The **financial network** is composed of policies, processes, and decision systems that obtain, allocate, and apportion fiscal resources to acquire and maintain distribution capabilities and to execute the global distribution mission. The **information network** consists of all data collection devices, automatic identification technology, automated data and business information systems, decision support tools and applications, and asset visibility (AV) capabilities supporting or facilitating global distribution. The **communications network** links every facet of military operations affecting the ability of the Armed Forces to control and influence the outcome of military operations.

Movement Control Capabilities - Intertheater

Movement control entails the coordination of all modes of transportation assets, terminals, Services, commands, and host-nation assets during deployment, sustainment, and redeployment.

The Defense Transportation System (DTS) is that portion of global distribution infrastructure that supports DOD common-user transportation needs across the range of military operations. USTRANSCOM is responsible for providing common-user transportation and terminal management for DOD as well as non-DOD agencies upon request. Its three subordinate transportation component commands (TCCs), Air Mobility Command (AMC), Military Sealift Command (MSC), and Military Surface Deployment and Distribution Command (SDDC), work in concert to enable global mobility.

Movement Control Capabilities - Intratheater

The coordination of the intertheater and intratheater movement control systems is the shared responsibility of USTRANSCOM and the supported combatant command.

Air Mobility Capabilities - Intertheater

Air mobility capabilities are provided by AMC, Navy-unique fleet essential aircraft, and the Civil Reserve Air Fleet. As a TCC of USTRANSCOM, AMC is the designated lead major command for air mobility issues and standards and is responsible for all continental United States (CONUS)-based common-user air mobility assets.

Air Mobility Capabilities - Intratheater	Air mobility operations are defined by geographic boundaries. Air mobility forces assigned or attached to that GCC normally conduct these operations.
Sealift Capabilities - Intertheater	Sealift capabilities are provide by MSC and foreign-flagged ships. MSC is the ocean transportation component of USTRANSCOM and provides worldwide ocean transportation of equipment, fuel, supplies, and ammunition during peacetime and war with a fleet of government-owned and chartered US-flagged ships.
Sealift Capabilities - Intratheater	Army watercraft platforms provide lift associated with waterborne operational maneuver and the intratheater sealift of units, equipment, and supplies. The US Navy's MSC operates the joint high-speed vessel in support of CCDRs' intratheater lift requirements. The high-speed vessel provides intratheater lift for the United States Marine Corps.
Surface Capabilities - Intertheater	SDDC is the surface transportation component of USTRANSCOM and is DOD's single port manager (SPM) for all common-user seaports of embarkation and SPODs. SDDC performs SPM functions necessary to support the strategic flow of the deploying forces' equipment and supplies to and from the theater.
Surface Capabilities - Intratheater	The commercial transportation industry has substantial capability available to meet the CONUS transportation needs of DOD across the range of military operations. For outside the continental US, assigning responsibility for common-user land transportation (CULT) is a function of the GCC's directive authority for logistics, and it is up to each GCC to outline this in the operation plan (OPLAN) and supporting plans. Under CULT, land transportation assets are normally under the operational control of the Army component commander, who coordinates all planning and requirements for the use of DOD-controlled land transportation equipment and facilities designated as common-use in theater.
Equipment/Stock Pre-Positioning and Forward Stocking	DOD pre-positioned force, equipment, or supplies (PREPO) programs are both land-based and sea-based. They are critical programs for reducing closure times of combat and support forces needed in the early stages of a contingency and also contribute significantly to reducing demands on the DTS. The US Army and US Marine Corps pre-positioning programs consist of combat, combat

support, and combat service support capabilities, to include in-stream discharge and joint logistics over-the-shore capabilities. Other Service and Defense Logistics Agency (DLA) PREPO programs are logistics oriented.

Distribution Planning

Planning Functions

From a logistician's perspective it is important for the CCDRs and operations planners to understand the capabilities and limitations of available core logistic capabilities. To that end, the joint logistician is deeply involved in each of the planning functions and assists in preparing the logistic portion and/or supplement for a plan supporting the CCDR's strategic context and assumptions, global priorities, and missions.

Key Joint Deployment and Distribution Enterprise Planning Tasks

Distribution planning tasks provide guidance to logistic planners assessing the adequacy and feasibility of concepts of support for campaign plans and OPLANs. Distribution planning should address the following tasks: analyze force requirement and sourcing, verify sustainment, analyze transportation, assess networks and distribution network limitations, refine logistic support, review logistics support analysis, develop commodity distribution concepts, ensure protection, and plan for retrograde.

Distribution Planning Considerations

The essence of distribution planning is determining the joint force requirements and identifying the needed capabilities. Distribution planning considerations include: deployment/redeployment and sustainment/retrograde, surge planning, planning focus, planning balance, use of intermodal platforms, movement control planning, strategic to theater distribution interface, and multinational operations.

Execution and Assessment

Distribution Framework

Performing intertheater distribution operations involves a unity of effort among CDRUSTRANSCOM; Director, DLA; and each of the Services. DLA is the primary operator of the defense supply and depot system and is responsible for acquisition, receipt, storage, issuance, and generation of source data for all materiel (other than materiel procured by the individual Services) flowing in the defense distribution pipeline. USTRANSCOM assumes responsibility for the movement of materiel as it enters the DTS. Distribution execution at the intratheater level is the

The primary organizations involved in the

distribution management functions are the joint deployment and distribution operations center, joint logistics operations center, theater-joint transportation board, Joint Transportation Board, and other management boards, as required.

responsibility of the GCC and the forces assigned, and occurs in that part of the distribution pipeline extending from intermediate staging bases and ports of debarkation throughout the OA. The GCC's logistics directorate of a joint staff directs and manages the effectiveness of the distribution system in theater. Each Service is responsible for the logistic support of its own forces. Services can augment organic logistic capabilities by agreements with national agencies or allies, or by participating in common, joint, or cross-servicing agreements.

Supplier, Strategic, and Theater Distribution

The JDDE COI must optimize organic and commercial capabilities from the point of origin/source of supply through the point of need to the point of employment or consumption. While some distribution continues to be made from producers and vendors through the military depot system, particularly for munitions and repair parts, commercial contracts for some materiel support now require customer-direct delivery to the military customers on a global basis. Other contracts require delivery by the vendor to the DTS for movement into the overseas areas, where either the contractor takes possession to make the delivery or the shipment is moved by US military capability to the final destination.

End-to-End Asset Visibility and In-Transit Visibility

AV throughout the JDDE provides the CCDR the capability to see and redirect strategic and operational commodity/force flow in support of current and projected priorities. It also provides users with timely and accurate information on the location, movement, status, and identity of units, personnel, equipment, and supplies so that they may act upon that information to improve DOD logistic practices supporting operations. In-transit visibility is the ability to track the identity, status, and location of DOD units, nonunit cargo, passengers, patients, and personal property from origin to consignee or destination across the range of military operations.

Management and Control of Intermodal Platforms

Container management is the planning, organizing, directing, controlling, and executing of functions and responsibilities required to provide for positive and effective use of DOD and Military Department owned, leased, or controlled International Organization for Standardization containers. Management and control of intermodal platforms is accomplished by global, Service, and theater container and pallet managers.

Controlling Distribution

Control of movements across the entire distribution pipeline is achieved through the ability to coordinate and synchronize processes, business rules, systems/tools, and organizations.

Control over the distribution pipeline means the ability to track and shift—and potentially reconfigure (per supported commander's requirements and priorities)—forces, equipment, and supplies, even while en route, and to deliver tailored packages directly to the CCDR. Application of centralized control and decentralized execution among the JDDE COI produces the flexibility necessary to adapt logistic structures and procedures to changing situations, missions, and concepts of operation to support fluid joint operations.

Authorities and Responsibilities

USTRANSCOM serves as the DPO, responsible for coordinating and overseeing the DOD distribution system to provide interoperability, synchronization, and alignment of DOD-wide, end-to-end distribution.

Common-user assets within the DTS are under the combatant command (command authority) (COCOM) of CDRUSTRANSCOM, excluding Service-organic or theater-assigned transportation assets. Theater-assigned common-user transportation assets are under the COCOM of the respective GCC.

The supported commander is the commander having primary responsibility for all aspects of a task assigned by the Joint Strategic Capabilities Plan or other joint operation planning authority. For distribution purposes, supported organizations are JDDE customers that need something moved. JDDE customers define movement requirements—what, where, and when.

The supporting commander is the commander who provides augmentation forces or other support to a supported commander or who develops a supporting plan. For distribution purposes, supporting organizations are JDDE partners with resources and responsibility to provide movement capability and are, as such, supporting.

Distribution Control Functions

Distribution control occurs within the continuous operations cycle of planning, preparing, executing, and assessing. This continuous cycle ensures that all elements of the JDDE (organizations, terminals, lift assets, and lines of communications) are arranged in time, space, and purpose to deliver the supported CCDR's deployment and distribution requirements at the right time to allow the CCDR to accomplish the mission.

Movement Control Operations

Movement control spans the strategic, operational, and tactical levels of war to ensure that the distribution pipeline is fully coordinated and operating effectively and efficiently. Execution of joint distribution operations to satisfy movement requirements is built on the underpinning movement plans that allow active coordination, as necessary, to allow fulfillment of the movement requirement.

Multinational, Interagency, Intergovernmental Organization, and Nongovernmental Organization Arrangements

In order to enhance movement support to multinational operations, the establishment of a combined movement coordination center (CMCC) is viewed as a critical enabler in coordinating the optimal employment of movement and transportation assets. If in a fully functional combined environment where a multinational joint logistics component (MNJLC) has been established, the CMCC should be established as a cell in the MNJLC. If no such component is established, then the CMCC should reside alongside the lead nation logistic component.

CONCLUSION

This publication provides doctrine for the planning, execution, and assessment of joint distribution operations.

CHAPTER I
DISTRIBUTION OPERATIONS OVERVIEW

> *"Combat operations cannot succeed without secure, mature lines of logistics."*
>
> **Admiral Michael Mullen, US Navy,**
> **17th Chairman of the Joint Chiefs of Staff, 2008**

1. Introduction

a. **Distribution includes the ability to plan and execute the movement of forces for deployment and redeployment as well as sustainment and retrograde.** This publication provides joint force commanders (JFCs), the Services, combat support agencies, and other organizations a doctrinal framework for planning, executing, and assessing distribution operations during joint operations. Distribution is a critical element of joint operations that enables the projection and sustainment of our Nation's military power. It is the operational process of synchronizing all elements of the logistic system to deliver the right things to the right place at the right time to support the JFC. The Secretary of Defense (SecDef)-directed joint deployment and distribution enterprise (JDDE) community of interest (COI) connects Service, Department of Defense (DOD), and other government agency movements under the end-to-end distribution coordinating authority exercised by Commander, United States Transportation Command (CDRUSTRANSCOM) as the distribution process owner (DPO). In addition, United States Transportation Command's (USTRANSCOM's) Unified Command Plan mission as Global Distribution Synchronizer designates CDRUSTRANSCOM as responsible for synchronizing planning for global distribution operations in coordination with other combatant commands (CCMDs), Services, and, as directed, DOD agencies. Distribution includes the collective activities of combatant commanders (CCDRs), Services, DOD, other United States Government (USG) departments and agencies, and commercial sectors to meet the required delivery date (RDD) or to achieve time-definite delivery (TDD).

b. This publication also sets forth doctrine that governs joint activities to facilitate unity of effort during joint distribution operations. In this context, joint distribution operations cover the joint end-to-end movement of forces and sustainment from point of origin to the designated point of need within an operational area (OA). In distribution operations, the point of need is the physical location within an OA designated by the geographic combatant commander (GCC) or subordinate commander as a receiving point for forces or materiel for subsequent use or consumption. Joint distribution operations must also cooperate in the production of a seamless interface between the joint distribution pipeline and onward movement to the point of employment, thus generating a global distribution pipeline (see Figure I-1). Movements past the point of need are not a joint distribution responsibility. However, the common operational picture (COP) for distribution operations provides shared, common visibility of requirements and capabilities beyond the point of need that increases the ability to provide coordinated and synchronized support. Distribution operations also include the movement of forces for reconstitution and movement of retrograde materiel for proper disposition. The ultimate intent of this global distribution process is effective and efficient accomplishment of the joint force mission.

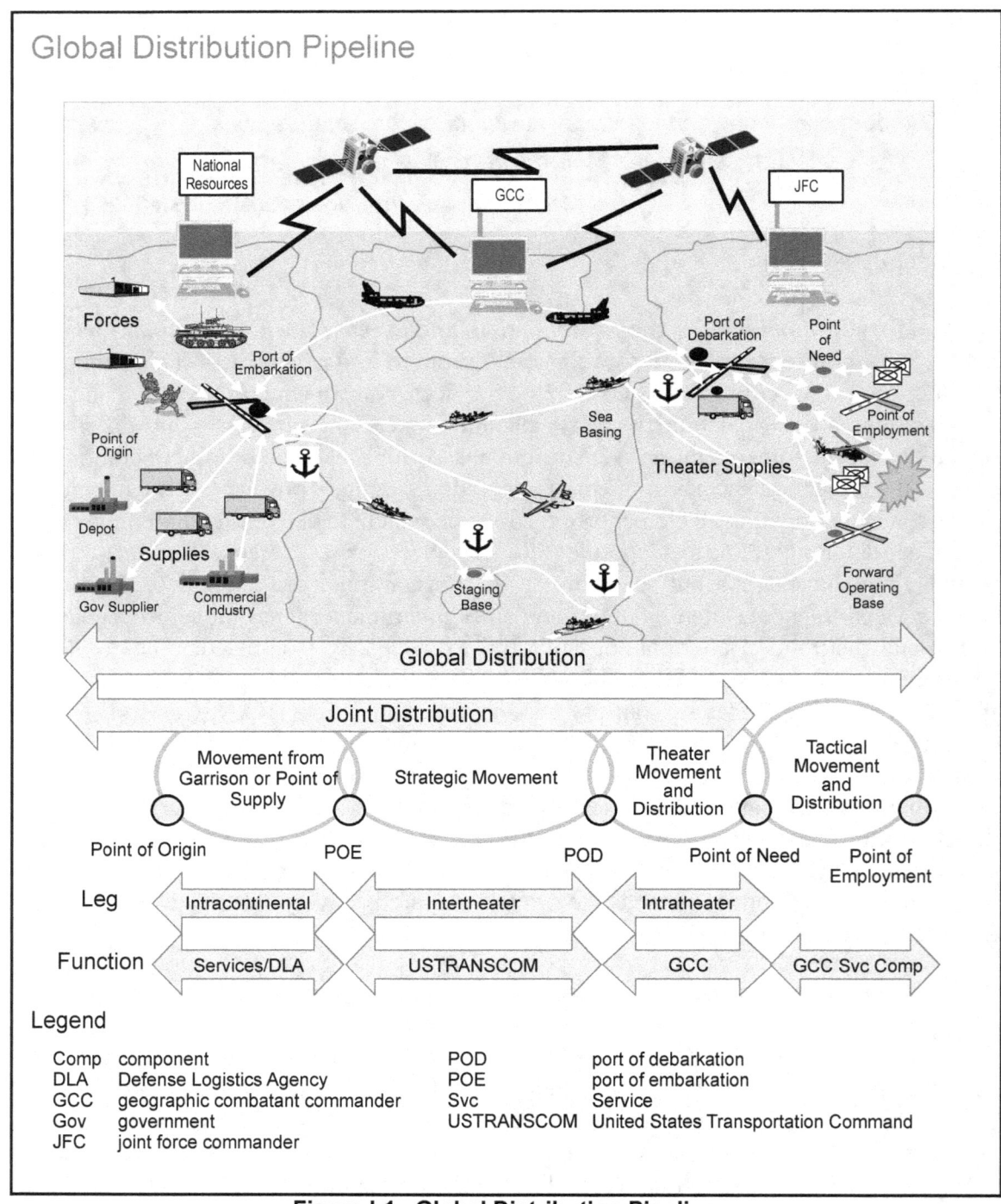

Figure I-1. Global Distribution Pipeline

c. Finally, authorities and responsibilities for distribution are described to underscore their importance in implementing joint distribution.

(1) Title 10, United States Code (USC), and Department of Defense Directive (DODD) 5100.01, *Functions of the Department of Defense and Its Major Components*, describe the statutory requirements for each Military Department to provide logistical support to assigned forces. Title 10, USC, also describes the basic authority to perform the

functions of command that include organizing and employing commands and forces, assigning tasks, designating objectives, and "giving authoritative direction to subordinate commands and forces necessary to carry out missions assigned to the command." This authority includes all aspects of military operations, joint training, and logistics.

(2) **Directive Authority for Logistics (DAFL).** CCDRs exercise DAFL, in accordance with (IAW) Title 10, USC, Section 164, and may delegate directive authority for as many common support capabilities to a subordinate JFC as required to accomplish the assigned mission. This is normally accomplished in coordination with the Services and, for some commodities or support services common to two or more Services, one provider may be given DOD executive agent (EA) responsibility by SecDef or Deputy Secretary of Defense. However, the CCDR must formally delineate this delegated authority by function and scope to the subordinate JFC or Service component commander. The exercise of DAFL by a CCDR includes the authority to issue directives to subordinate commanders, including peacetime measures necessary to allow the following: effective execution of approved operation plans (OPLANs), effectiveness and economy of operation, and prevention or elimination of unnecessary duplication of facilities and overlapping functions among the Service component commands.

For additional information on DAFL, refer to Joint Publication (JP) 1, Doctrine for the Armed Forces of the United States; *for joint logistics-related DAFL, refer to JP 4-0,* Joint Logistics.

(3) **EA.** SecDef or the Deputy Secretary of Defense may designate a DOD EA and assign associated responsibilities, functions, and authorities within DOD. The head of a DOD component may be designated as a DOD EA. The DOD EA may delegate to a subordinate designee within that official's component the authority to act on the official's behalf for any or all of those DOD EA responsibilities, functions, and authorities assigned by SecDef or Deputy Secretary of Defense. The nature and scope of the DOD EA responsibilities, functions, and authorities shall be prescribed at the time of assignment and remain in effect until SecDef or Deputy Secretary of Defense revokes or supersedes them. DOD EA designations are related to, but not the same as, CCDR lead Service designations.

For additional information on EA, refer to JP 1, Doctrine for the Armed Forces of the United States, *and DODD 5101.1,* DOD Executive Agent; *for joint logistics-related EAs, refer to JP 4-0,* Joint Logistics.

2. Distribution Operations in the Joint Logistics Environment

a. Military operations are conducted in a complex, interconnected, and increasingly global operational environment characterized by uncertainty and surprise. These operations are also distributed and conducted rapidly and simultaneously across multiple joint operations areas (JOAs) within a single theater or across boundaries of more than one area of responsibility (AOR) and can involve a large variety of military forces and multinational and other government organizations. The joint logistics enterprise (JLEnt) is a multitiered matrix of key global logistics providers cooperatively engaged or structured to achieve a common purpose without jeopardizing the integrity of their own organizational missions and goals.

The JLEnt is characterized by a web of relationships among global logistic providers and supporting and supported organizations.

For more information on the JLEnt, refer to JP 4-0, Joint Logistics.

b. The JLEnt describes an approach to working across organizational boundaries to generate improved levels of logistics support and core logistics functions, such as supply, maintenance operations, deployment and distribution, health services, engineering, logistic services, and operational contract support. JLEnt key distribution stakeholders manage end-to-end processes that provide joint logistic capabilities to the supported JFCs and link their requirements to process outcomes. DOD executes its JLEnt role through the JDDE.

c. Joint distribution is the operational process of synchronizing all elements of the joint logistic system using the JDDE. DOD employs the JDDE to deliver joint end-to-end movement of forces and material, through the Defense Transportation System (DTS), from point of origin to the designated point of need in support of the JFC. Effective joint logistics depends on clear roles, responsibilities, and relationships between the key distribution stakeholders in the JDDE.

d. **The Joint Staff J-3 [Operations Directorate].** The Joint Staff J-3 serves as the DOD joint deployment process owner (JDPO) and is responsible for maintaining the global capability for rapid and decisive military force power projection. As the JDPO, the Joint Staff J-3 is responsible for leading the collaborative efforts of the joint planning and execution community to improve the joint deployment and redeployment processes, while maintaining the overall effectiveness of these processes so that all supported JFCs and supporting DOD components can execute military force power projection more effectively and efficiently.

e. **Services.** IAW Title 10, USC, the Army, Marine Corps, Navy, Air Force (under their respective departmental Secretaries) and the United States Coast Guard (USCG) (under the Department of Homeland Security [DHS] in peacetime, or when transferred to the Department of the Navy in wartime, during a declared national emergency, or when the President otherwise directs) are responsible to organize, train, equip, and provide logistic support to their respective forces.

f. **CCMDs**

(1) **GCCs.** GCCs are responsible for the development and production of CCMD plans and orders in response to mission taskings, as well as integrating military activities with interagency/diplomatic activities in their AOR. The GCC is responsible for articulating theater requirements and issuing guidance for theater business rules and optimum lift. GCCs exercise DAFL for assigned forces within their AOR to include developing and maintaining an effective theater distribution system that is consistent with established policies and procedures as well as prescribing specific policies and procedures unique to that theater.

(2) **Functional Combatant Commanders (FCCs).** An FCC is a commander of a CCMD with transregional responsibilities. Because of the numerous global distribution

stakeholders, successful operations require high levels of integration. Normally, more than one functional CCMD is involved in every phase of a joint operation.

(a) **USTRANSCOM.** CDRUSTRANSCOM has the following assigned responsibilities:

1. Serve as the DOD single manager for transportation (other than Service-unique or theater-assigned assets) responsible for providing common-user and commercial air, land, and sea transportation, terminal management, and aerial refueling to support the global deployment, employment, sustainment, and redeployment of US forces.

2. Serve as the mobility joint force provider, identifying and recommending to the Chairman of the Joint Chiefs of Staff (CJCS) global joint sourcing solutions, in coordination with the Services and other CCDRs, from all mobility forces and capabilities, and supervising implementation of sourcing decisions.

3. Serve as the DOD single manager for patient movement, providing global patient movement through the DTS in coordination with the GCCs.

4. Serve as DPO with the responsibility to coordinate, sustain, and improve distribution processes. The DPO is assigned the following specific responsibilities:

a. Oversee the overall effectiveness, efficiency, and alignment of DOD-wide distribution activities, including force projection (force movement), sustainment, and retrograde operations.

b. Establish the concepts and operational frameworks relating to planning and execution of DOD transportation operations.

c. Develop and implement distribution process improvements that enhance DOD's joint and global distribution.

d. Serve as the DOD single coordination and synchronization element on behalf of and in coordination with the JDDE COI.

e. Serve as the DOD information technology (IT) distribution portfolio manager for that subset of logistics systems providing key capabilities in support of distribution-related (force movement and sustainment) activities. This includes establishing distribution-related IT standards, data standards (including those in support of asset and in-transit visibility [ITV]), shipping standards, enterprise performance standards, and metrics.

f. Serve as lead functional proponent for automatic identification technology (AIT) in the DOD supply chain and for ITV.

5. Synchronize planning for global distribution operations in coordination with other CCMDs, the Services, and, as directed, appropriate USG departments and agencies. Specific responsibilities are to:

a. Provide DOD representation to USG departments and agencies, US commercial entities, and international agencies for global distribution operations, as directed.

b. Advocate for global distribution capabilities.

c. Integrate theater security cooperation activities, deployments, and capabilities supporting global distribution, in coordination with the GCCs and making priority recommendations to SecDef.

6. Provide mission-tailored, ready joint capability packages, as directed, which are capable of short-notice, limited duration deployments to assist CCDRs in establishing, organizing, and operating a joint force headquarters, including deployable communications and public affairs support.

For additional information on the roles and responsibilities of USTRANSCOM, see DODD 5158.04, United States Transportation Command (USTRANSCOM), *and for additional information on the roles and responsibilities of the DPO, see Department of Defense Instruction (DODI) 5158.06,* Distribution Process Owner (DPO).

(b) **United States Special Operations Command (USSOCOM).** USSOCOM is responsible for training, equipping, and providing combat-ready personnel for employment by GCCs; synchronizing DOD's global campaign planning against terrorist networks, including their use of weapons of mass destruction; and for conducting global operations as directed. Most special operations forces (SOF) operations require non-SOF support. This support includes intertheater lift for deployment and intratheater lift for onward movement and sustainment. SOF are usually employed and distributed beyond the last theater distribution node. Coordination for support of these special operations is done by the logistics directorate of a joint staff (J-4) within the theater special operations command (TSOC) and the theater joint deployment and distribution operations center (JDDOC), air operations center (AOC), or joint air operations center (JAOC).

(3) **Joint Task Forces (JTFs).** A JTF is one of the command options used for joint force operations. It is the principal structure when the mission has a specific limited objective. Logistic functions normally remain the responsibility of the Service components. The JTF is normally subordinate to a supported GCC who will manage the overall theater distribution system. The JTF J-4 coordinates logistic support through the supported CCDR. The principal distribution responsibilities of the JTF are to determine distribution requirements and capabilities for the operation and coordinate JTF distribution operations to exercise control of the distribution network in the JTF's JOA. A CCDR may designate common support capabilities for the JTF. It is critical that the JTF J-4 determines what, if any, logistic directive authority for a common support capability the CCDR should delegate to the JTF commander and if the scope of the authority meets JTF requirements.

g. **Support Agencies and Organizations**

(1) **Defense Contract Management Agency (DCMA).** DCMA is the combat support agency responsible for ensuring major DOD acquisition programs (systems, supplies, and services) are delivered on time and within projected cost or price, and meet

performance requirements. DCMA's major responsibility in contingency operations is to provide contingency contract administration services for external and theater support contracts and for selected weapons system support contracts with place of performance in the OA and theater support contracts when contract administration services are delegated by the procuring contract officers.

(2) **Defense Logistics Agency (DLA).** DLA is the combat support agency of DOD responsible for providing integrated materiel management for assigned items of supply and services. DLA functions as an integral element of DOD by providing worldwide logistic support to the Military Departments and the CCMDs across the range of military operations, as well as to other DOD components, USG departments and agencies, foreign governments, and intergovernmental organizations (IGOs). DLA manages or distributes a significant amount of defense materiel stocks including physical distribution of Service-owned and -managed stocks and nearly all fuel and petroleum products for military use. DLA coordinates and performs the procurement, management, and supply of clothing and textiles DOD wide. DLA is also the designated DOD EA for Class I (subsistence), Class III (bulk petroleum), Class IV (construction and barrier materiel), and Class VIII (medical materiel) supply chains.

(3) **General Services Administration (GSA).** GSA is an independent agency of the USG established to help manage and support the basic functioning of federal agencies. The GSA supplies products and communications for USG offices, provides transportation and office space to federal employees, develops government-wide cost-minimizing policies, and performs other management tasks.

(4) **Commercial Transportation Industry.** Commercial transportation providers contribute a substantial capability to support distribution movement requirements. The wide range of options obtained through the commercial transportation industry is managed under USTRANSCOM as part of the total distribution process to allow coordinated and synchronized efforts to meet JFC requirements. Vendor-supported shipments play a major role in sustaining the JFC. The JDDE requires visibility of these shipments to ensure they are integrated into the overall distribution effort and that their delivery meets JFC requirements.

(5) **Program Executive Office Ammunition.** The Program Executive Office Ammunition within the Department of the Army is the Single Manager of Conventional Ammunition (SMCA). SMCA is a Class V support organization of DOD responsible for providing wholesale integrated Class V materiel management for assigned items of supply and services. The SMCA functions as an integral element of DOD by providing worldwide support to the Military Departments and DOD agencies. SMCA manages or distributes a significant amount of existing Class V stocks of defense materiel including physical distribution of Service-owned and managed stocks and nearly all demilitarization and disposal of Class V wholesale stocks. SMCA coordinates and performs the procurement, management, and supply of conventional ammunition (except Service retained items, missiles, torpedoes, etc.) and foreign military sales (FMS) ammunition.

For more information, see DODD 5160.65, Single Manager for Conventional Ammunition (SMCA).

3. Joint Deployment and Distribution Enterprise

a. The JDDE includes equipment, procedures, doctrine, leaders, technical connectivity, information, organizations, facilities, training, and materiel necessary to conduct joint distribution operations. As such, it provides JFCs with the ability to rapidly and effectively move and sustain forces across the range of military operations. The JDDE also provides logistic solutions to the JFC to minimize seams in the joint distribution pipeline from the point of origin through the point of need. Furthermore, the JDDE complements, interacts with, and augments Service or JFC-unique theater distribution responsibilities and capabilities to ensure distribution is coordinated and synchronized all the way to the point of employment. The JDDE is a critical part of the JLEnt and its governance is the primary responsibility of the DPO in coordination with the Joint Staff J-3 and other members of the JDDE.

For additional information on deployment operations, see JP 3-35, Joint Deployment and Redeployment Operations.

b. The JDDE COI is the collaborative network of JDDE partner organizations, to include DOD components, sharing common distribution-related goals, interests, missions, and business processes, which comprise end-to-end distribution, in support of CCDRs. The JDDE includes organizations and partnerships from the Services, CCMDs, and JTFs, other USG departments and agencies, and the private sector. The JDDE operates across the strategic, operational, and tactical continuum with a set of integrated, robust, and responsive physical, information, communication, and financial networks. At the tactical level, the JDDE complements, interacts with, and augments Service-unique, supporting CCMD, or theater-assigned distribution capabilities and responsibilities. It has the capability to establish and maintain infrastructure whenever and wherever it is needed.

c. USTRANSCOM serves as the single coordination and synchronization element on behalf of and in coordination with the JDDE COI to establish processes to plan, apportion, allocate, route, schedule, validate priorities, track movements, and redirect forces and materiel per the supported commander's intent. This coordination and synchronization does not usurp the supported CCDRs' Title 10, USC, responsibilities but drives unity of effort throughout the JDDE to support CCDRs. The supported CCDR is responsible to plan, identify requirements, set priorities, and redirect forces and materiel as needed to support operations within the respective AOR. Coordination and synchronization also promote shared situational awareness, providing the leaders and personnel in the JDDE with the ability to understand the supported commanders' intents and be aware of the impact and consequences that distribution decisions have on supporting the commanders and the stakeholders that comprise the JDDE. Visibility through the JDDE provides the CCDR, in conjunction with the global providers, the capability to see and redirect intertheater and intratheater force and commodity flow in support of current and projected priorities.

4. Logistic Imperatives Applicable to Distribution Operations

a. The value of distribution operations can be measured by how well the JDDE attains the following three logistic imperatives: unity of effort, JLEnt visibility, and rapid and precise response. See JP 4-0, *Joint Logistics,* for descriptions of the logistic imperatives. The applicability of logistic imperatives to distribution follows:

(1) Unity of effort in joint distribution is described as the coordination and cooperation toward common objectives. The JDDE leaders and organizations act in response to requirements and priorities established by the supported CCDR/JFC and other supported organizations. Unity of effort achieved by JDDE organizations is reflected in effective distribution control—the coordination and synchronization of actions of JDDE organizations.

(2) JLEnt visibility, as it applies to distribution, is the awareness of requirements, resources, and capabilities across the joint distribution pipeline, as well as the capability to determine status, location, and direction of flow for forces, requirements, and materiel. Visibility requires the availability of timely, accurate, and usable information.

(3) Rapid and precise response within the JDDE is described as the accuracy, speed, and composition with which delivery of forces, requirements, and materiel occurs at the right time, the right place, and the right amount. Rapidity involves fulfilling requirements at the right speed and means that synchronization of speeds of various aspects of the distribution process is required in order to maximize effectiveness. Speed also incorporates the ability of elements of the JDDE to forecast, anticipate, and plan distribution execution. Precision also addresses the ability of the JDDE to minimize deviation from acceptable standards as it responds to dynamically changing conditions and requirements.

For additional information on joint logistics imperatives, see JP 4-0, Joint Logistics.

b. Joint distribution operations are also informed by the enduring logistic principles of responsiveness, simplicity, flexibility, economy, attainability, sustainability, and survivability. These serve as guides for planning, organizing, managing, and executing joint logistic operations. They are not a set of rigid rules, nor will they apply in every operation. Applying creativity, insight, and boldness in the application of these logistic principles is essential to successful JDDE operations—balancing these principles with the application of sound judgment and decision-making skills is the basis of the art of logistics.

For additional information on logistics principles, see JP 4-0, Joint Logistics.

5. Fundamental Considerations for Movement Control

a. The JDDE leaders and organizations act in response to requirements and priorities established by the supported GCC and other supported organizations. USTRANSCOM is responsible for overseeing the effectiveness, efficiency, and alignment of DOD-wide distribution activities.

b. The most basic element of movement control is the movement requirement—a stated movement mode and time-phased need for the transport of units, personnel, and/or materiel from a specified origin to a specified destination. An understanding of the movement requirement is necessary so its priority can be established. It also provides the ability to affect mode determination early in the planning process—not after a requirement has been validated by the supported commander. Control of the distribution system is defined as the ability to coordinate and synchronize activities that track movements, monitor performance, and respond to movement requirements according to priorities. The following movement considerations provide the foundation for management and control of joint distribution operations:

(1) **Centralized Control and Decentralized Execution.** The GCC, supported by and in coordination with USTRANSCOM and DLA, controls movement planning and resource allocation. The GCC establishes operational priorities and then normally delegates control of movements to the Service component having the required assets or capabilities to fulfill the mission. This delegation of authority achieves two objectives: it satisfies requirements at the lowest level possible and it frees the GCC to focus on theater-wide critical issues.

(2) **Regulated Movements.** Movement control authorities must regulate movements to prevent terminal congestion and scheduling conflicts between Service components. Proper management of transportation assets and the transportation network is critical. Advances in technology have increased both the capability and requirement to regulate movements. Highly mobile forces, longer distances, increased consumption rates, fewer ports of debarkation, and shared lines of communications (LOCs) are a few of the challenges.

(3) **Optimum Use of Carrying Capacity.** Transportation capacity is a limited resource. Therefore, planners must understand when to use a specific mode of transport and how to optimize the use of each mode's unique capabilities by balancing their capacity and availability with distribution effectiveness and efficiency objectives that meet CCDR requirements. This approach involves the simultaneous, synergistic use of all transportation resources to meet the CCDR's requirements with respect to such factors as priority of shipment, impact on JFC operations if delayed, cost of shipment to both the customer and distribution network, speed of shipment, and means/mode of shipment.

(4) **Forward Support.** Forward support includes fast, reliable transportation to provide support as far forward as possible. Forward-oriented transportation support is a combat multiplier; it allows the commander to concentrate all forces on the enemy. The key to forward support is the reception and clearance capabilities at the destination units. These units may require equipment and personnel augmentation to enhance their reception and clearance capabilities. Forward support may entail temporary allocation of theater-level transportation assets to meet specific user requirements. However, any requirement for forward support that relinquishes centralized control for an extended time must be balanced against the efficiency of the transportation system and its ability to influence the operation.

(5) **Fluid and Flexible Movements.** The transportation system must provide an uninterrupted flow of supplies, and it must be flexible enough to change with mission modifications. The key to successful execution is the ability to regulate and manage the transportation system.

6. Supply Chain

a. The DOD supply chain is a global network of DOD and commercial supply, maintenance, and distribution activities that acquires and delivers materiel and logistic services to the joint force. Its fundamental goal is to maximize force readiness while optimizing the allocation of limited resources. Distribution is an integral component of supply chain operations—the vital part of the supply chain that provides for the delivery of the right thing to the right place at the right time.

b. Supply chain operations require that DOD's key global providers coordinate and synchronize their end-to-end supply chain business processes to meet JFC requirements for the full range of military operations. The objective is efficient end-to-end supply chain planning, supply sourcing, acquisition of material, making/maintaining (production/kitting operations and maintenance of equipment), fulfillment of commodity requisitions, distribution operations, the return and retrograde of materiel, and the movement and retrograde of repairable items to support maintenance activities, while effectively meeting the JFC requirements. The supply chain satisfies requirements through appropriate sourcing, maintenance, and/or distribution of materiel and equipment to the requirements generators. Commanders and their staffs are key to optimizing supply chain operations and must strive to rapidly identify and communicate requirements. It is important that commanders establish mission priorities, assess the risk to and plan for the protection of materiel and forces as required, and establish JLEnt visibility of materiel requirements, distribution operations, resource availability/shortfalls, and shared processes.

7. Global Distribution

a. Global distribution is the process that coordinates and synchronizes fulfillment of joint force requirements from point of origin to point of employment. The ultimate objective of this process is the effective and efficient support of the joint force mission. Effective and efficient fulfillment of joint operational requirements is dependent on the deliberate coordination and synchronization of multiple logistic processes. USTRANSCOM, as the DPO, must coordinate and synchronize a joint distribution tempo that is responsive to the requirements, capabilities, and military limitations in the OA.

b. The JDDE leaders and organizations respond to requirements and priorities established by the supported GCC. The GCC determines the point of need, which can be a major aerial port of debarkation (APOD) or seaport of debarkation (SPOD), an austere airfield, a sea base, or any forward location within the OA (e.g., open fields, parking lots, highways). The global distribution pipeline is comprised of the following:

(1) The intracontinental leg includes the movement of unit forces, equipment, and supplies from their point of origin to the port of embarkation (POE) as well as movement of

supplies from a vendor to a defense distribution depot and then to the POE. This leg represents the distribution functions normally performed by DLA and the Services.

(2) The intertheater leg includes force and sustainment movements between theaters in support of GCCs. The intertheater leg extends from the POE to the port of debarkation (POD) in the GCC's AOR. It may also include forces and materiel delivered directly to the point of need, bypassing normal strategic ports or strategic airfields in the desired OA.

(3) Some intertheater movement may consist of only sequential intracontinental legs (e.g., when forces or sustainment move overland from US European Command to US Central Command). In these cases, GCCs are responsible for ensuring movement, and coordinating with adjacent GCCs, while troops and supplies transit their theaters toward the final destination in the supported GCC's AOR.

(4) Intratheater movements are force and sustainment movements within a theater. Intratheater movements are optimized and synchronized by a JDDOC. The intratheater leg extends from the POD or the point of origin (internal to a theater) to the point of need in the desired OA. Operation of the intratheater leg of the joint distribution pipeline is the responsibility of the supported GCC. Movement that extends beyond the point of need to the point of employment is a Service-specific responsibility as designated by the GCC.

(5) Theater movement processes encompass end-to-end force and sustainment movements that interface with the intertheater leg. They also support intratheater movement demands. Consequently, the theater pipeline is continually changing to meet both intertheater- and theater-generated demands as well as responding to forces and sustainment delivered directly to the point of need, bypassing strategic ports or airfields. Intratheater movements are characterized by frequent changes, an operational view that is typically 24-48 hours, and relatively short LOCs driving rapid cycle times and decision cycles. For this reason, supported GCCs and staffs are essential to the end-to-end global distribution process and must be able to coordinate the intertheater and intratheater distribution interface.

(6) The JDDOC is the GCC's staff element that coordinates, synchronizes, and optimizes strategic and theater deployment and distribution operations within the GCC's AOR. The JDDOC enhances unity of effort throughout the entire JDDE.

c. **Joint Operational Activities.** The JDDE provides operational mission support across the range of joint operational activities: mobilization, deployment, employment, sustainment, and redeployment. The JDDE provides national resources to the logistic activities in direct support of operations and, in some cases, directly to the joint force. DOD agencies, the Services, CCMDs, other USG departments and agencies, and the US industrial base (as well as multinational partners) may, at one time or another, all participate in this system. The following paragraphs describe the relationship of global distribution to the joint operational activities.

For more information on joint operations, see JP 3-0, Joint Operations.

(1) **Mobilization.** Mobilization is the act of assembling and organizing national resources to support national objectives in time of war or other emergencies. Mobilization includes bringing all or part of the industrial base and the Armed Forces of the United States to the necessary state of readiness to meet the requirements of the specific contingency.

For more information, see JP 4-05, Joint Mobilization Planning.

(2) **Deployment.** Deployment is the relocation of forces and materiel to desired OAs. Deployment encompasses all activities from origin or home station through destination, specifically including intracontinental US, intertheater, and intratheater movement legs, staging, and holding areas. The deployment process has four phases: planning; predeployment activities (e.g., force sourcing and selection); movement; and joint reception, staging, onward movement, and integration (JRSOI).

For more information on joint deployment, see JP 3-35, Deployment and Redeployment Operations; Chairman of the Joint Chiefs of Staff Manual (CJCSM) 3122.01A, Joint Operation Planning and Execution System (JOPES) Volume I, Planning Policies and Procedures; CJCSM 3130.03, Adaptive Planning and Execution (APEX) Planning Formats and Guidance; and CJCSM 3122.02D, Joint Operation Planning and Execution System (JOPES) Volume III (Time-Phased Force and Deployment Data Development and Deployment Execution).

(3) **Employment.** Employment is the application of force or forces to attain specified national strategic objectives. Employment concepts are developed by JFCs and their component commands during the planning process. These concepts provide the foundation and determine the scope of mobilization, deployment, sustainment, and redeployment processes. Joint operation planning prescribes how logistics is integrated and synchronized with operations. Global distribution supports employment of the joint force through effective coordination and synchronization of the intertheater and intratheater legs to meet the needs of the operating force.

For more information on arrangement of operations and logistics, see JP 3-0, Joint Operations, and JP 4-0, Joint Logistics.

(4) **Sustainment.** Sustainment is the provision of logistics and personnel services required to maintain and prolong operations until successful mission accomplishment. The distribution process provides sustainment to employed forces allowing them to remain engaged as required to achieve the JFC's objectives. This allows the joint force to maintain a higher operational tempo and agility resulting in an operational advantage. Sustainment is conducted for the duration of the joint mission. A logistic concept of support must complement the overall concept of operations (CONOPS). Logistic planners accomplish this by tailoring the JDDE, including incoming stock, theater excess stock and disposal requirements, or devising new distribution capabilities to be responsive, timely, and accurate in providing logistic support to the JFC and integrating and synchronizing logistics and operation planning to maintain readiness and competitive advantage.

For more information on sustainment of joint operations, see JP 4-0, Joint Logistics.

(5) **Redeployment.** Redeployment is the transfer of forces and materiel to support another JFC's operational requirements, or to return personnel, equipment, and materiel to the home and/or demobilization stations for reintegration and/or outprocessing. Similar to deployment, redeployment operations encompass four phases; these are redeployment planning, pre-redeployment activities, movement, and JRSOI. Redeployment operations are dependent on the supported CCDR's defined end state, concept for redeployment, or requirements to support another CONOPS. Redeployments to home or demobilization stations take place either because of an end-of-mission or in response to Service force rotation requirements. Redeployment also includes units that redeploy to their sustainment base for Service force generation before being deployed back into the same theater to continue operations as part of prolonged conflict. Units may also be reconstituted and redeployed to a different theater in support of another GCC. Commanders must plan and execute redeployment in a manner that optimizes readiness, security, and mobility of redeploying forces and materiel to meet new contingencies or crises. Global distribution supports the redeployment objectives including reconstitution and reorganization of the force prior to redeployment; movement of personnel, equipment, and materiel; and disposal of unwanted materiel and hazardous waste (HW).

For additional information on redeployment of the joint force, see JP 3-35, Deployment and Redeployment Operations.

CHAPTER II
DISTRIBUTION OPERATIONS CAPABILITIES

> *"As we select our forces and plan our operations...we must understand how logistics can impact on our concepts of operation...Commanders must base all their concepts of operations on what they know they can do logistically."*
>
> **Lieutenant General Alfred M. Gray, Jr., United States Marine Corps**
> ***Marine Corps Gazette*, July 1987**

1. Introduction

Chapter I, "Distribution Operations Overview," established that global distribution is a critical capability necessary to project and sustain joint forces. Resident within the JDDE are numerous capabilities that enable the movement of forces and the delivery and positioning of sustainment from any point of origin to the supported commander's designated point of need. This chapter will discuss those capabilities in the context of the four JDDE networks as well as provide information on key intertheater and intratheater Service, DOD agency, and commercial distribution capabilities.

2. Joint Deployment and Distribution Enterprise Networks

The four networks of the JDDE are the physical, financial, information, and communications networks. The information and communications networks form the communications system. Understanding the interdependencies and interrelationships of these networks is essential in planning for global distribution. It is imperative that the critical infrastructures that support each of the networks be assessed continuously to determine whether their capability is sufficient and to identify any vulnerabilities that might disrupt the continuity of global distribution operations. Assured access to these networks is critical; the effectiveness and efficiency of global distribution is improved or diminished by their performance levels.

a. **Physical Network.** The physical network of the distribution system consists of the quantity, capacity, and capability of fixed structures and established facilities supporting distribution and redistribution operations. It includes roads, railroads, structures (such as warehouses, depots, or storage facilities), ports, waterways, and pipelines. The physical network also encompasses physical resources such as personnel, equipment, and materiel and the capabilities to physically move these assets. It includes organic capabilities of military organizations and those of commercial partners as well as those of multinational and interagency participants. General engineer capability can be used to expand the capacity of the physical network (e.g., terminals, airfields, roads, waterways). Transportation and engineering intelligence provides information on the capacities of the physical system as well as potential barriers or bottlenecks.

(1) **Facilities and Infrastructure.** Global distribution operations rely on modern and efficient military and civilian facilities and supporting infrastructure. Facilities include the real estate and physical plant, such as buildings, equipment, and IT systems to support

operations. Supporting infrastructure is also vital to global distribution operations and includes ports, roads, airfields, railroads and railheads, and staging areas. The quantity and quality of these facilities and infrastructure, particularly outside the continental United States (OCONUS), may not always be adequate. Global distribution operations leverage existing facilities and infrastructure at the commencement of operations. Initially, distribution operations may require the use of labor- or equipment-intensive methods to overcome facility and infrastructure inadequacies. Over the course of an operation the condition of distribution facilities and infrastructure, including essential ports, airfields, and roads, may be upgraded by US military engineer forces through use of rapid construction methods and techniques such as runway repair, temporary bridging and bypasses, construction of prefabricated shelters, and beddown construction. Major facility improvements, however, are contracted commercial projects that require significant investment in both time and money and may not be feasible for short-term accomplishment when measured against the expected duration of campaigns or operations and distribution requirements.

(a) **Transportation Infrastructure.** DOD-owned transportation infrastructure consists of ammunition terminals, aerial ports, and limited surface transportation capability. DOD heavily leverages commercial transportation infrastructure to support global distribution operations. Planners must identify commercial transportation infrastructure support required and work closely with the commercial industry to ensure support.

(b) **Depots, Arsenals, and Maintenance Facilities.** In addition to transportation infrastructure, the network of DOD and Service depots, arsenals, and maintenance facilities provides the strategic distribution functions of supply and maintenance. The Military Departments operate arsenals, maintenance depots, and naval shipyards as well as ammunition plants and storage areas.

1. DLA Distribution, a critical element of the DOD distribution system, provides a full range of worldwide services in support of DOD and other USG departments and agencies during military operations. The depots are responsible for managing and providing DOD-owned commodities to all branches of the Armed Forces of the United States, by conducting distribution functions of receipt, storage, and issue.

2. Within this network of depots, there are five strategic distribution platforms (SDPs), which are located in San Joaquin, California; Oklahoma City, Oklahoma; Red River, Texas; Robins Air Force Base, Georgia; and New Cumberland, Pennsylvania (SDP Susquehanna). These sites provide strategic support to both the continental United States (CONUS) and OCONUS customers. SDPs are separate from forward distribution points (FDPs) because they operate consolidation and containerization point (CCP) operations. CCPs receive, consolidate, containerize, and ship to a designated customer base. CCPs also build pallets for air shipment and containers for surface intermodal movement to customers. Shipments originate from other depots, prime vendors (PVs), GSA, and other government supply sources. FDPs focus on the receipt, storage, and issuance of inventory for local/regional customers. Some FDPs are collocated with Service-owned industrial sites where repair and maintenance occur. SDP San Joaquin operates a CCP supporting United States Pacific Command customers (OCONUS), SDP Susquehanna operates a CCP supporting United States European Command, United States Africa Command, and United

States Central Command (OCONUS), SDP Warner Robins operates a CCP supporting Southeastern customers (CONUS), SDP Oklahoma City operates a CCP supporting customers in the Midwest and Central North (CONUS), and SDP Red River operates a CCP supporting customers in the South and Southwest (CONUS).

(2) **Host Nation (HN) Distribution Infrastructure Support.** US forces frequently operate in areas, or require en route support, necessitating reliance on HN resources to successfully execute global distribution operations. Preexisting multilateral joint logistic support plans and other similar joint support plans can serve as useful tools in identifying HN committed infrastructure support capabilities. HN agreements, such as status-of-forces agreements (SOFAs) and multinational or bilateral agreements negotiated before crises arise facilitate needed access to HN resources. HN coordination should be centralized as much as possible to effectively use the assistance provided by the HN and other nations in the region. The GCC should address HN sensitivity issues as early as practicable to ensure theater distribution operations are not adversely affected. Planners must be aware of creating competition with the local population or government for scarce distribution-related facilities. Clearances for convoys, air and rail movement, and hazardous material may be required and should be coordinated in advance of anticipated operations.

b. **Financial Network.** The financial network is composed of policies, processes, and decision systems that obtain, allocate, and apportion fiscal resources to acquire and maintain distribution capabilities and to execute the global distribution mission. These fiscal assets enable investment in materiel inventory, facilitate necessary physical distribution capabilities, and provide the critical linkage to commercial distribution capabilities.

c. **Information Network.** The information network consists of all data collection devices, AIT, automated data and business information systems, decision support tools and applications, and asset visibility (AV) capabilities supporting or facilitating global distribution. The optimum integration of these information systems and their data provides tools critical to the effectiveness and efficiency of global distribution operations to enable improved situational awareness and management processes.

d. **Communications Network.** The communications network links every facet of military operations affecting the ability of the Armed Forces to control and influence the outcome of military operations. It carries the data of the information network. The capacity, reliability, and security of communications networks, principally those that support the rapid transmission of global distribution data, significantly affect the tempo and effectiveness of global distribution operations. These communications requirements increase proportionally with the distribution task and/or priority. Real-time communications are an absolute requirement for successful execution of distribution operations. Modern military and commercial communication technology and capabilities, combined with information systems, comprise the "central nervous system" of global distribution and enable a common logistic operating environment.

3. Movement Control Capabilities

Movement control is a critical capability of the JDDE. It entails the coordination of all modes of transportation assets, terminals, Services, commands, and HN assets during deployment, sustainment, and redeployment. Furthermore, it spans the strategic, operational, and tactical levels to ensure that transportation capabilities are fully coordinated in order to enhance combat effectiveness and meet the priorities of the supported CCDR.

a. **Intertheater.** The DTS is that portion of global distribution infrastructure that supports DOD common-user transportation needs across the range of military operations. USTRANSCOM is responsible for providing common-user transportation and terminal management for DOD as well as non-DOD agencies upon request. Its three subordinate transportation component commands (TCCs), Air Mobility Command (AMC), Military Sealift Command (MSC), and Military Surface Deployment and Distribution Command (SDDC), work in concert to enable global mobility.

b. **Intratheater.** The coordination of the intertheater and intratheater movement control systems is the shared responsibility of USTRANSCOM and the supported CCMD. The GCC's movement control plan is key to a sound movement control system and should coordinate the transportation capabilities of component commands to produce a movement control system with centralized control and decentralized execution.

For more information on the transportation and movement control capabilities of each joint force component, see Chapter V, "Controlling Distribution," paragraph 4, "Movement Control Operations."

4. Air Mobility Capabilities

a. **Intertheater**

(1) **AMC.** As a TCC of USTRANSCOM, AMC is the designated lead major command for air mobility issues and standards and is responsible for all CONUS-based common-user air mobility assets. AMC is also responsible for maintaining the worldwide express (WWX) small parcel contract. C-5, C-17, KC-10, and KC-135 aircraft operate through a combination of active duty, Air Force Reserve, and Air National Guard resources to provide common-user air mobility under the combatant command (command authority) (COCOM) of CDRUSTRANSCOM. Additionally, AMC trains, equips, and operates CONUS-gained C-130s and operational support airlift (OSA) air mobility assets until they are assigned or attached to a GCC. During a contingency or major operation, of long or indeterminate duration, a number of these shorter-range airframes would normally be assigned to a GCC to establish or augment the theater air mobility capability. AMC air mobility forces conduct both intertheater and intratheater common-user operations. Under certain conditions, AMC aircraft may be temporarily attached to a GCC to provide additional theater capability. Airlift programs include the following:

(a) **Airlift Channels.** Channel airlift missions support global distribution operations over established worldwide routes (CCMD or Service-validated) that are served by scheduled DOD aircraft under AMC control or commercial aircraft contracted and scheduled by USTRANSCOM. These missions provide airlift services from aerial ports of embarkation (APOEs) to APODs to meet customer needs. AMC establishes some channel airlift missions to support service between two or more points on a recurring basis, with actual movements dependent upon the volume of traffic. Other channel airlift missions are established to support operational necessity and quality of life requirements in remote areas. Airlift missions operate daily from CONUS APOEs to OCONUS APODs. Additional channels are established to move materiel within theater. Channel cargo moves on a cost per pound basis, billed to the owner of the cargo.

(b) **Special Assignment Airlift Missions (SAAMs).** SAAMs require special consideration due to the number of passengers involved, weight or size of cargo, urgency of movement, sensitivity, or other valid factors that preclude the use of channel airlift. SAAMs support DOD users as well as other government agencies such as the US Secret Service, Federal Bureau of Investigation, and Drug Enforcement Administration. Service is from origin to destination and the customer is billed for mission operating costs.

(c) **OSA.** OSA is comprised of organic airlift assets that are an integral part of a specific Service, component, or major command and primarily support the priority movement of personnel and cargo with time, place, or mission-sensitive requirements. The Services equip and operate OSA assets and provide the training required to do so. During contingency or war a number of these airframes would normally be provided to a JFC to create or supplement the theater's air mobility capability.

(d) **Routine Aerial Distribution (RAD).** RAD requirements are identified by the GCC as part of the operations deployment and sustainment plan. The common-user airlift portion as well as the intertheater leg of distribution are provided through the commander, Air Force forces (COMAFFOR).

(e) **US/Republic of Korea Mutual Airlift Support Agreement.** The Mutual Airlift Support Agreement allows USTRANSCOM and DOD access to Korean commercial aircraft to augment US airlift capacity in case of hostilities in the Republic of Korea.

(f) **Cooperative Military Airlift Agreements and Acquisition and Cross-Servicing Agreements (ACSAs) with Implementing Arrangement.** The Royal Australian Air Force, Canadian Air Force, Royal New Zealand Air Force, Royal Air Force (United Kingdom), and AMC move traffic for each other under these agreements. Travel by implementation of these agreements is on a space-required, reimbursable basis.

(2) **Navy-Unique Fleet Essential Aircraft (NUFEA).** NUFEA are Service-organic distribution assets that accomplish the final link in the delivery chain from AMC channel distribution hubs to the mobile or afloat customer unit. NUFEA perform the critical fleet support role of destination flexible replenishment of high-priority air-eligible items or passengers.

(3) **Commercial Airlift Augmentation.** Commercial airlift augmentation capabilities include both AMC-controlled and -contracted airlift to increase the agility and flexibility that airlift provides to global distribution.

(a) **Charter.** Category A is a contract with the commercial air carrier industry allowing cargo to be individually waybilled between CONUS and OCONUS stations or between OCONUS stations. Category B is an AMC-procured "planeload" charter on commercial aircraft. Cargo moves in full planeload lots on other than a carrier's regularly scheduled commercial flights.

(b) **Civil Reserve Air Fleet (CRAF).** DOD uses the contractually committed capability of commercial air carriers to augment the military airlift capability of AMC to satisfy DOD airlift requirements. CRAF can be incrementally activated by CDRUSTRANSCOM with approval of SecDef in three stages in response to defense-oriented situations, up to and including a declared national emergency or war, to satisfy DOD airlift requirements. When CRAF is activated, the air carriers continue to operate and maintain the aircraft with their resources; however, USTRANSCOM controls the aircraft missions.

For more information on CRAF and its activation stages, refer to JP 3-17, Air Mobility Operations.

(c) **Express Service.** During a contingency, the vast majority of airlift sustainment will move on channel missions. However, USTRANSCOM can establish, upon request of the supported GCC, an express service to move GCC-designated high priority items into the AOR. The supported GCC will direct what portion of the CJCS-allocated strategic lift will be used for express service. For express service to be effective, the supported GCC must dedicate theater distribution capabilities to deliver express service cargo from the APOD to final destination at an "express" level of service. Depending on the speed and volume of cargo, space will be allocated to each joint force component by one of two processes:

1. Dedicated pallet positions on designated channel missions

2. Dedicated express aircraft

(d) **WWX.** WWX is the USG time-definite, door-to-door commercial express package service for high priority packages up to and including 300 pounds. Features of the service include: door-to-door pickup and delivery, TDD, customs clearance, and ITV through the Integrated Data Environment/Global Transportation Network Convergence (IGC).

(e) **Air Tenders.** Air tenders are voluntary or negotiated offers by qualified CRAF carriers to provide transportation services at specific rates that are negotiated for each traffic lane (established air route). Customers negotiate directly with carriers to establish or modify rates, charges, rules, and accessory services. Tenders must be approved by USTRANSCOM prior to use. This support is based on commercial carrier capabilities into geographic areas or lanes.

(f) **Military Air Lines of Communications (MILALOCs) and Commercial Air Lines of Communications (COMALOCs).** MILALOC shipments are single consignee, full air pallet shipments consolidated at DLA CCPs and trucked to AMC APOEs for air shipment to designated OCONUS military activities. The COMALOC program moves consolidated air pallets under Category A contracts with commercial air carriers from CCPs directly to the recipient, bypassing AMC aerial ports.

b. Intratheater

(1) **Theater Airlift Augmentation.** Intratheater air mobility operations are defined by geographic boundaries. Air mobility forces assigned or attached to that GCC normally conduct these operations. The inventory of these aircraft is dependent on documented wartime requirements validated annually by the CJCS. However, when intratheater air mobility requirements exceed the capability of assigned or attached forces, other mobility forces can either be assigned to the GCC or support intratheater airlift using a support relationship. Under certain conditions, AMC aircraft may be temporarily attached to a GCC to provide additional theater airlift capability. For instance, although intratheater air mobility assets are normally scheduled and controlled by the AOC or the JAOC, C-17s dwelling in an AOR are normally scheduled and controlled by the AMC 618th Air Operations Center (Tanker Airlift Control Center) (618 AOC [TACC])in support of theater requirements. The ability to identify and coordinate movement requirements visible in JDDE-common systems is critical to providing theater reachback support from the 618 AOC (TACC). The supported commander may also request augmentation from SecDef through the request for forces/request for capabilities (RFF/RFC) process.

(2) **Army Component**

(a) The Army theater aviation command has helicopters (UH-60/CH-47) and a limited number of fixed-wing aircraft (C-23) that can be used for intratheater transportation of ground forces and critical cargo during operational movement and maneuver, shaping, and sustainment operations. These aircraft meet time-sensitive transport requirements for urgently needed personnel, equipment, and supplies that are not otherwise available through ground transport systems.

(b) Airdrop Company. Heavy airdrop supply companies are normally assigned to combat sustainment support battalions (CSSBs). Their mission is to pack parachutes and temporarily store and rig equipment and supplies for airdrop by the Army, Air Force, or other Services. Their capabilities include the ability to airdrop up to 200 short tons (STONs) of materiel daily. The heavy airdrop supply company also assists in loading supplies and equipment into aircraft and in release of supplies and equipment from aircraft in flight. The company also provides personnel parachute support (packing and unit maintenance) for 450 Soldiers during a 45-day period. It provides technical advice and assistance in recovery and evacuation of airdrop equipment. The company also performs technical/rigger inspection of airdrop equipment upon initial receipt from supply sources and performs the Army portion of the joint inspection of airdrop loads.

5. Sealift Capabilities

a. Intertheater

(1) **MSC.** MSC is the ocean transportation component of USTRANSCOM and provides worldwide ocean transportation of equipment, fuel, supplies, and ammunition during peacetime and war with a fleet of government-owned (GO) and chartered US-flagged ships.

(a) **Sealift Programs.** Historically, over 90 percent of joint force materiel is transported by sealift—the fastest and most cost-effective method for transporting large quantities of materiel to OCONUS locations. However, cargo shipping for DOD is subject to the Military Cargo Preference Act of 1904, which requires that items procured for, intended for use by, or owned by Military Departments or DOD agencies must be carried exclusively on US-flagged vessels, if available at reasonable rates. Use of foreign-flagged shipping is permitted IAW the terms of an applicable law or treaty, when US-flagged ships are not available to meet the cargo requirements, or when the Secretary of the Navy or the Secretary of the Army determines that rates charged are excessive or otherwise unreasonable pursuant to Subpart 247.5 of the Defense Federal Acquisition Regulation Supplement.

(b) There are a variety of capabilities that enhance sealift support to global distribution operations. These programs are:

1. **Dry Cargo Operations**

a. **Controlled Fleet.** MSC has a fleet of dry cargo ships to satisfy roll-on/roll-off (RO/RO) and long-term cargo lift requirements that cannot be filled by US-flagged commercial liner operators. The fleet is sized based on the forecast of special category and exercise cargo (by type and route) that cannot be carried by regular commercial liner services.

b. **Commercial Maritime Industry.** USTRANSCOM establishes contracts with the ocean carrier industry for ocean and intermodal transportation services for the worldwide movement of cargo. Where contract services are not available or do not meet the particular customer's service requirements, special or dedicated service contracts are established by USTRANSCOM and its components. All agreements and long-term contracts are with US-flagged carriers, preferably those participating in the Voluntary Intermodal Sealift Agreement (VISA) program, unless such service is not available.

c. **VISA.** VISA, the primary sealift mobilization program, was developed through a unique partnership between DOD, the Department of Transportation, and the commercial sealift industry. VISA is an intermodal, capacity-oriented program vice a ship-by-ship oriented program. It provides contractually committed, time-phased, sealift capability to meet DOD contingencies when commercial service is not adequate to meet OPLAN requirements for joint operations. The worldwide shipping services provided by these commercial carriers provide extensive and flexible capabilities to DOD. VISA provides the process for DOD and industry to develop flexible concepts of operations for contingency sealift in support of CCDR concept plans (CONPLANs) and OPLANs. The majority of the dry cargo fleet is enrolled in VISA. The types of ships enrolled include container ships, RO/RO ships, combination RO/RO and container ships, heavy lift ships, breakbulk ships, tugs, and barges.

d. **US/Republic of Korea Flag Shipping Arrangement.** The Korean Flag Shipping Arrangement allows USTRANSCOM and DOD to gain operational control (OPCON) of specified Korean commercial vessels in the event of hostilities on or near the Korean peninsula.

2. **Combat Logistics Force (CLF).** The CLF are those units, under the OPCON of a CCDR, that service or replenish combatant vessels forward-deployed or underway in the GCC's AOR. These vessels are Service-organic assets and directly support US Navy operations.

3. **MSC Petroleum Tanker Fleet.** The MSC petroleum tanker fleet is a fleet of chartered or GO, contract operated ships providing worldwide point-to-point movement of DOD bulk petroleum products. Primary customers are DLA Energy and the Navy. Service can be from, to, and between commercial sources or storage locations and military base storage sites, and for special delivery to Navy ships at sea.

4. **Contingency Support Fleet.** The contingency support fleet is composed of three categories of vessels: large, medium speed roll-on/roll-off ships (LMSRs), the afloat pre-positioning force (APF), and the Maritime Administration Ready Reserve Force (MARAD RRF). All are strategic sealift resources that provide rapid response and worldwide strategic pre-positioning. These assets and capabilities are used to satisfy exercise, surge, and contingency requirements only and cannot be used for routine movement of peacetime cargo.

a. **LMSRs.** LMSRs each carry approximately twice the amount of cargo as a fast sealift ship (FSS), but are slower at 24 knots. They are civilian contract operated and lay berthed on the US East, Gulf, and West Coasts to be within a few days transit of their loading ports, or they may be pre-positioned afloat.

b. **APF.** APF ships provide mobile materiel storage and delivery capabilities that defer the need for strategic lift (both air and sea) and serve as a vital source of inventory during the critical early stages of joint force operations. The APF includes: maritime pre-positioning force (MPF) ships; Army pre-positioned stocks (APS) ships; and Navy, DLA, and Air Force pre-positioning ships.

c. **MARAD RRF.** The MARAD RRF is a fleet of ships maintained in a reduced operating status (ROS) for use by DOD when required. These ships are civilian contract operated and lay berthed on the US East, Gulf, and West Coasts to be within a few days transit of their loading ports. They are in ROS-5, along with one offshore petroleum discharge system (OPDS) tanker which is in ROS-10, and can be activated in order to carry combat-surge and follow-on cargo under the OPCON of USTRANSCOM (exercised through MSC). Included in the MARAD RRF are FSSs. With more than 27-knot capability and installed RO/RO ramps, the FSSs can rapidly transport military equipment to contingency locations around the world. Additionally, some MARAD RRF vessels have unique features to support joint logistics over-the-shore (JLOTS), where fixed-ports may be inadequate, damaged, or nonexistent. The MARAD RRF outporting program places some of the high readiness ships at commercial and government layberths near their activation yards and load ports to improve response time.

For more information on the types and capabilities of MSC ships and MSC-gained vessels, see JP 4-01.2, Sealift Support to Joint Operations. *For more information on JLOTS, see JP 4-01.6,* Joint Logistics Over-the-Shore.

(2) **Foreign-Flagged Ships.** When US-flagged ships are unavailable, foreign-flagged ships can be acquired for DOD use by three methods:

(a) **Voluntary Charter.** During peacetime, MSC will charter foreign-flagged ships whenever US-flagged ships are unavailable. This ability allows MSC to enter the foreign charter market and quickly expand its fleet whenever the need arises.

(b) **Allied Shipping Agreements.** Allied shipping agreements, arranging for vessels received through allied nations, can either be prenegotiated and in existence or they can be drawn up on an emergency basis as the need arises.

(c) **Effective United States-Controlled Ships (EUSCS).** EUSCS are ships owned by US citizens or companies that are registered in countries that have no prohibition on requisitioning of these vessels by the US. These ships may be requisitioned by the US under authority of Section 902, Merchant Marine Act of 1936 (Title 46, USC, Chapter 563).

b. **Intratheater**

(1) **Army Component**

(a) **Army Watercraft Units.** Organized into the units shown below, these Army watercraft platforms provide lift associated with waterborne operational maneuver and the intratheater sealift of units, equipment, and supplies. They support marine terminal and sea-based operations to conduct force closure and to execute distributed support and sustainment of employed forces. Operating as part of the joint force, these watercraft and the organizations to which they belong provide critical capability in mitigating an adversary's antiaccess strategy and in overcoming area denial challenges present in the theater of operations.

(b) **Types of Army Watercraft Organizations:**

1. Theater support vessel detachment

2. Transportation medium boat detachment

3. Transportation heavy boat company

4. Transportation modular causeway company

5. Transportation floating craft company

<u>6.</u> Transportation watercraft maintenance company

<u>7.</u> Logistic support vessel detachment

<u>8.</u> Transportation harbormaster detachment

(2) **Navy Component.** The US Navy's MSC operates the joint high-speed vessel in support of CCDRs' intratheater lift requirements. The high-speed vessel provides intratheater lift for the United States Marine Corps (USMC). MSC provides life cycle management for these platforms used by the CCDRs to provide over ocean lift in support of mission requirements.

6. Surface Capabilities

a. Intertheater

(1) **SDDC.** SDDC is the surface transportation component of USTRANSCOM and is DOD's single port manager (SPM) for all common-user seaports of embarkation (SPOEs) and SPODs. SDDC performs SPM functions necessary to support the strategic flow of the deploying forces' equipment and supplies to and from the theater. SDDC is also responsible for providing management of all port operations to include coordinating workload requirements, waterside port security, and port support activities with the GCC's theater sustainment command (TSC).

(2) **Land Programs.** Virtually all movement of forces and materiel begins and ends with land transportation, regardless of the strategic lift method. SDDC provides CONUS traffic management support for freight movements on surface carriers, operates the Defense Freight Railway Interchange Fleet (DFRIF) of more than 1,000 special-use railcars, and administers the DOD highways, railroads, ports, and intermodal programs for national defense. SDDC also monitors the status of worldwide infrastructure, including seaports, inland waterways, and pipelines. SDDC, through its Transportation Engineering Agency, coordinates force movement to seaports both in CONUS and OCONUS, prepares the ports for ships and cargo, and supervises loading operations. SDDC administers the contingency response program (CORE), serves as SPM to CCDRs, develops integrated traffic management systems, and provides transportation engineering services to DOD.

b. Intratheater

(1) **CONUS Commercial Resources.** The commercial transportation industry has substantial capability available to meet the CONUS transportation needs of DOD across the range of military operations.

(a) CORE supports the acquisition of domestic civil transportation resources during military deployments. This voluntary program provides DOD commercial transportation service support and priority for commercial transportation prior to and during contingency and mobilization. CORE supports acquisition of commercial transportation resources for DOD, coordinates hazardous materials (HAZMAT) movement, provides liaison to the USCG for port security support, and performs source identification for emergency lease or purchase of commercial heavy equipment transporters.

(b) **Defense Transportation Coordination (DTC).** The DTC integrates DOD logistics to become more responsive to joint force readiness while achieving greater efficiencies. DTC is a third-party transportation service which improves reliability, predictability, and efficiency of DOD materiel moving within CONUS by managing the CONUS-wide distribution of freight of all kinds.

(c) **Dedicated Truck Delivery.** Dedicated truck delivery programs enable time-definite service supporting customers receiving numerous shipments on a regular basis from DLA Distribution depots. Agreements are made to deliver all cargo, regardless of priority or size, via regular truck service. The delivery schedule is based on volume and can be every day or as little as once a week. The depot and the customer determine the best delivery schedule. Customers specify the receiving location and time of day for delivery. Regular deliveries on a set schedule save transportation costs and allow customers to schedule receiving workloads. Dedicated truck arrangements are best suited for customers with consistent volumes of cargo.

(2) **OCONUS Common-User Land Transportation (CULT).** Assigning responsibility for CULT is a function of the GCC's DAFL, and it is up to each GCC to outline this in the OPLAN and supporting plans. Under CULT, land transportation assets are normally under the OPCON of the Army component commander, who coordinates all planning and requirements for the use of DOD-controlled land transportation equipment and facilities designated as common-use in theater. Service component commanders, however, maintain control and authority over their Service-owned assets that are not designated as common-use to facilitate accomplishment of their mission. The Navy and Air Force components provide organic land transportation support within their installations and activities and submit peacetime requirements for common-use theater or area transportation to the Army component for those theaters where the Army has been assigned CULT responsibility. Wartime CULT requirements are the GCC's responsibility and normally the JDDOC or a component assigned the CULT mission will consolidate and coordinate planned wartime movement requirements for all component commands. Nonmilitary transportation resources can include host-nation support (HNS), multinational civil organizations, indigenous commercial transportation providers, and third-party logistic organizations.

(3) **Army Component**

(a) **Motor Transportation Capabilities.** The Army provides motor transport through the use of motor transport battalions. Motor transport battalions are assigned to the TSC and are normally attached to sustainment brigades (SUST BDEs) responsible for conducting theater distribution missions. A motor transport battalion's core capabilities include motor transportation and inland terminal operations. Motor transport battalions are composed of three to seven motor transport or cargo transfer companies responsible for conducting distribution.

(b) **Rail Transportation Capabilities.** The Army provides an expeditionary railway center to a senior logistics headquarters (TSC or expeditionary sustainment command [ESC]). This unit provides: rail network capability and infrastructure assessments; rail mode feasibility studies; advice on employment of rail capabilities; coordination of rail and bridge safety assessments; assistance with rail planning; and coordination of use of HN or contracted rail assets.

(c) **Petroleum Distribution Capabilities.** The Army distributes petroleum through petroleum, oils, and lubricants (POL) supply battalions and petroleum pipeline and terminal operating (PPTO) battalions. The POL supply battalion provides command and control (C2) and administrative, technical, and operational supervision for two to five POL support companies and POL truck companies. PPTO battalions provide C2 for PPTO companies. Each PPTO company can operate up to 90 miles of pipeline. POL supply battalions plan for the storage, distribution, and quality surveillance of bulk petroleum products. POL supply battalions maintain the theater petroleum reserve and operate a mobile petroleum products laboratory. They are normally assigned to a TSC or petroleum group. POL supply companies are assigned to either a CSSB or POL supply battalion, each capable of providing bulk fuel storage. A POL supply company with three 50-thousand (k)-bag platoons can store 1.8 million gallons of fuel, receive/issue 600k gallons daily, and establish and operate six hot refueling sites. Its area support sections can store/receive/issue 360k gallons daily, and its distribution sections can distribute 146,250 gallons daily. A POL supply company with three 210k-bag platoons can store 58 million gallons of fuel, receive/issue 900k gallons daily, and establish and operate six hot refueling sites. Its area support sections store/receive/issue 360k gallons daily and its distribution sections can distribute 146,250 gallons daily.

(4) **Theater Resources**

(a) **HNS.** A frequently used means of augmenting or expanding the GCC's distribution capability is HNS. HNS, negotiated through bilateral or multilateral agreements, provides for a nation to either accept responsibility for a particular function within its borders (e.g., APOD cargo clearance) or designate civilian and/or military resources to be used in that capacity under military control. HNS offers the GCC a proven means to meet theater distribution requirements and offset force structure shortfalls.

(b) **ACSAs.** CCDRs may negotiate and conclude ACSAs when authorized by the CJCS. Negotiated bilaterally, usually with US allies or partner nations and sometimes with other eligible countries, ACSAs allow for the exchange of logistic support, supplies, and services during combined exercises, training deployments, operations, contingencies, and unforeseen circumstances. Some examples include: food, billeting, clothing, communication services, medical services, spare parts and components, training services, POL, transportation (including airlift), ammunition, and, in limited cases, other items of military equipment. ACSAs are not to be used to procure goods and services reasonably available from US commercial sources and are military-to-military exchange only.

(c) **Commercial Ocean Carriers.** Under USTRANSCOM contracts, commercial ocean carriers often have an existing infrastructure in developed areas that can transport containerized cargo from SPOD to designated destinations. The theater traffic manager in concert with SDDC can use these services to ease demands on military and HNS assets. However, the theater traffic manager must allow the release and return of container assets under terms of the container agreement to obtain maximum system efficiency.

(d) **Contracted Support Operations.** Contracted support operations can provide additional resources to GCCs when they are properly coordinated with intratheater transportation policies, requirements, and contingency procedures. C2 of the movement of materiel arriving in, and departing from, a theater on civilian contractor assets must be fully integrated into the commander's OPLAN to ensure that transportation requirements are met and to offset transportation force structure shortfalls. Fully integrated plans should address contractual compliance with DOD policies regarding CRAF and/or VISA participation, contingency validation procedures, time-phased force and deployment data (TPFDD) procedures, ITV, and coordination of civilian operations within the DTS. Proper contracted support integration will enable timely movement coordination, transportation assets validation, and required ITV of vital support requirements while easing demands on limited space requirements and essential cargo or materials handling equipment (MHE).

7. Port Capabilities

a. Fixed

(1) **SPM.** Operational experience has shown that the SPM construct is necessary to improve the planning and execution of port management operations and allows the seamless transfer of cargo and equipment in any given theater. As a result, USTRANSCOM was designated by SecDef as the single worldwide manager for common-user POEs and PODs. As such, it performs those functions necessary to support the strategic flow of deploying and redeploying forces, unit equipment, and sustainment supply in the SPOEs and APOEs and hand-off to the GCC in the SPODs and APODs.

(a) **SDDC.** As USTRANSCOM's surface TCC, SDDC performs SPM functions necessary to support the strategic flow of the deploying forces' equipment and sustainment supply in the SPOE and hand-off to the GCC at the SPOD. SDDC has port management responsibility through all phases of the theater port operations continuum, from a bare beach (e.g., JLOTS) deployment to a commercial contract fixed-port support deployment. When necessary, in areas where SDDC does not maintain a manned presence, an SDDC deployable port management team will direct water terminal operations, including supervising movement operations, contracts, cargo documentation, ITV, support arrangements, and security operations. As the SPM, SDDC is also responsible for providing strategic deployment status information to the CCDR and for managing the workload of the SPOD port operator based on the CCDR's priorities and guidance.

The specific roles and functions of both the port manager and port operator are summarized in JP 4-01.5, Joint Terminal Operations.

(b) **AMC.** As USTRANSCOM's air TCC, AMC performs SPM functions necessary to support the strategic flow of the deploying forces' equipment and sustainment supplies and materiel in the APOE and hand-off to the GCC in the APOD. AMC has port management responsibility through all phases of the theater aerial port operations continuum, from a bare base deployment to a commercial contract fixed-port support deployment. In areas not served by a permanent USTRANSCOM presence, AMC will, through its contingency response wing (CRW), deploy contingency response forces to open and initially operate expeditionary airports. In its SPM role, AMC uses cargo cross-docking to the maximum extent possible to expedite materiel through the distribution pipeline.

(2) **OCONUS Seaports and Airports.** PODs in the supported theater are the points from which materiel flows from the intertheater to intratheater leg of joint distribution. OCONUS ports can be the most constraining aspect of all facilities affecting global distribution lanes. Selection and operation of port facilities are critical to distribution support of joint forces. Port capabilities, facilities, physical security, and proximity to adequate roads, rail lines, inland waterways, and pipelines are important factors in port selection. The true measure of port effectiveness is throughput. Some factors affecting throughput include: facilities, labor, MHE, port capacity, and connectivity to other transportation infrastructure and information systems. USTRANSCOM, AMC, MSC, and SDDC are the primary DOD agencies that determine and assess port throughput capabilities.

(a) **SPODs.** The flow from strategic sealift to theater distribution capabilities using intratheater air, highway, rail, barge, and pipeline occurs at SPODs. Seaport adequacy is based on physical considerations that are often difficult to improve in the short term. Navigability, channel depths, numbers and sizes of ship berths, intermodal cargo handling equipment, and explosive handling limitations are significant factors that will affect materiel throughput. Another significant consideration is the impact of simultaneous commercial transportation, industrial operations, and other activities in the port area. Expansion of fixed-port facilities by US forces requires a long lead time and significant resources. Another alternative, much faster to implement, is to augment inadequate SPODs through the employment of JLOTS capabilities until other infrastructure enhancements can be realized.

(b) **APODs.** Many factors impact throughput capacity and aerial port operations. Communications systems, navigation aids, runway length and weight bearing capacity, taxiway systems, ramp space, MHE, personnel, aircraft servicing and maintenance, fuel and refueling capacity, and the maximum (aircraft) on the ground (MOG) play an integral part in aerial port effectiveness. A significant consideration in determining capabilities of an APOD to support global distribution operations is the impact of commercial transportation, industrial operations, and other activities in the port area. Construction or rehabilitation efforts can overcome some APOD shortcomings.

b. **Expeditionary.** Expeditionary theater opening capabilities provide GCCs critical initial actions for rapid insertion/expansion of force capabilities into an OA that directly affects the JFC's ability to expand and adjust force flow to allow flexible, agile response to asymmetric and dynamic operations requirements. Expeditionary theater opening capabilities support the first critical OA entry missions with eventual transition of theater POD operations to a JFC-designated Service component and establishes conditions to facilitate the arrival of larger Service theater distribution and sustainment forces where/when appropriate.

(1) **Joint Task Force–Port Opening (JTF-PO).** Although all Services have the organic capability to execute theater opening functions, traditional Service port opening/operating forces may not be sufficient in situations that require rapid response or joint integration. JTF-PO provides the supported GCC with a rapid assessment of potential aerial ports and seaports and their associated distribution infrastructures as well as a port opening capability to facilitate crisis response in established or austere environments that is designed to be in place in advance of a deployment of forces, sustainment, or humanitarian/relief supplies. JTF-PO is a joint expeditionary capability that enables USTRANSCOM to rapidly establish and initially operate and clear a POD and conduct cargo handling operations to a forward distribution node, facilitating port throughput in support of a GCC-executed contingency. APOD forces are ready to deploy within 12 hours, SPOD forces within 36 hours, and both are designed to operate for up to 60 days and then redeploy or be relieved by follow-on forces. JTF-PO is designed to address the historic shortcomings associated with the rapid opening of ports worldwide, including ad hoc C2 and lack of continuous visibility of cargo moving from the PODs through the theater of operations. Consistent and deliberate joint training, a robust C2 suite including ITV, and dedicated surface movement control units enable JTF-PO to effectively and efficiently address previous deficiencies of port opening. The deployment of JTF-PO is conducted under the authority of the CDRUSTRANSCOM (as authorized in the Unified Command Plan and SecDef standing execute order [EXORD]) in direct support of the supported GCC.

(a) **JTF-PO (APOD)**

1. JTF-PO is one of the capabilities designed to rapidly establish and initially operate an APOD in a theater of operations. JTF-PO (APOD) further adds the ability to operate a forward distribution node. Modular and scalable, JTF-PO (APOD) capabilities are mission tailored IAW their intended use.

2. Comprised of Air Force contingency response groups (CRGs) and Army transportation detachment–rapid port opening elements (RPOEs), JTF-PO (APOD) is capable of providing C2, aircraft maintenance support, passenger and cargo handling/transfer, movement control, ITV and radio frequency identification and node and container/pallet management.

3. JTF-PO (APOD) facilitates JRSOI and theater distribution by providing near-real-time ITV of arriving passengers and cargo and expeditiously clearing the APOD. JTF-PO forward distribution node operations are a critical component of GCC efforts to rapidly establish a distribution network within a theater of operations.

4. Enabled by AIT and ITV systems, JTF-PO (APOD) is able to rapidly and reliably communicate deployment and sustainment flow. JTF-PO (APOD)-generated ITV data provides the JDDOC and other theater distribution managers with the information necessary to coordinate and synchronize distribution operations IAW GCC requirements.

5. Depending upon the GCC intended long-term use of the APOD, and as follow-on theater logistic capabilities arrive, JTF-PO (APOD) may begin transferring

mission responsibilities of the forward distribution node to arriving forces or contracted capabilities to facilitate the seamless continuation of aerial port and distribution operations.

(b) **JTF-PO (SPOD)**

1. JTF-PO (SPOD) is one of the capabilities to rapidly assess, establish, and initially operate SPODs. It also provides the GCC with a forward distribution node capability consistent with the SPM concept and is tailorable to support varying situations within the GCC's AOR, including austere seaports with limited contract support capabilities.

2. Comprised of Army seaport command element (CE), RPOE and Navy cargo-handling battalion (NCHB) elements, JTF-PO (SPOD) deploys as an integrated and tailorable joint team with robust communications systems and automated information systems (AISs) capable of synchronizing onward surface movements associated with the SPOD deployment and distribution processes. JTF-PO (SPOD) provides the added functionality to coordinate cargo movement control activities and position cargo at a forward distribution node to minimize distribution backlogs and facilitate cargo throughput from the strategic to the theater levels.

3. JTF-PO (SPOD) establishes and operates joint ITV at the SPOD and a forward distribution node. This capability supports the accountability and management of materiel assets such as twenty-foot equivalent unit (TEU) containers, rolling stock, and tie down devices.

4. JTF-PO (SPOD) capability eliminates historical gaps and seams between port opening, operating, and management. USTRANSCOM planners are involved from the onset with joint planning for seizure operations to ensure that all seams are eliminated. As follow-on theater logistic capabilities arrive, JTF-PO (SPOD) begins transferring mission responsibilities of the forward distribution node to arriving forces or contracted capabilities to allow the seamless continuation of seaport and distribution operations. JTF-PO (SPOD) can also support future JLOTS operations and help facilitate cargo movement and ITV from the beach area to the forward distribution node.

(2) **Army Component**

(a) **Transportation Brigades/Battalions.** Transportation brigades/battalions assigned to SDDC plan and execute common-user water terminal and surface distribution operations within a geographic area. Their core functions include predeployment planning; HN liaison; ITV and documentation; cargo booking; container management; port security planning and coordination; issuing port call messages; as well as receiving, staging, and transshipping cargo. Additionally, they monitor ocean carrier performance and compliance with MSC shipping and container agreements and contracts.

(b) **Terminal Battalions.** Terminal battalions are assigned to the TSC and are normally attached to a transportation brigade (expeditionary) that has the theater opening mission. The terminal battalion provides C2 and technical supervision of three to seven companies (mix of seaport operating companies and watercraft companies) at ocean and inland waterway terminals, and JLOTS sites in the theater. The terminal battalion staff translates mission orders from the transportation brigade (expeditionary) into specific requirements, enabling the effective and efficient flow of materiel and personnel into and out of theater.

(c) **Seaport Operating Company.** The seaport operating company performs seaport terminal service operations to discharge and load containerized cargo and wheeled/tracked vehicles in fixed seaports or in logistics over-the-shore (LOTS) sites. In a fixed port, they can discharge or load up to 375 containers, or 750 wheeled/tracked vehicles, or 1,875 STONs of breakbulk cargo per day. In a LOTS operation they can discharge or load up to 150 containers, or 750 STONs of breakbulk cargo per day, or 450 wheeled/tracked vehicles. They can be assigned to a TSC, a SUST BDE, transportation brigade (expeditionary), or a transportation terminal battalion.

(d) **Heavy Boat Company.** Heavy boat companies perform intratheater waterborne transportation of personnel, cargo, and equipment during water terminal operations, waterborne tactical operations, and joint amphibious, inland waterway, or JLOTS operations. Their capabilities include providing up to eight landing craft, utility (LCU)-2000 for transport missions on a 24-hour basis. During that time, each LCU-2000 can move five M-1 main battle tanks or twenty-four 20-foot containers at one time. They can transport 2,800 STONs of cargo consisting of vehicles, containers, and/or general cargo. Heavy boat companies are assigned to a TSC and are normally attached to a transportation terminal battalion.

(3) **Navy Component**

(a) **Naval Beach Group (NBG).** The mission of the NBG is to put landing force equipment and supplies ashore during and following an amphibious assault or an MPF offload. The NBG provides the JFC with beachmaster traffic control, pontoon lighterage, causeways, ship-to-shore bulk fuel systems, limited construction capabilities, landing craft, beach salvage capability, and communications to properly facilitate the flow of troops, equipment, and supplies ashore.

(b) **Navy Expeditionary Logistic Support Group (NAVELSG).** NAVELSG is an active duty command with active and reserve cargo handling battalions organized and staffed to provide a wide range of supply and transportation support critical for peacetime support, crisis response, humanitarian operations, and combat service support missions. NAVELSG consists of active duty and selective reserve support staff, one active and three reserve expeditionary logistics regiments, and one active and six reserve NCHBs. The NCHBs are active and reserve Navy commissioned units tasked with loading and unloading all classes of cargo, except bulk petroleum. They are an active and reserve advanced base functional component (ABFC) unit of NAVELSG, capable of worldwide deployment in its entirety or in specialized detachments. The NCHB is organized, trained, and equipped to: load and off-load Navy and Marine Corps cargo carried in maritime pre-positioning ships (MPSs) and merchant or container ships in all environments; operate an associated temporary ocean cargo terminal; load and off-load Navy and Marine Corps cargo carried in military-controlled aircraft; and operate an associated expeditionary air cargo terminal.

(4) **Air Force Component**

(a) **CRW.** AMC's single CRW is organized, trained, and equipped to employ rapidly deployable cross-functional teams to open forward airbases and/or extend AMC infrastructure in an expeditionary environment. The CRW as an organization does not deploy; however, it provides the resources for and coordinates the deployment of its subordinate units. CRW elements are designed for a decreased transportation and logistic footprint and are not designed as long-term assets.

(b) **CRG.** CRGs rapidly survey, assess, open, and establish contingency air base lodgments and expand existing air mobility support infrastructure worldwide. The CRG performs expeditionary aircraft quick-turn maintenance, airfield management, passenger and cargo movement, C2, threat assessment, force protection, air traffic control, weather support, airfield systems maintenance, finance services, and contracting.

(c) **Contingency Response Element (CRE).** Each CRE is a mobile organization responsible for providing continuous on-site air mobility operations management. CREs deploy to provide air mobility mission support when C2, mission reporting, and/or other support functions at the destination do not meet operational requirements. CREs provide aerial port, logistics, maintenance, weather, medical, force protection, and intelligence services, as necessary.

8. **Equipment/Stock Pre-Positioning and Forward Stocking**

a. **Pre-positioning.** DOD pre-positioned force, equipment, or supplies (PREPO) programs are both land-based and sea-based. They are critical programs for reducing closure times of combat and support forces needed in the early stages of a contingency and also contribute significantly to reducing demands on the DTS. The US Army and USMC pre-positioning programs consist of combat, combat support, and combat service support capabilities, to include in-stream discharge and JLOTS capabilities. Other Service and DLA PREPO programs are logistics oriented.

(1) **APF.** In addition to sealift ships, MSC operates the APF, a fleet of pre-positioned ships strategically placed around the world and loaded with equipment and supplies to sustain Army, Navy, Marine Corps, and Air Force operations. These ships are chartered commercial and GO vessels and remain at sea, ready to deploy on short notice. The APF consists of MPSs, the APS-3 ships, and the Navy and Air Force ships.

(2) Summaries of DOD land- and sea-based PREPO programs are as follows:

(a) **APS**

1. The primary purposes of APS are to reduce the initial amount of strategic lift required to support a predominately CONUS-based force projection Army, and to sustain the soldier until sea LOCs are established. Accordingly, APS are located at several land-based locations, as well as aboard ships, to quickly project power to contingency areas. APS are owned by Headquarters, Department of the Army. Their release for use is approved by CJCS, SecDef, or the President. The four categories of APS are:

a. **Pre-Positioned Unit Sets.** Equipment, configured into unit sets (to include authorized stockage list, shop stock, and unit basic load), is positioned ashore and afloat in order to reduce deployment response times by meeting the Army's global pre-positioning strategy requirements to provide simultaneous support to more than one contingency in more than one theater.

b. **Operational Project (OPROJ) Stocks.** OPROJ stocks are materiel above normal table of organization and equipment, table of distribution and allowances, and common table of allowance authorizations tailored to key strategic capabilities essential to the Army's ability to execute its force projection strategy. OPROJ stocks are designed to support one or more Army operations, plans, or contingencies.

c. **Army War Reserve Sustainment Stocks.** The Army procures sustainment stocks in peacetime to meet increased wartime requirements. They consist of major and secondary materiel designated to satisfy the Army's wartime sustainment requirements. They provide minimum essential support to combat operations and post-mobilization training beyond the capabilities of peacetime stocks, industry, and HNS. Army war reserve sustainment stocks are pre-positioned in or near a theater of operations to be used until wartime production and supply lines can be established. These stocks consist of major end items and secondary items to sustain the operation by replacing operational combat losses.

d. **War Reserve Stocks for Allies (WRSA).** WRSA is a program directed by the Office of the Secretary of Defense (OSD) and facilitates US preparedness to assist designated allies in case of war. WRSA assets are pre-positioned in the appropriate theater and owned and financed by the US. They are released to the proper Army component commander for transfer to the supported multinational force (MNF) under provisions in the Foreign Assistance Act and under existing country-to-country memorandums of agreement.

2. APS are positioned and contain categories of stocks as follows: APS-1 (CONUS), OPROJ stocks and sustainment stocks; APS-2 (Europe), OPROJ stocks and WRSA; APS-3 (Afloat), pre-positioned sets and sustainment stocks; APS-4 (Pacific and Northeast Asia), pre-positioned sets, OPROJ stocks, sustainment stocks, munitions, and watercraft; APS-5 (Southwest Asia), pre-positioned sets, OPROJ stocks, sustainment stocks, munitions, and watercraft.

(b) **USMC.** The Marine Corps depends heavily on afloat pre-positioning known as the MPF. MPF is a strategic deployment option that quickly combines MPF equipment and sustainment loaded aboard the ships of a maritime pre-positioning ships squadron (MPSRON), as part of the assault follow-on echelon, to establish a formidable combined arms force capable of sustained operations. The Marine air-ground task force (MAGTF) and Navy support element (NSE) personnel, selected equipment, and combat aircraft are flown into the objective area where the MPS operations occur. The MPS are specifically constructed or modified RO/RO ships that are forward deployed in two self-contained MPSRONs. Each MPSRON (except for the maritime PREPO force enhanced ships which have no bulk liquid capabilities) carries the unit equipment and approximately 30 days of supplies for one brigade-size MAGTF. Each ship carries a spread load of unit equipment, supplies, POL, and potable water, thereby eliminating the need to discharge all vessels in order to obtain required types and quantities of equipment and cargo. Additionally, each ship is outfitted with NSE equipment consisting of the camp support and lighterage needed to discharge cargo over unimproved ports or over the beach. MPSRON 2 is positioned in the Indian Ocean (Diego Garcia), and MPSRON is positioned in the Western Pacific (Guam, Saipan, and Korea). MPS cargo may be discharged pier-side in three days or "in stream" in five days by NSE personnel composed of NBG and cargo handling battalion personnel, as well as Marine Corps personnel airlifted to the objective area. The Marine Corps also maintains land-based pre-positioned assets in Norway sufficient to support a Marine expeditionary brigade (MEB) with equipment and supplies.

(c) **US Air Force.** The Air Force pre-positions equipment and supplies both afloat and on land. The current Air Force pre-positioned fleet consists of two ammunition carriers under MPSRON OPCON. On land, the Air Force pre-positions standard air munitions packages, theater ammunition stocks, and life support and flightline support complexes. A unique capability also pre-positioned by the Air Force is the bare base life support system intended for use in war, contingencies, and natural disasters. The Air Force Base Expeditionary Airfield Resources system is an air or surface transportable system composed of small and medium shelters, and a suite of equipment designed to overcome climate and infrastructure limitations for an extended period of time. It is expandable and scalable to a variety of configurations.

(d) **US Navy.** The Navy pre-positions one ship for use as a floating OPDS pumping station, which can hook up with any tanker of opportunity to pump fuel ashore. The ship and its installed system can provide fuel during contingencies when land-based petroleum is either unavailable or insufficient. OPDS can pump 1.7 million gallons of fuel in a 20-hour day (four hours maintenance) from up to eight miles offshore. Service or HN petroleum distribution systems ashore help complete the conveyance of petroleum from ship to shore and store petroleum products until transferred to tankers for inland transportation. In addition, two aviation support vessels are pre-positioned for the Marine Corps; one each is stationed on the East Coast and the West Coast of the US.

b. **Forward Stocking.** DLA's OCONUS distribution sites are located in Germany, Italy, Bahrain, Korea, Japan, Guam, and Hawaii. These depots offer OCONUS customers opportunities to forward position stock and enhance the in-theater distribution system by enabling more timely delivery of parts and supplies. DLA Distribution sites in Southwest Asia, Germany, and Korea also have theater consolidation and shipping point (TCSP) capabilities.

(1) **DLA Defense Distribution Expeditionary Depot (DDED).** The DDED is an integral component of DLA's integrated distribution strategy, which combines land-based forward stocks, CONUS depots, and a deployable distribution center for expeditionary operations. The DDED provides a deployable DLA distribution management and warehouse capability to support GCC operational requirements from within a theater. Fixed-base forward stock locations and DLA CONUS depots are potential sources of supply for the DDED.

(2) The DDED provides an in-theater DLA face to the GCC and Service component logistic headquarters that enables better control, management, and visibility of materiel flowing from national sources to the theater and ultimately the end user. It is scalable to GCC requirements and is capable of supporting troop densities up to 120k. It provides distribution, forward stocking, and information management capabilities over Class I, II, IIIP, IV, VIII, and IX supplies. In addition to forward positioning selected DLA-managed items, the DDED also stocks selected fast-moving Service and GSA-managed items.

(3) The forward deployment of the DDED reduces the friction that normally occurs at seams in the JDDE. Placing this capability forward results in DLA's supporting role taking on added significance and making it a stakeholder in theater distribution operations.

(4) Specific DDED capabilities include a forward stocking capability; breakbulk operations; TCSP operations; in-theater distribution expertise; receipt, storage, and issue of wholesale supplies; and materiel visibility. Forward positioning these capabilities reduces overall customer wait time (CWT), improves joint theater logistic capabilities, and reduces requirements for scarce strategic lift resources.

9. Intermodal Operations and Capabilities

Deployment operations can involve intermodal movement of personnel and equipment by air, land, and sea from unit installations or depots to the theater of operations. Intermodalism is simply the transferring of passengers or transshipping of cargo among two or more modes of transportation (e.g., sea, highway, rail, and air). In concert with intermodalism, containerization facilitates and optimizes carrying cargo via multiple modes of transport without intermediate handling of the container contents. Efficient and effective use of intermodalism and containerization is critical for mobility and transportation support to single-Service or joint operations worldwide. The following considerations apply to intermodal platform use:

a. **Mobility and Readiness.** The objective of joint planning and execution is to prepare, deploy, employ, support, sustain, and redeploy forces assigned or committed to an AOR. To the greatest extent possible, DOD uses commercial and organic intermodal transportation that is flexible and fast to accomplish this mission.

(1) The DOD airlift system is keyed to fast response using both military aircraft and contracted commercial aircraft, as required. Common-user organic military aircraft and certain commercial aircraft can be configured to rapidly load equipment using RO/RO ramps and standard 463L pallet systems.

(2) The surface transportation system uses highway, rail, and inland waterway systems to move materiel to APOEs or SPOEs for loading on intertheater airlift and sealift assets. Rolling stock can be loaded directly on railcars using end or side ramps; this facilitates fast loading at installations and discharge at POEs during deployment operations. Intermodal containers can be quickly loaded or unloaded from railcars using container-handling equipment (CHE) or gantry cranes. Containers moved by highway can proceed

directly to pier-side for loading aboard containerships using container terminal gantry cranes or ship's cranes. They also may be offloaded from the chassis by specially designed CHE and positioned in the terminal's container yard for loading aboard ship. Containers moved by railcar, which normally do not have direct pier-side access, require CHE for off-load and transfer to pier-side.

(3) The DOD sealift system is designed to provide rapid support using GO and chartered vessels. A significant number of the vessels are self-sustaining RO/RO vessels, characterized by large cargo capacities and rapid loading and discharge rates. Commercial containership capability is available to DOD through time or voyage charters and on a day-to-day basis via commercial contracts with US flag ocean carriers. These contracts, managed by USTRANSCOM, provide complete door-to-door intermodal services that include use of containers/flatracks, line haul transportation for positioning containers at installations/depots, moving loaded containers to SPOEs, port/terminal services, space aboard carrier's vessels, and offload/onward movement in theaters of operations. Containerships can be rapidly loaded using intermodal systems. Training, planning, and preparation to deploy unit equipment, ammunition, and follow-on sustainment using RO/RO vessels and containerships allow responsive and effective support to the GCC.

b. **Synchronized Flow of Materiel and Information.** Assets and systems have been designed and employed to facilitate the rapid movement of personnel, equipment, supplies, and information with minimum impediments to the deployment flow.

(1) In the surface transportation system, RO/RO vessels and containerships are linked to land transportation (highway or rail) through port and water terminal systems that provide for a smooth, seamless flow of equipment and materiel from mode to mode. RO/RO vessels provide the primary means of strategic sealift for initial unit deployment and unit equipment (e.g., tanks, towed artillery, armored infantry fighting vehicles, and rolling stock), whereas containerships are the ideal means of transport for sustainment, ammunition, and resupply. However, due to the limited numbers of RO/RO vessels, all forces must be prepared to deploy using containerships to the maximum extent possible. Accompanying supplies and equipment, to include ammunition, are well suited for containerization and rapid deployment using containerships. While other ship types (e.g., breakbulk, barge carriers) also represent intermodal sealift assets, they primarily augment RO/RO vessels and containership capability when this is insufficient for the operation being undertaken, when theater infrastructure constraints dictate, or when the tactical mission or situation precludes use of containers in delivering materiel and equipment.

(2) In the air transportation system, military assets are configured to allow for RO/RO of equipment or rapid loading or unloading using the 463L pallet system. The pallet and net resources are in high demand during deployment surge and sustainment operations, but while it is preferred that 463L assets remain in the airlift system, some system components may have to move intermodally via surface transportation in support of the GCC's objectives and priorities. However, due to the intermodal utility of the pallet system and the significant cost to replace these assets, it is critical that plans be made for their return from end destination locations back into the DTS. Responsibility for controlling and returning 463L equipment to the airlift system remains with the GCC.

(3) DOD AISs are designed to interface with commercial transportation information systems to receive and pass required personnel, unit, and cargo movement data and other transportation information to appropriate commands and agencies throughout the DTS. This capability exists to the extent that commercial carriers have formatted their electronic data interchange (EDI) reports to DOD standards or through use of AIT.

c. **Origin to Destination.** Effective intermodal movement of personnel, equipment, and supplies begins at the origin and continues unimpeded to the final destination.

d. **Standardization.** Intermodal containers are transportation assets designed to maximize cargo throughput with minimum handling of cargo at mode transfer points. This capability demands standardization for ease of handling.

(1) Intermodal containers used within the DOD surface transportation system for international trade are designed to conform to the American National Standards Institute (ANSI) and International Organization for Standardization (ISO) specifications.

(2) Intermodal containers and airlift pallets used within the airlift system conform to the military 463L pallet standard.

e. **Container Status and ITV**

(1) Container status and ITV of cargo are essential for effective and efficient use of intermodal platforms. GCCs and their components need to know where their critical resources are and when those resources will arrive. This provides the situational awareness required to execute or modify courses of action (COAs), the CONOPS, and schemes of maneuver during joint operations. GCCs are also responsible for managing the use of AIT and AISs within the AOR. The supporting CCDRs and other DOD agencies use this information to prioritize, allocate, and reroute resources between theaters.

(2) The visibility of all containers moving in the DTS (DOD-owned, leased, or commercial) and their contents must be available to the CJCS, CCMDs, Services, and supporting components via an automated capability. This includes containers that contain excess property which is available for redistribution in the theater. Identification and status information should include type of ISO container, location, and status (loaded or empty). DOD has developed and continues refining IT systems to provide ITV capability. These must be interoperable with commercial systems and other DOD supply, transportation, and in-theater systems supporting movement of materiel from origin outload, through distribution operations, to the end user in theater.

f. **Cargo Integrity, Security, and Safety.** The large size of containerships, along with state-of-the-art commercial and developing DOD ITV systems and the inherent security of ISO containers, facilitates unit integrity and cargo security. When using modern intermodal lift capability, adhere to unit integrity objectives of the shipping Service and maintain them at the highest level possible consistent with cargo types and capability and/or capacity of vessels involved. Intermodal containers decrease pilferage, injury to personnel, and damage to equipment and supplies. This is particularly important when moving unit basic loads and resupplying quantities of ammunition.

10. Commercial Distribution Capabilities

DOD has increased its reliance on the commercial sector to perform specific or multiple supply chain functions and, to that end, global distribution operations leverage numerous commercial sector capabilities.

a. **Vendor Support.** Increased use of vendor capabilities is a major method of increasing the value, velocity, and efficiency of distribution support to the joint force while also decreasing the "footprint" of logistic support. The transfer of government inventory and distribution capabilities to vendors decreases requirements on organic military assets. However, the potential exists for commercial distribution channels to become constrained or restricted under wartime conditions, resulting in an influx of commercial-origin materiel entering at a variety of points into the DOD distribution system. Vendor support contractual agreements should include control provisions that allow shipment schedules to be adjusted to promote a smooth interface of vendor shipments into the distribution pipeline. These contracts should also ensure contractors provide the JDDE with required movement visibility throughout the shipment process.

(1) **PV.** PV is a vendor support process that provides commercial products to regionally grouped military activities and federal customers from commercial distributors using electronic commerce methods. The process uses long-term contracts that set forth price, product, and delivery agreements for a variety of goods. Customers order directly from the vendor and receive materiel through the vendor's commercial distribution system. The subsistence and medical PV programs, for example, take advantage of the existing industry infrastructure and inventory to achieve rapid direct shipment from vendor to customer. Receiving fresher, brand name products faster increases customer satisfaction and significantly reduces DOD inventory holding and distribution costs. PV programs are widely used in CONUS and have been implemented OCONUS for selected commodities.

(2) **Virtual Prime Vendor (VPV).** VPV is a vendor support technique to provide a complete logistic solution covering numerous commodity and product lines to the customer. VPVs are integrators who make use of commercial and government inventories, contracts, and other means to provide logistic support within DLA and the Services for both maintenance and supply functions ranging from aircraft component repair to recruit training uniform issue. VPV functions include forecasting requirements, inventory control, mechanical engineering support, technical services, storage, distribution, and any other functions required to satisfy customers' needs. Like PV arrangements, VPV is also enabled by electronic commerce.

(3) **Customer Direct (CD).** CD (formerly direct vendor delivery) is a streamlined distribution method that requires vendor delivery directly to a customer or DTS transshipment point. CD may reduce both CWT and the workload on the military distribution system. CD complements some or all of the JDDE. As an added benefit, CD can eliminate DOD depot shelf-life and handling problems inherent in some commodities, such as light bulbs (fragile), camera and X-ray film (short shelf-life and special storage), and motor oil (hazardous material storage and handling). CD efforts include a customer-transparent paperless ordering interface with military standard requisitioning and issue

procedures (MILSTRIPs). CD may present the joint and Service logistic planners and operators with significant challenges in integrating CD into theater-level distribution operations.

(4) **Civil Augmentation Programs.** Civil augmentation programs enable peacetime planning for the use of civilian contractors in wartime and other contingencies. These contractors can perform selected distribution services to support US forces in support of DOD missions. Civil augmentation programs are primarily designed for use in areas where no bilateral or multilateral agreements exist. However, these programs may provide additional support in areas with formal HNS agreements, where other contractors are involved, or where peacetime support contracts exist. They are also available during CONUS mobilizations to assist the CONUS support base and help units get ready for deployment. Civil augmentation programs, such as the Army's logistics civil augmentation program (LOGCAP), the Navy's Global Contingency Construction Contract Program (operated by the Naval Facilities Engineering Command), and the Air Force contract augmentation program (AFCAP) (operated by the Air Force Civil Engineer Support Agency), also play a significant role in mission accomplishment by providing the JFC and joint force engineer with additional options and flexibility in general/civil engineering and logistic support. If use of a civil augmentation program is contemplated, planners must consider the impact of contractor logistic needs on limited transportation and infrastructure assets.

b. **Government Purchase Card (GPC).** The cardholder uses the GPC to make purchases from commercial or selected government sources, up to the authorized limit for the user. The GPC reduces requisition processing time and facilitates decentralized buying by nonprocurement personnel. Caution should be exercised when using the GPC during contingency or wartime due to lack of ITV and purchases moving outside of the approved distribution networks, which may preclude delivery to final destination or disrupt the flow of more critical materiel. Cardholders should contact their transportation officer to ensure commercial or government sources apply proper packaging, documentation, and shipment funding to shipments entering the DTS. Transportation should be most advantageous to the government.

c. **Contract Surge and Sustainment Requirements.** As DOD continues to downsize and reduce materiel inventories, new strategies must be used to assure access to commercial inventories and production capabilities to satisfy surge and sustainment needs. In forming partnerships to develop surge and sustainment capabilities with contractors, it may be essential to require efforts beyond, and sometimes inconsistent with, contractors' customary business practices. This necessitates the consideration of surge and sustainment requirements in business arrangements and long-term contracts. These requirements include processes to ensure that contractor capabilities actually exist and to validate those capabilities through testing and DOD exercises.

d. **Internet Materiel Ordering.** DOD Internet-based materiel ordering systems have consolidated previously separated functions, for both customers and providers, into fast, convenient electronic outlets that are accessible worldwide and available around the clock. For example, the DOD Internet-based electronic mall provides a single point of entry for customers to find and acquire off-the-shelf, finished goods from the commercial marketplace with point, click, and ship GPC buying from commercial catalogs.

Intentionally Blank

CHAPTER III
DISTRIBUTION PLANNING

> *"Logistic considerations belong not only in the highest echelons of military planning during the process of preparation for war and for specific wartime operations, but may well become the controlling element with relation to timing and successful operation."*
>
> **Vice Admiral Oscar C. Badger, United States Navy**
> **Address to the Naval War College, 1954**

1. Introduction

a. **Purpose.** This chapter outlines the planning considerations for effective distribution operations.

b. **Overview.** Distribution planning is an important part of the overall joint operation planning process (JOPP) and is integrated into all seven JOPP steps. It must include detailed analysis and evaluation of the distribution networks and functions supporting the end-to-end distribution process, as well as encompass the full range of activities necessary to plan for national mobilization, deployment, employment, sustainment, and redeployment requirements of forces and materiel.

c. The products of successful distribution planning are distribution plans that are articulated in the annexes and supporting plans of a CCDR's OPLANs/CONPLANs and operation orders (OPORDs). CCMD distribution plans must guide the planning of other supporting commands and organizations within DOD, as well as USG departments and agencies, and HNs that will be supporting the CCMD. Appendix C, "Commander's Checklist for Distribution of Materiel and Movement of Forces," contains a generic list of issues or questions that distribution planners should consider when they integrate distribution activities into OPLANs/CONPLANs or OPORDs. The questions in this checklist can be used to develop a distribution appendix to annex D (Logistics) to an OPLAN/CONPLAN.

2. Planning Functions and Key Joint Deployment and Distribution Enterprise Planning Tasks

a. **Planning Functions.** Planning and resultant activities or operations should aim to defuse strategic problems before they become crises and resolve crises before they reach a critical stage requiring large-scale operations. Steady-state activities should support these ends and, at the same time, set the conditions for success should military operations become necessary. The theater campaign plan and campaign support plans are designed to do this. Theater campaign plans provide the vehicle for linking steady-state shaping activities to current operations and contingency plans. Planning should translate strategic guidance and direction into OPLANs and OPORDs for contingency or crisis action response. From a logistician's perspective it is important for the CCDRs and operations planners to understand the capabilities and limitations of available core logistic capabilities. To that end, the joint logistician is deeply involved in each of the planning functions and assists in preparing the logistic portion and/or supplement for a plan supporting the CCDR's strategic context and assumptions, global priorities, and missions.

(1) **Strategic Guidance.** The Guidance for Employment of the Force (GEF) and the Joint Strategic Capabilities Plan (JSCP) are the principal sources of guidance for CCDR steady-state campaign, contingency, and posture planning efforts. The GEF consolidates and integrates DOD planning guidance related to operations and other military activities into a single, overarching guidance document. The JSCP implements the strategic policy direction provided in the GEF and initiates the planning process for the development of campaign, campaign support, contingency, and posture plans. USTRANSCOM, DLA, and other logistics supporting organizations conduct strategic dialogue with the supported CCMD planners to inform the process earlier and provide near real-time planning factors. Key distribution planning input includes detailed information on airfields, seaports, road, rail, fuel, and bridging capabilities, and other critical infrastructure. Key information required for distribution planning and operations should also be identified in the commander's critical information requirements, including priority intelligence requirements (PIRs), articulated in the annexes and supporting plans of the CCDR's OPLANs, CONPLANs, and OPORDs.

(2) **Concept Development.** Logistic support concept development must begin at the inception of maneuver concept development and continue in parallel throughout COA development. This includes identifying requirements and critical items and services needed while being fully aware of force structure planning, TPFDD development, and JRSOI operations. Within this planning function concepts of support (addressing supply, maintenance, deployment and distribution, health services, engineering, logistic services, and operational contract support) are developed in order to meet sustainment requirements from theater entry and operations, through redeployment and reset. It is not uncommon for logistic and support operations to begin prior to, or concurrent with, planning. Thus logistic planners need to remain flexible and sensitive to the ever-evolving operational requirements and changing force structure/organization of the joint force.

(3) **Plan Development.** A clear understanding of the CONOPS is essential to the joint logistician's ability to meet joint force requirements. Because logistic support is provided through a variety of organizations, joint logistic planning provides the coordination mechanism to achieve synergy and unity of effort from all sources of distribution support. The joint logistic concept of support specifies how capabilities will be delivered over time, it identifies who is responsible for delivering a capability, and it defines the critical logistical tasks necessary to achieve objectives during the phases of the operation. The logistic concept of support coordinates the capabilities of joint forces and MNFs, the HN, other USG departments and agencies, IGOs, and nongovernmental organizations (NGOs). The deliverable product at the conclusion of plan development is a completed joint logistic concept of support which resides in the base plan and logistic annex to an OPLAN/OPORD.

(a) **Support Plan Development.** The purpose of support planning is to determine the sequence of the personnel, logistics, and other support required to provide supply, maintenance, deployment and distribution, health services, engineering, logistic services, and operational contract support IAW the CONOPS. Support planning is conducted in parallel with other planning, and encompasses such essential factors as lead agent or EA (if designated) identification; assignment of responsibility for base operating support; airfield and seaport operations; health services; aeromedical evacuation (AE); personnel services; handling of detainees; theater general engineer construction standards and policy; logistic-related environmental considerations; support of noncombatant evacuation operations and other retrograde operations; disposal operations; and HN assistance.

(b) Support planning is primarily the responsibility of the Service component commanders and begins during CONOPS development. Service component commanders identify and update support requirements in coordination with the Services, DLA, and USTRANSCOM. They initiate the procurement of critical and low-density inventory items; determine HNS availability; develop plans for AV; and establish phased delivery plans for sustainment in line with the phases and priorities of the CONOPS. They develop plans for battle damage repair; retrograde of reparables; container management; force and LOCs protection; and transportation and support that are aligned with the CONOPS. Service component commanders continue to refine their sustainment and transportation requirements as the force providers identify resources and source force requirements.

(c) During distribution planning, the supported CCDR and USTRANSCOM resolve gross transportation feasibility questions impacting intertheater and intratheater movement and delivery of sustainment supplies. USTRANSCOM and other transportation providers identify air, land, and sea transportation resources to support the approved CONOPS. These resources may include apportioned intertheater transportation, GCC-controlled theater transportation, and transportation organic to the subordinate commands. USTRANSCOM, its TCCs, the supported CCMD, and in specific cases a designated network owner or contributor (e.g., the Northern Distribution Network), other CCMDs, and the Department of State (DOS) must assess the availability of LOCs and their impact on deployment, sustainment, and redeployment/retrograde of personnel and equipment. This includes the potential requirement for the use of commercial transportation assets in lieu of Service or CULT assets.

(d) Alternative LOCs should be a critical planning factor during phase 0 distribution planning negotiations between USTRANSCOM, in its global distribution operations role, and the geographic CCMDs. USTRANSCOM synchronizes distribution planning through the Global Campaign Plan for Distribution, specifically across the GCC's theater campaign plans, to set conditions during phase 0 for successful global distribution operations. USTRANSCOM and other transportation providers develop transportation schedules for movement requirements identified by the supported commander. A transportation schedule does not necessarily mean that the supported commander's CONOPS is transportation feasible; rather, the schedules provide the most effective and realistic use of available transportation resources in relation to the phased CONOPS.

For more information on deployment planning and shortfall identification, see JP 5-0, Joint Operation Planning.

(4) **Assessment.** CCDR campaign plan assessments are integrated into the CJCS deliberate assessment process. This provides the CJCS an assessment on how well the

command is executing the strategic guidance provided in the GEF and JSCP. The assessment includes the most pressing issues, force and resource limitations, risk drivers, and mitigation requirements. Guidance concerning assessments of campaign support plans is provided in each of the appendices tasking campaign support plans. The use of war games, simulations, or exercises often enables joint logisticians to work directly with the operations planners as they seek to conduct assessments and identify risk. Rehearsals are used as another tool to assess the effectiveness of the concept of support, to familiarize supporting joint forces with the concept, and to provide all concerned with confidence in the selected concept. In order to monitor the progress or effectiveness of plans in execution, logisticians and various subject matter experts identify expected outcomes from the concept of support that will be used to assess logistic progress.

b. **Key Distribution Planning Tasks.** Distribution planning tasks provide guidance to logistic planners assessing the adequacy and feasibility of concepts of support for campaign plans and OPLANs. Distribution planning should address the following tasks:

(1) **Analyze Force Requirement and Sourcing.** Operational planners conduct deliberate planning, crisis action planning (CAP), and ongoing operational planning for rotational and emergent force requirements. Specific procedures for how these types of planning occur and shortfalls are addressed and specified in JP 5-0, *Joint Operation Planning*; CJCSM 3122, *Joint Operation Planning and Execution System (JOPES) Series*; CJCSM 3130, *Adaptive Planning and Execution (APEX) Series*; and SecDef's *Global Force Management Implementation Guidance.* During the planning process, personnel and logistic requirements are evaluated to assess force sustainability and transportation feasibility and to develop an end-to-end distribution concept. This process involves coordination and cooperation with supporting commands and agencies. Supporting CCDRs and agencies confirm resource availability and support materiel requirements during execution planning. Knowledge of force sourcing decisions is critical to the acceptability, adequacy, and feasibility of the concept of support and sustainment planning. All planners must understand the relationship between the employment of forces and current distribution concepts for various sustainment and commodity supply chains. This allows logistic planners to be able to incorporate new distribution capabilities.

(2) **Verify Sustainment.** Sustainment planning is directed toward providing and maintaining levels of forces, materiel, and consumables required to sustain the planned type of activity for the appropriate duration and at the desired level of intensity. **Sustainment planning is the responsibility of the supported CCDRs, in close coordination with USTRANSCOM, the Services, and DOD agencies.** Detailed planning is necessary to determine sustainment requirements from the beginning of the deployment force flow, determine available resources to fill identified sustainment requirements, and validate and reconcile sustainment shortfalls. Sustainment planning is an iterative and continual refinement process. **With the increased emphasis on reduced Service logistic footprints, the importance of up-front sustainment planning cannot be overstated.** Sustainment requirements included in CCMD plans and orders must be realistic and reflect the detailed distribution analysis required to allow timely materiel support. An additional requirement of sustainment planning is a mechanism to capture and provide visibility of intratheater excess property, especially expendable items such as Class IV construction materiel.

NORTHERN DISTRIBUTION NETWORK

When Pakistan's government halted United States ground shipments through Pakistan to Afghanistan in late November 2011, United States Transportation Command (USTRANSCOM) had already increased its use of the Northern Distribution Network (NDN), several integrated supply routes deliberately established as an alternative surface transportation option in 2009 and expanded in 2010-2011. From 2002 on, US forces supporting Operation ENDURING FREEDOM in Afghanistan relied on the Pakistan ground lines of communication as the most direct and least expensive surface transportation route. In 2011, more than 35,000 containers were delivered from the Pakistan port of Karachi to Afghanistan via commercial trucks using Pakistan's roads. The NDN started with a "proof of principle" test shipment from Latvia through Russia to Afghanistan completed on 14 March 2009. NDN became an ongoing supply operation of commercial goods by private commercial carriers in May 2009. NDN points of entry expanded from the Latvia/Russia route to include a total of seven routes. In 2011, 27,000 containers of supplies were sent to troops in Afghanistan over the NDN, an increase of 15 percent over 2010. The proven flexibility the NDN provided in supporting troops in theater is now being expanded to support current force levels in Afghanistan and to facilitate the planned drawdown. USTRANSCOM is working with United States Central Command, United States European Command, and industry partners and the nations supporting the NDN to build capacity and velocity in movements out of the area of operations. As of January 2013, all NDN routes have agreements in place and proofs of principle either complete or in progress, validating the ability of the NDN to reverse flow.

SOURCE: Various Sources

(3) **Analyze Transportation.** Supported CCDRs develop concepts of deployment based upon mission taskings found in Chairman of the Joint Chiefs of Staff Instruction (CJCSI) 3110.01, *Joint Strategic Planning System,* and detailed guidance contained in CJCSI 3110.03, *Logistics Supplement to the Joint Strategic Capabilities Plan* (classified SECRET with limited distribution). During planning, subordinate component commanders are tasked to determine specific forces (unit) and materiel (nonunit) requirements (including personnel replacements) and recommended time-phasing of these requirements. Component command force and support requirements are submitted to the supported CCDR who coordinates these requirements with other requirements to develop the TPFDD. Strategic movement requirements are analyzed against apportioned transportation lift by USTRANSCOM, to determine gross transportation feasibility of plans and operations as well as a cost estimate. Refinements are made to the total movement plan, as required, and the TCCs prepare movement tables for the plan or operation.

(4) **Assess Networks and Distribution Network Limitations.** Distribution network limitations are the factors that place limits on global distribution networks and functions through mobilization, deployment, JRSOI, employment, sustainment, and redeployment during joint operations. Logistic planners must determine and understand

these factors so they are capable of offsetting potential network constraints or can make informed tradeoff decisions to adapt to potential constraints.

(a) **Physical Network Limitations.** Physical network limitations are **restrictions in the flow of materiel for CONUS, intertheater, and intratheater movements.** These restrictions also can be described as bottlenecks or conditions that limit or degrade the ability of the distribution system to support a campaign or operation. Planners must identify and offset or adapt to these limitations. Identifying limitations en route to or within the theater is the first step in coordinating activities to avoid overloading theater LOCs. Historically, limited numbers of ports and airfields, limited unloading capacity at ports and airfields, lack of AV, and limited inland transportation have negatively affected logistic support of combat forces. During Operation ENDURING FREEDOM, the main limitation was the inability to secure a ground line of communications (GLOC) to/from Afghanistan. GLOC limitations impact not only the physical distribution of cargo, but also geopolitical associations and financial planning. Distribution and deployment planners must anticipate congestion and seek solutions to these limitations. **An infrastructure assessment is essential to understanding the capabilities and limitations of the theater to support distribution operations.** It serves as the basis to determine the amount and type of support personnel and materiel that must be deployed early to facilitate the deployment of combat forces, as well as for determining facility upgrades required to enhance operations. The supported CCDR, with assistance as required from USTRANSCOM, determines whether the theater is adequate for employment of assets, forces, facilities, and supporting systems. In cases where the theater is inadequate, distribution options available to the supported CCDR include increasing the infrastructure capacity, reducing the distribution flow, or extending allowable force closure times.

(b) **Financial Network Limitations.** Financial network limitations are **factors that may restrict fiscal resource availability for distribution operations.** The immediate concern to planners is the adequacy of funding, the authority and ability to access that funding, and the ability to disburse financial resources to obtain needed distribution capabilities and materiel. The compartmentalized nature of DOD financial apportionment between the Services and DOD agencies may affect both long-term and short-term elements of global distribution. Planners may influence long-term financial apportionment through the establishment of materiel and capabilities requirements in CCMD campaign plans, OPLANs, and CONPLANs.

(c) **Communications System Limitations**

1. **Information Network Limitations.** Information network **limitations may affect the flow of information or the utility of that information.** Planners must identify potential information network limitations and take action to offset or adapt to them. **Compatibility limitations, particularly when dealing with multinational, HN, or commercial partners, may affect information network operations.** Capacity limitations may arise when network operations surge from peacetime to wartime, contingency operations, or humanitarian assistance/disaster relief levels. Restrictions imposed for operations security purposes may shut down or limit access to some peacetime information networks used in the global distribution process.

2. **Communications Network Limitations.** Communications network limitations are **physical or administrative restrictions within the communications network** that may limit the amount of logistic information flow over communications systems below that which is needed to effectively conduct logistic operations. Planners must recognize these potential limitations and take action to increase the network capacity available for logistic communications and information flow, or establish alternative communications methods, which are not in competition with higher priority users. Joint communications systems such as Global Command and Control System (GCCS)–Joint and Global Combat Support System–Joint (GCSS-J), in concert with Service communications capabilities, provide the means to achieve the unity of effort necessary to conduct distribution operations.

(5) **Refine Logistic Support.** Logistic refinement is the **process of resolving shortfalls in logistic support during the planning process.** Service sourcing agencies, DLA, CCMD components, and supporting CCMDs conduct it under the overall direction of the Joint Staff and the supported CCDR during deliberate planning and CAP. During deliberate planning, USTRANSCOM hosts force flow refinement conferences for the Joint Staff and supported CCMDs to review OPLAN logistic support. **The purpose of the force flow refinement conference is to confirm sourcing of logistic requirements IAW GEF, JSCP, Joint Staff, and Service guidance and to assess the adequacy of resources determined by support planning.** The deployment and distribution community begins refinement of a TPFDD when the supported CCMD provides a completely sourced and adequate TPFDD. Sourcing includes identification of facilities and materiel support requirements. During the force flow refinement conferences, the CCMDs, Services, and DOD agencies will resolve problems related to unit and nonunit personnel, cargo, retrograde, medical evacuation, and resupply. At the conclusion of the force flow refinement conference, USTRANSCOM will reassess gross transportation feasibility for the supported CCDR to ensure that the TPFDD can be executed. **The refined TPFDD articulates the CCDR's distribution concept and highlights joint force materiel requirements.** If the TPFDD fails transportation feasibility analysis, deployment and distribution planners must consider alternative actions to achieve deployment and sustainment goals within the envelope of transportation capability. Creating or increasing theater materiel stocks and shifting pre-positioning ships are potential responses to transportation shortfalls. Refinement of logistic support during CAP is conducted using the same considerations as deliberate planning, with the fundamental difference being constraints on the time available to conduct refinement.

(6) **Review Logistics Support Analysis (LSA). LSA is a continuous process during the development and maintenance of CCDR OPLANs and CONPLANs that assesses requirements and sourcing of requirements at all levels.** LSA provides a broad assessment of key logistic factors by documenting the results of a process that assures an integrated evaluation of key logistic capabilities, identifying logistic support deficiencies, assessing their risks, and providing a baseline for the Joint Monthly Readiness Review (JMRR) process. **LSA describes and assesses combined support capabilities, and validates planned distribution concepts.** Preparation of this analysis is a two-step process. It begins with the Services' and DOD agencies' assessment of their ability to support a CCDR's plan, followed by the CCDR's assessment of the inputs along with analysis of

theater requirements and capabilities. Where other portions of the JMRR assess the readiness of the commodity stocks against the total requirement, LSA identifies possible shortcomings in the distribution system. During the planning process, only the commodity requirements that would actually enter the TPFDD on execution should be considered, including all substitutions and secondary stock. LSA assesses the impact on the distribution system as reflected in the movement of large numbers of substitute and secondary weapons that carry significantly different logistic requirements.

(7) **Develop Commodity Distribution Concepts.** Logistic planners must develop a distribution concept for each commodity's supply chain. This is accomplished by determining the impact of each element of global distribution on the commodity's supply chain and adjusting or adapting as necessary to meet the requirements of the supported CCDR's CONOPS and concept of support. It is critical to tie all commodity supply chains together by adding up all the requirements, and then comparing the sum total to resources needed to execute the distribution plan.

(8) **Ensure Protection.** Comprehensive protection requires the employment of the full array of active and passive measures and the integration and coordination of intelligence and security programs, information operations, risk management techniques, and safety programs to increase individual awareness of potential threats. Planning for weapons of mass destruction effects, operating in a chemical, biological, radiological, and nuclear (CBRN) environment, and decontamination operations should also be considered, especially when supporting CBRN consequence management operations.

(9) **Plan for Retrograde.** The retrograde and redistribution of materiel occurs in almost all operations. Unserviceable assets that cannot be repaired in the field should be rapidly returned to the appropriate repair centers (sometimes CONUS) or depots for repair. Ensuring rapid, effective, and traceable retrograde shipment for repairable spares is a vital part of planning and operating a distribution system. Whether a unit is redeploying and is leaving some equipment behind, or is trying to redistribute its serviceable excess materiel, or is trying to dispose of its unserviceable excess and/or HW, it must plan and coordinate its actions as a part of the distribution system. Larger movements for retrograde require more assets, time, and planning. Where exposure to CBRN contamination is possible, plans should include decontamination prior to unit movement.

See JP 3-11, Operations in Chemical, Biological, Radiological, and Nuclear Environments, *and JP 3-41,* Chemical, Biological, Radiological, and Nuclear Consequence Management, *for additional guidance on operations in CBRN environments and CBRN consequence management.*

3. Distribution Planning Considerations

Distribution planning is a form of support planning completed using the CCDR's guidance and mission statement as stated in the supported commander's CONOPS. The essence of distribution planning is determining the joint force requirements and identifying the needed capabilities. Sourcing and resourcing for both must be verified. Requirements to be distributed and the associated capabilities needed must be integrated into the formal joint operation planning processes and systems frameworks. The product of successful distribution planning is a supply and distribution scheme able to anticipate operational requirements regardless of the environment. This concept must be supported by current, relevant, and accurate planning factors. This enables continuous planning and transportation analysis during the strategic guidance, concept development, plan development, and plan assessment phases. These distribution planning considerations must be articulated in distribution annexes within CCMD plans and orders. These distribution plans must guide the planning of supporting commands and organizations within DOD, external departments and agencies, and HNs that will be supporting mission execution.

a. **Deployment/Redeployment and Sustainment/Retrograde.** Planners must avoid focusing solely on deployment tasks at the expense of distribution and retrograde actions needed to sustain the employment concept of the campaign or operation. If the campaign or operation extends beyond a single unit rotation, planners must take into account the requirement to sustain the force while conducting deployment and redeployment operations. Depending on the length of the operation, factors such as the use of theater-provided equipment vice each unit deploying/redeploying with its own equipment must be weighed. Distribution planners must be prepared to meet the delicate balance required to execute these tasks while supporting the CCDR. In addition, the ability to capture and provide visibility of theater excess and its redistribution requirements will have an impact on lift planning. Finally, retrograde shipping of repairable assets must be given the appropriate level of planning, visibility, and resources to ensure a viable repair pipeline to and from repair centers at all echelons.

See JP 3-35, Deployment and Redeployment Operations, *for additional planning guidance on deployment, redeployment, sustainment, and retrograde.*

b. **Surge Planning Considerations. Surge is the ability to meet increased requirements for goods or services caused by rapidly increased demands during war or other contingencies.** Typically, surge requirements are directed at the industrial base and the transportation industry. Identified surge requirements are communicated to the industrial base and transportation industry and analyzed to determine a COA to rapidly meet the emergent demand. Planners must understand the following: surge capabilities, the avenues available to fulfill initial demands, the surge requirements that the transportation system can support, and what special requirements or procedures need to be put in place to accommodate surge demand. **With limited DOD-owned inventories, the reliance on the industrial base for timely resupply has grown.** In addition to incoming surges of goods and personnel, planners must also consider surges associated with redeployment, retrograde of repairable items, and theater redistribution requirements. While the impact on the supply system may be different, the impact on the transportation system can be just as significant and possibly even more complex.

See JP 4-10, Operational Contract Support, *for additional information.*

(1) **Industrial Base Surge.** Strategic level organizations and CCMD distribution planners must factor response times for mobilization of the industrial base into plans to support their operations. Definitive DOD plans to support a CCMD must be in place prior to

the start of any campaign or operation to facilitate timely response from the Services, DLA, and industry. Although the greatest demand normally occurs within the first 30 to 60 days of an operation, industrial surge to meet the demands of more prolonged operations or campaigns requires significant additional time to build to maximum output. DOD will frequently compete with private sector customers for a manufacturer's industrial capacity and inventories.

(2) **Transportation Surge.** USTRANSCOM, in conjunction with its TCCs and the commercial transportation industry, determines lift availability and assesses the need for mobility augmentation based on projected movement requirements to support proposed COAs. **Shortfalls in strategic common-user transportation assets may cause activation of several stand-by programs** to augment military capability. In addition, depending on movement control requirements, port support activities, and the theater reception capability required for a particular operation, USTRANSCOM assets might be required to facilitate and manage transportation. For example, SDDC will assess CONUS surface transportation and common-user water terminal management requirements for both CONUS and OCONUS. AMC will assess anticipated CRAF requirements. SDDC, MSC, and the Maritime Administration will review the MARAD RRF and VISA for possible augmentation requirements.

c. **Planning Focus.** Distribution planners must understand the supported CCDR's CONOPS and be intimately familiar with the major activities that occur in each phase of the joint force projection scenario as well as understand the unique implications on movement requirements. Early involvement by the logistic staffs and planners during deliberate planning and CAP is paramount. Distribution planning focuses on the transition from peacetime military and associated commercial distribution techniques to those required for contingency or wartime operations. Planners must consider the impact and limitations that their distribution CONOPS will have on war or contingency operations on each of the distribution networks and functions involved in the flow of materiel. The product of distribution planning is an appendix to a logistic annex of a plan. The appendix should be prepared by supporting and supported commanders and must be designed to provide a versatile and continual flow of materiel to support dynamic operational requirements.

d. **Planning Balance. Distribution planning must synchronize and balance materiel distribution flow with the other operational processes,** such as deployment of military units and their accompanying logistic resources, to bring them together at the decisive place and time. Moreover, distribution planning must ensure that intertheater and intratheater deployment and sustainment including redistribution of excess assets and disposal requirements are balanced and compatible with the theater's JRSOI and distribution capabilities. In addition, distribution planning should ensure that these requirements can be satisfied within the resource constraints imposed on the supported commander for mission execution. Collaboration sessions with USTRANSCOM, force providers, Services, and supporting/supported commands are necessary to carefully coordinate the movement of materiel and forces in a balanced approach. Integration of distribution requirements and force projection occurs during TPFDD force flow conferences, is further refined through the validation phase of the TPFDD, and is continuously fine-tuned through the execution phase through collaborative meetings between the stakeholders.

(1) **Balance between the Services and Other Organizations.** Distribution balance issues become more complex when MNFs, US Service components, and international organizations/NGOs operate simultaneously within the theater and the LOCs approaching the theater. **Coordination of distribution functions among all affected commands, nations, agencies, and organizations is essential** to gain control of networks, avoid congestion at critical nodes, and reduce duplication of effort.

(2) **Balancing Distribution Requirements with Operational Requirements.** Planners will be continuously challenged to provide the proper balance of combat forces, support forces, and materiel support within the time constraints imposed by the mission and consistent with the supported CCDR's intentions. Supported CCDRs may have to increase US military capability or seek non-US military resources such as multinational partners or contracted sources to expand the infrastructure, facilities, and capabilities to support current or future distribution operations. These choices are made throughout an operation and range from the subtle to the direct. Devoting intertheater airlift to deploy military port opening forces is a distribution decision that has operational implications. That same intertheater airlift also may be used to transport additional combat forces or materiel for protection or other mission requirements. In a direct choice, a commander may use combat power to seize forward operating bases or protect main supply routes from adversary forces to expand logistic capability and gain freedom of action. **Planning decisions concerning the in-theater balance of operational requirements and distribution support requirements have an impact at the strategic level.** Tradeoffs on theater distribution capabilities may require compensating application of strategic level resources. For example, limitations on 40-foot container handling and transporting capabilities in-theater may require additional investments in 20-foot containers to be used at the origin.

(3) **Understanding Tradeoffs. Planning global distribution of materiel requires the calculation of tradeoffs between requirements, inventory, and the capability to provide materiel when, where, and in the quantity required.** Tradeoff decisions are a function of the warning time prior to commencement of operations, resources available, fiscal considerations, and constraints and restraints imposed on a JFC by the mission. These tradeoff decisions involve choices among the numerous variables present within materiel supply chains. Requirement variables include differing physical characteristics of materiel (e.g., volume and special handling characteristics) and RDDs to support the joint operation. Inventory variables include source, location, and quantity of the required materiel. Physical distribution variables include distance, velocity, and the capacity and capability to move or store materiel. Combinations of these variables are present in every materiel distribution transaction, with flexibility in one variable capable of offsetting constraints imposed by reality or intentionally reduced capability in another. The use of premium air transportation, for example, can offset low inventory levels and provide materiel from geographically dispersed sources. In assessing these tradeoffs, distribution planners must consider numerous constraints such as finite resources in money, materiel, and forces.

e. **Use of Intermodal Platforms.** Effective and efficient use of intermodal platforms requires that all aspects (e.g., loading, deployment, reception, onward movement, unloading, distribution, and associated force structure) of intermodal operations be factored into support plans developed from the CCDR's CONOPS.

(1) Intermodal platform use must be prioritized. Developing a theater distribution CONOPS that prioritizes use of GO or government-leased (GL) containers and containers owned by ocean carriers for the deployment of unit equipment and movement of ammunition and sustainment is an example of planning actions aimed at ensuring the effective and efficient use of intermodal platforms. Another example is planning for the use and management of special types of containers or platforms which may be in short supply, such as ammunition grade containers, refrigerated (reefer) containers, ISO-configured or palletized load system (PLS) flatracks, and system 463L pallets and nets.

(2) During deliberate planning, all unit equipment suitable for containerization must be identified and appropriately coded for inclusion in the OPLAN TPFDD consistent with in-theater infrastructure capabilities, force structure, and the GCC's CONOPS. The cargo increment numbers for sustainment, ammunition, and resupply cargo are not included in a TPFDD being readied for execution; hence sustainment and resupply are only estimated for transportation feasibility. Estimates for the volumes of containerized cargo required for the force being deployed can be made using the appropriate models and provided to the CCDRs for development of theater distribution plans.

(3) Containerships and intermodal systems may improve force closure when surge capability is insufficient. Closure profiles using containerships for movement of unit equipment should be made available to the supported CCDR during the planning process, particularly when sealift shortfalls are identified.

(4) Commercial intermodal container liner service available to DOD through USTRANSCOM is the primary means used to ship sustainment cargo. These contracts provide end-to-end intermodal transportation services (e.g., spotting containers, line haul to SPOE and terminal services, strategic sealift, offload at SPOD, and line haul to theater destinations when appropriate). However, commercial containers provided by this service must be unstuffed and returned expeditiously to the DTS to support continuous industry shipping requirements and to avoid costly financial penalties for container detention. Use of DOD-owned or leased containers is preferred over using containers provided directly by ocean carriers since these assets do not incur detention penalties. Maximum benefit and efficiency are achieved when compatible cargo is loaded into containers at the cargo origin (or as near as practical) and delivered as far forward in the OA as practical.

(5) DOD/Service-owned or leased containers will normally be used to ship accompanying supplies and certain unit equipment in support of deploying forces in the early stages of a deployment, particularly when the operation is being conducted in an undeveloped, austere environment. Under extreme circumstances these assets can be retained for use as temporary storage, protection barriers, and other uses if approved by the GCC.

(6) Aircraft 463L pallet and net resources are in high demand during deployment surge and sustainment operations. These resources are often used to facilitate onward surface movement from the APOD. It is critical that logistic planners at all levels plan for the rapid return of these assets to the AMC transportation system for continued use.

CONTAINER MANAGEMENT PLANNING FOR OPERATIONS

Distribution planners should consider the availability of existing infrastructure within the theater and the expected duration of the operation when developing strategy to use commercial and government containers to support the combatant commander. Detention occurs when carrier-owned containers are held longer than the contractual agreement between the government and the commercial ocean carrier to unload the container, and either notifies the carrier that the container is available for pick-up or returns the container to the carrier. During Operation IRAQI FREEDOM (OIF) and Operation ENDURING FREEDOM (OEF), commercial ocean carrier containers were delivered to the forward areas and subsequently used by forces as storage facilities, force protection barriers, and other base operating support enablers. This practice resulted in excessive detention, maintenance, port storage, and associated government "buy-out" charges for thousands of commercial containers within the United States Central Command area of responsibility. Container detention and buy-out costs for both OIF and OEF during the period 2003-2012 exceeded $700 million.

In an austere environment where operations are expected to exceed six months duration, distribution planners should consider the use of government-owned or leased containers during the initial stages of an operation to provide expeditionary storage and other essential base operating support capability. This approach sets conditions for the contents of carrier-owned containers to be unloaded, inventoried, and immediately issued or stored, and for containers to be returned to the carrier in a timely manner. The transfer of contents from one container to another container followed by additional transportation (transloading) should be avoided unless deemed temporarily essential by the supported joint force commander in coordination with United States Transportation Command.

Various Sources

f. **Movement Control Planning**

(1) **Strategic Movement Control.** Strategic movement control is primarily executed by USTRANSCOM, in conjunction with other JDDE partners, using organic and commercial lift assets, in response to the needs and intentions of the supported GCC. This movement control concentrates on the movement of forces, equipment, and materiel from a point of origin, or the supply source, to a designated theater POD, or point of need as specified by the supported CCDR. A primary control mechanism is the TPFDD, since it specifies the priority of movement and the dates by which cargo and passengers must arrive at the POEs for loading on strategic lift assets. USTRANSCOM provides airlift and sealift movement schedules to deploying units for compliance. Unit movement control teams monitor force movement from the origin to the ports and submit required reports through their respective Services to the Joint Staff J-3 as the joint force provider coordinator. This intracontinental leg includes movements by commercial rail and truck, which are coordinated by supporting GCCs and the Services with SDDC. Movements originating in theater

(retrograde and/or redeployment) that require strategic sealift/intertheater airlift assets require the same level of planning diligence as those arriving in the theater.

(2) **Intratheater Movement Control.** Intratheater movement control is the responsibility of the GCC and is executed by the Service components IAW priorities established by the GCC. Figure III-1 outlines the responsibilities of the movement planners at the senior movement headquarters, which will normally be the JDDOC or a TSC.

g. **Strategic to Theater Distribution Interface.** Operational planners must develop theater reception and distribution plans that are coordinated and synchronized with the deployment plan. The theater distribution plan may use established ports of debarkation or intermediate staging bases (if required), or establish other potential distribution nodes required to support the GCC's CONOPS. The theater distribution system is a complex set of networks, IT systems, and tools. These networks may use or overlap existing global commercial distribution capabilities as well as HN infrastructure (developed or underdeveloped) that must be shared with the HN and often with other military, civilian, and MNFs participating in the same operation. Combinations of US military, HN, multinational, and contractor organizations operate the nodes and modes of supply and transportation that distribute the forces and sustainment supplies. These organizations collect and report data to a network of operational and logistic headquarters responsible for processing the data into information and issuing instructions to the node and mode operators. This process ensures that the GCC's authoritative direction over all aspects of military operations and logistics within the AOR is carried out. Care must be taken to ensure joint distribution operations also plan for and are prepared to execute redeployment, retrograde, and theater closure operations.

(1) **Joint Distribution Operations.** Joint distribution operations are the collective activities necessary to plan, synchronize, and execute movement and sustainment tasks in support of military operations. Joint distribution operations have often competed for limited resources (e.g., insufficient sustainment commodities, lift assets, congestion at ports). The traditional way to deal with this competition has been through deconfliction. A better approach is to reduce the competition and smooth the flow through CCDR-assigned and -enforced supply and transportation priorities. The ideal approach is to ensure distribution networks are sufficiently robust and redundant to handle the CCDR's requirements for routine and surge distribution. The JFC determines a requirement and its point of need which can be a major strategic APOD/SPOD, an austere airfield, a sea base, or any forward location within the operational environment (e.g., open fields, parking lots, highway segments).

(2) **Joint Distribution in Support of Deployments.** The global distribution system requires the end-to-end synchronization of all elements of distribution. The deployment and distribution capability supports the movement of forces and unit equipment during the movement phase of the deployment and redeployment processes and supports materiel movement during the logistical sustainment of operations. The deployment and distribution capability moves forces and logistic support globally and on time meeting the RDD and providing TDD to meet the needs of the CCDR. Through sharing of critical information, it is possible to create unity of effort among diverse distribution organizations

---

Theater Movement Planning Responsibilities

1. Obtain advance intertheater arrival information.

2. Assess the movement requirements data such as required delivery date (RDD), priority of movement, equipment characteristics, and special requirements.

3. Group the requirements for each port of debarkation (POD) by destination geographic location in RDD sequence.

4. Obtain movement priority for requirements that have the same destination and RDD.

5. Determine available modes for onward movement based upon planning requirements. Consider the requirement, equipment characteristics, priorities, and modes servicing the PODs and staging areas/tactical assembly areas (SAs/TAAs).

6. Select and program the mode for each requirement for reporting to POD based upon estimated time for POD clearance. This is dependent on the type of strategic asset (airlift, sealift).

7. Determine availability of equipment for follow-on missions at the POD. Estimate uploading and processing time for each mode at the POD. Apply time/distance factors to estimate transit time to other transportation nodes or arrival at the SA/TAA. Determine total transit time, maintenance and crew rest, and return time.

8. Resolve conflicts by either rerouting, changing modes, or rescheduling or obtaining guidance from operational planners. Reconfirm that the selected route can accommodate any oversize or overweight cargo/equipment being moved.

9. Identify requirements for materials handling equipment and cargo/container handling equipment at the POD for each mode, cargo and trailer transfer points, and at destination.

10. Coordinate for holding and storage areas outside of POD staging areas if ports become congested due to transportation shortages or scheduling problems.

11. Identify en route supported requirements for fuel, mess, maintenance, and billeting.

12. Determine critical points where highway regulation or traffic control should be established to maintain the flow of traffic. Coordinate for en route communications.

Figure III-1. Theater Movement Planning Responsibilities

and provide end-to-end support to satisfy deployment execution and sustainment operations. Visibility through the JDDE provides the CCDR, in conjunction with the global providers, the capability to see and redirect strategic and operational commodity/force flow in support of current and projected priorities. In the context of this document, distribution does not include those aspects of the deployment process involving decisions about self-deploying

---

units, force readiness assessment, selecting units to deploy (sourcing), and priority of their deployment to satisfy JFC operational requirements.

(3) **Joint Distribution in Support of Sustainment.** The other key task of joint distribution operations is sustainment delivery. The timely and effective delivery (and return) of supplies, equipment, and services to the joint force requires a robust and agile joint distribution system inextricably linked to DOD's global supply chain. Supply chain operations include materiel planning, sourcing, making, delivering, redistributing and disposing of excess, and return process activities. Supply chain stock level and location decisions influence distribution processes and joint distribution performance directly affecting supply chain planning, sourcing, making, and return activities. DOD's global supply chain processes must strike an optimal balance regarding inventory levels, the positioning of stocks, and the robust capabilities of a distribution pipeline that moves those stocks to and from the theater. They also must have the ability to expand to meet surge requirements or to support distributed forces in an antiaccess environment. Finally, the supply chain also must coordinate sustainment distribution services among US forces and HNS, the interagency and multinational partners, NGOs, and contractors.

h. **Redeployment, Retrograde, and Theater Closure Planning**

(1) **Redeployment Planning.** Planning for redeployment can be as or more complex than planning for deployment. Each redeploying unit must plan and coordinate the movement of its equipment and personnel in the distribution system. It must plan what equipment it will be leaving with, what it will leave behind, how it will distribute or make visible its serviceable excess, its unserviceable excess, its HW, etc. Units also must plan how they will clean equipment to meet the United States Department of Agriculture (USDA) requirements or the requirements of the nation where it is going.

For more information on redeployment planning, see JP 3-35, Deployment and Redeployment Operations.

(2) **Retrograde Planning.** Retrograde of materiel either within the theater or from the theater to a source of supply must be planned and developed as a part of the distribution system. This planning considers the factors affecting the reverse distribution of reparable or excess materiel from the theater back to designated repair or storage points. It is used to determine requirements for repair and transportation capabilities and the necessary logistic management systems to administer the materiel flow. Retrograde planning must consider the type and amount of reparable components used by designated Service components, the maintenance concepts associated with these components, and the repair cycles that apply, particularly for major combat equipment items. Expeditious and visible movement of reparable items rearward, and a similar movement of repaired items forward to the joint force, is essential to maintain operational readiness. Strategic decisions on weapon system maintenance support must be reflected in corresponding distribution capabilities at all levels. Similar to redeployment planning, retrograde planning must include arrangements for cleaning and USDA inspection prior to shipment from the theater. Failure to do so may result in serious delays to the shipment, significant costs to the shipper Service, and

potentially significant damage to the agricultural and economic infrastructure of the US or other destination country.

(3) **Theater of Operations Closure Planning.** Most operations eventually end or draw down, leading to base closures and then closure of the theater as a theater of operations. These actions must be planned for. When a unit is responsible for the closure of a base in addition to its own redeployment, the planning requirements are significantly more complex. Support for a unit conducting a base or theater of operations closure may be limited at best, and will probably be more limited than that for the initial deployment. Therefore, the impact on the distribution system may vary. Theater of operations closure planning should also consider the transfer of real estate, real property and the remediation of HAZMAT or waste management sites (solid waste dumps, black water pits, etc.). Unserviceable items requiring demilitarization may remain at the location and either have to be demilitarized by the unit as a part of the closure process, or be retrograded to a location where appropriate demilitarization can be performed. The latter is an impact on the distribution system not normally incurred. Force protection requirements may also increase in a theater closure situation requiring additional planning and support.

i. **Multinational Operations.** Multinational operations is a collective term to describe military actions conducted by forces of two or more nations, usually organized within the structure of an alliance or coalition. The fundamental difference from unilateral US joint operations is that the participating forces represent sovereign nations. This fact has profound implications for how the multinational force commander (MNFC) may organize, plan, and execute global distribution in support of multinational operations. Unique command relationships, legal constraints on the transfer or provision of goods and services to foreign countries, and varying standards and capabilities in distribution networks and functions affect the broad nature of global distribution support to the MNF and complicate efforts to coordinate and synchronize C2, funding and reimbursement mechanisms, allied contributions, and other logistic support. **A key objective during multinational operations is to forge a partnership among participating nations executing global distribution of materiel.** Executed correctly, this partnership should improve operational support by allowing participating nations to share the burdens associated with participating in such operations.

For more information, see JP 4-08, Logistics in Support of Multinational Operations; *Allied Joint Publication (AJP)-4(A),* Allied Joint Logistics Doctrine; *and AJP-4.4(A),* Allied Joint Movement and Transportation Doctrine.

Intentionally Blank

CHAPTER IV
DISTRIBUTION EXECUTION

"Any amateur can shove tanks, planes, and infantry around a map. The real business of war is getting gas, ammunition, and spare parts to people that need them when they need them."

Lieutenant General Walter Bedell Smith, United States Army
Supreme Allied Headquarters
Europe, Chief of Staff, 1944

1. Introduction

a. This chapter will discuss the transition from planning to execution, describe the distribution framework, and highlight the complexity and variety of tasks required to effectively execute distribution operations. Additionally, it will discuss the unique aspects of retrograde, return, reutilization, and disposal of materiel as well as the integration of intermodal platforms and the need for control of these critical assets.

b. **Transition from Planning to Execution.** Since global distribution operations span the strategic, operational, and tactical levels of war, the transition from planning to execution is critical. In today's dynamic operational environments, planning and executing operations often occur simultaneously. But while these two functions may be running concurrently, it is still critical that planning outputs serve as inputs to executable actions. As such, an up-to-date logistic concept of support is the critical planning output that serves as the expectation against which distribution execution is measured. This necessitates the ability to monitor, assess, and direct distribution operations in order to assure that the concept of support is being effectively executed. It is during this transition that the logistic principles of responsiveness and flexibility become key. Global distribution operations must be responsive to evolving mission requirements and operate effectively across the range of military operations. Additionally, flexibility enables distribution operations to improvise and adapt structures and procedures to changing situations, missions, and operational requirements. It is reflected in how well distribution operations respond in an environment of unpredictability. Responsiveness is the JFC's expectation of distribution support; flexibility is the logistician's tool for achieving it.

2. Distribution Framework

The foundation of the distribution framework is the JDDE. The framework is designed around the intertheater and intratheater legs of the end-to-end distribution system.

a. **Intertheater Distribution.** Performing intertheater distribution operations involves a unity of effort among CDRUSTRANSCOM; Director, DLA; and each of the Services.

(1) **DLA.** DLA is the primary operator of the defense supply and depot system and is responsible for acquisition, receipt, storage, issuance, and generation of source data for all materiel (other than materiel procured by the individual Services) flowing in the defense distribution pipeline. DLA also controls worldwide disposal and defense reutilization.

(a) DLA Distribution operates distribution centers throughout the US and around the world, as well as CCPs at CONUS SDPs for loading cargo to intermodal platforms for onward movement to the GCCs' AORs.

(b) DLA operates primary-level field activities, each assigned as the lead center for a particular category of supply.

1. DLA Land and Maritime is the lead center for maritime and land-based weapons systems as well as construction and electronic spare parts.

2. DLA Troop Support is the lead center for general troop support, clothing and textile items, subsistence, medical supplies/pharmaceuticals, medicine, medical equipment, and general and industrial supplies. It supports US humanitarian assistance and disaster relief efforts. It also serves as the EA responsible for end-to-end management of subsistence, construction and barrier material, and medical materiel. Delivery of medical materiel support is executed through a CJCS designated theater lead agent for medical materiel which remains under the C2 of the Service or GCC task organization such as the JDDOC or similar organization.

3. DLA Aviation is the lead center for aerospace weapons systems and environmental logistics support.

4. DLA Energy is the lead center for DOD energy products. It also serves as the EA responsible for end-to-end management of bulk petroleum.

(c) DLA Disposition Services provides worldwide reuse, recycling, and disposal support to DOD. DLA Disposition Services provides HW management and disposal services in addition to disposal of scrap and redistribution of excess material. DLA Disposition Services also provides demilitarization advice and services for most property.

(d) Defense Logistics Agency support teams (DSTs) provide worldwide logistic support for conflicts, natural disasters, emergencies, mobilizations, and other contingency operations.

(2) **USTRANSCOM.** USTRANSCOM assumes responsibility for the movement of materiel as it enters the DTS. The DTS includes contracts with various domestic and international commercial carriers for air, ground, inland and coastal waterways, and sea transportation support. USTRANSCOM maintains and updates the in-transit status of the shipments within the DTS using a single database, IGC, the DOD system of record for ITV. IGC is used for recording and archiving the movement that occurs from the shipping activity (depot, vendor, or installation), regardless of mode or carrier, through POEs/PODs, to the final destination. AISs are used by the GCCs to determine the location and shipping status of materiel within the DTS. The USTRANSCOM Deployment and Distribution Operations Center (DDOC) directs the global air, land, and sea transportation capabilities of the DTS to meet national security objectives. The DDOC fuses capabilities of multimodal deployment and distribution operations, intelligence, force protection, capacity acquisition, resource management, and other staff functions to collaboratively provide distribution options to the CCDR. C2 of the majority of intertheater lift forces and logistic infrastructure is

accomplished through the DDOC, which tracks the movement requirement from lift allocation and initial execution through closure at final destination. USTRANSCOM, as DPO, will have influence in stock positioning and sourcing decisions, while integrating efforts of materiel providers and lift providers, to optimize throughput. It also will offer materiel providers influence in lift asset positioning and capacity management/generation. Specific tasks include:

(a) Establish TCC distribution policy (including commercial/organic transportation resource use).

(b) Source lift capacity through TCCs.

(c) Compare aggregated/specific requirements to available capacity.

(d) Analyze requirement for and develop multimodal, end-to-end COAs.

(e) Make initial and final mode selection recommendations to customers, including commercial versus organic options.

(f) Identify the need for integrated distribution lanes (IDLs) and other supply chain performance standards and mechanisms.

(g) Measure delivery performance against CCDR's requirements and refine distribution system as needed.

(h) **Movement from Origin to POE.** Movements to the SPOE/APOE include materiel from the installation, vendor or supplier, storage activity, or depot. GCC visibility of these movements enables adjustments to the flow of materiel prior to the loading of strategic lift assets. For materiel originating in OCONUS supporting commands, the Service transportation component coordinates with the JDDOC and SDDC forward operating elements to plan and execute the movement of materiel to the POE.

(i) **Movement from the POE to POD.** MSC, SDDC, and AMC are the primary mode operators for this movement phase.

<u>1</u>. **Sealift.** As the USTRANSCOM single manager for common-user seaports worldwide, SDDC directs water terminal operations including supervising movement operations, contracts, cargo documentation, security operations, and the overall flow of information. SDDC also will select the SPOE, make recommendations to the GCC as to the SPOD, and coordinate vessel selections with MSC. SDDC provides visibility data to IGC, the enterprise ITV system, as well as to enterprise-level business systems, and transmits necessary advance cargo-related information (e.g., manifests) directly to the theater for planning purposes. Theater port personnel and movement control organizations use the advance information to preplan the reception, staging, onward movement, and integration of unit equipment and sustainment supplies. This preplanning is a critical aspect of JRSOI.

<u>2</u>. **Airlift.** In coordination with the GCC, differing levels of air movements may be offered, to include force deployment missions, normal channel missions,

and TDD options such as WWX. A unique aspect of these operations is their reliance upon the Global Air Mobility Support System and the worldwide C2 capabilities of the 618 AOC (TACC). In that capacity, AMC selects APOEs and makes recommendations to the GCC as to the APOD. The cargo documentation functionality and processes in the APOE are very similar to the SPOE. Using the Global Air Transportation Execution System (GATES) and Service unit move execution systems, AMC documents cargo that is being prepared and airlifted to a theater. This advanced visibility is used in the same manner as described above.

b. **Intratheater Distribution.** Distribution execution at the intratheater level is the responsibility of the GCC and the forces assigned, and occurs in that part of the distribution pipeline extending from intermediate staging bases and PODs throughout the OA. The primary staff responsibility for the execution of theater distribution rests with the GCC J-4 and the associated centers and boards, bureaus, cells, and working groups that perform day-to-day distribution functions. These staff elements monitor the necessary information in the various Service and joint systems, and integrate the management products of the Service components into a COP. Each level of command and operational unit plays a unique part in the overall distribution process; these roles are as follows:

(1) **Geographic CCMD J-4.** The GCC's J-4 directs and manages the effectiveness of the distribution system in theater. The J-4 uses a series of boards, offices, and centers to prioritize and accomplish management tasks. The primary organizations involved in the distribution management functions are the JDDOC, joint logistics operations center (JLOC), theater-joint transportation board (T-JTB), Joint Transportation Board (JTB), and other management boards, as required. The GCC's logistic planning element is responsible for the development and management of the four networks of the theater distribution system. They develop the logistic portion of the OPLAN and prepare the theater distribution plan IAW the OPLAN. The J-4 monitors the execution of all aspects of theater distribution—inbound, outbound, and internal. The J-4 also coordinates theater priorities and coordinates those plans with the other logistic commands and agencies located in CONUS or other theaters. Additional responsibilities include:

(a) Balances and synchronizes overall movement requirements based on the GCC's priorities and available transportation capabilities.

(b) Identifies significant variances between programmed movements and actual movements throughout the distribution system.

(c) Recommends to the GCC, as appropriate, COAs with respect to allocation of common-user transportation when movement requirements exceed capability or when competing requirements result in unresolved conflicts.

(d) Directs lateral distribution and reconsignment in support of theater high priority requirements. Captures visibility of and directs redistribution of intratheater excess assets in support of theater operations.

(e) Monitors noncombatant evacuation operations to facilitate the sufficiency of transportation and logistic support.

(f) Makes a recommendation to the GCC concerning who should be appointed the theater container manager (TCM) (see paragraph 6d, "Theater Container Management").

(2) **JDDOC.** As part of a supported GCC's staff, the JDDOC develops deployment and distribution plans, integrates multinational and/or interagency deployment and distribution, and coordinates and synchronizes supply, transportation, and related distribution activities. Therefore, in consonance with the GCC's overall priorities, and on behalf of the GCC, the JDDOC coordinates common-user and theater distribution operations above the tactical level. The JDDOC's strength is its ability to resolve potential deployment and distribution problems through coordination of available theater logistical support capabilities and collaborative reachback to national partners (USTRANSCOM, DLA, individual Service organizations), agencies, and other organizations (multinational, NGOs) deemed critical to the GCC's operational mission. See Figure IV-1 for JDDOC relationships.

(3) **JLOC.** The GCC will usually form command centers and operational planning teams that are supported by a JLOC under the direction of the J-4. The JLOC performs the following key functions:

(a) Monitors current and evolving theater logistic capabilities to determine potential impact on planned operations.

(b) Coordinates logistic support with upcoming operations by:

<u>1.</u> Recommending shifts of logistic support from one Service component or one geographic area to another in the theater.

<u>2.</u> Assessing materiel commonalities among the Services for possible cross-leveling. This function includes review of intratheater excess to determine what may be cross-leveled.

<u>3.</u> Maintaining a COP of the location and status of Service component distribution resources and information networks.

<u>4.</u> Tracking materiel en route and within the theater.

<u>5.</u> Interpreting the various Service-unique means of measuring supply levels.

<u>6.</u> Assessing multinational/combined logistic support.

(c) Advises the GCC on the supportability of various COAs by:

<u>1.</u> Coordinating with Service components as they perform their supportability analysis.

<u>2.</u> Providing gross transportation feasibility analyses.

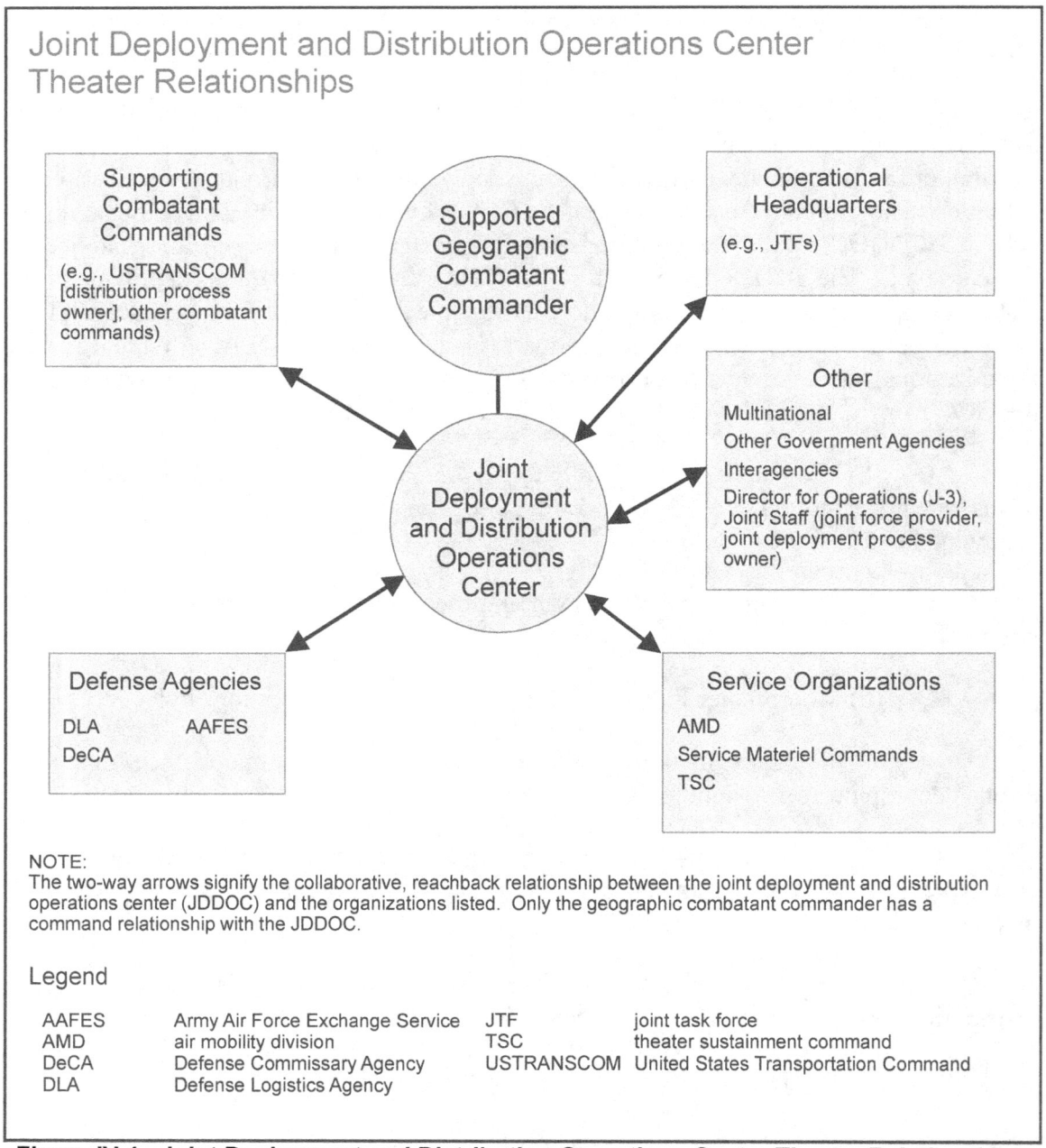

Figure IV-1. Joint Deployment and Distribution Operations Center Theater Relationships

(d) Acts as the GCC's agent and advocate to nontheater logistic organizations by:

1. Reporting logistic status to the Joint Staff J-4.

2. Requesting additional resources, if needed.

3. Overseeing priorities conveyed to supporting organizations.

4. Overseeing adjustments to the flow of forces and supplies.

<u>5.</u> Coordinating logistics with allies and partner nations.

(4) **T-JTB.** CCMD and subordinate organizations need the capability to rapidly change transportation resource allocation to adjust to changing circumstances or immediately react to emergency or unanticipated situations. One recommendation for effective control of theater transportation assets is the establishment of a supported GCC's T-JTB. Procedures for establishing the T-JTB are developed during peacetime to facilitate rapid stand-up and execution under emergency or wartime conditions. The T-JTB's role is to resolve contentious transportation issues within the command, such as allocating transportation capability among components for unit movement, nonunit movement, resupply, and disposal. The T-JTB is normally co-chaired by the director of the JDDOC and the GCC's J-4.

For additional information on the JTB, see JP 4-0, Joint Logistics.

c. **Service Component Commands.** Service component commands execute distribution operations. Each Service is responsible for the logistic support of its own forces. Services can augment organic logistic capabilities by agreements with national agencies or allies, or by **participating in common, joint, or cross-servicing agreements. Service component commands are responsible for direct communications with appropriate headquarters on all logistic matters. The Service component commands are responsible for operating their assigned/attached units within the physical network IAW the supported GCC's established theater distribution system.**

(1) **Army Service Component Command (ASCC).** Each CCMD has an ASCC assigned to it. GCCs have theater Army headquarters assigned to them as their ASCCs. The theater Army includes the theater Army commander, the theater Army headquarters, and all Army forces—organizations and units, personnel, and installations assigned or attached to the CCMD. The theater Army is designed to perform the functions of the ASCC to the GCC, including the Title 10, USC, administrative control, common-user logistics (CUL), and Army EA responsibilities. These responsibilities extend to the support of any JOAs opened within the AOR, including theater opening, and Army support to other Services and USG departments and agencies. With additional joint augmentation provided by an approved joint manning document, the organization provides a fully functional operational level headquarters capable of effectively commanding and controlling joint forces or MNFs engaged in sustained military operations. The ASCC is responsible for preparing Army forces for effective military operations IAW integrated joint operations and mobilization plans.

(a) **TSC.** The TSC is the logistic C2 element assigned to the ASCC and is the single Army sustainment (less medical) headquarters within a theater of operations (see Figure IV-2). It is responsible for executing logistics and distribution capabilities for port opening, theater opening, theater surface distribution, and sustainment functions in support of Army forces. Additionally, the TSC may provide lead Service and EA support for designated CUL to other government agencies, MNFs, and NGOs as directed. The TSC manages theater distribution and executes distribution operations IAW ASCC component logistics staff officer (G-4) priorities. It develops the ASCC's distribution plan and synchronizes materiel and movement management, and is also responsible for coordinating

Chapter IV

```
┌─────────────────────────────────────────────────────────────────────┐
│ Theater Sustainment Command                                         │
│                                                                     │
│   Theater Sustainment Command (TSC)                                 │
│                                                                     │
│     ● Army Sustainment headquarters (less medical) for Army Service │
│       component command (ASCC), joint force commander (JFC).        │
│     ● Regionally focused; globally employable.                      │
│     ● Uses its distribution management command (DMC) to integrate   │
│       distribution from the strategic to tactical.                  │
│     ● Joint capable; provides logistics command and control (less   │
│       medical) for multiple operational areas.                      │
│                                                                     │
│   Expeditionary Sustainment Command (ESC)                           │
│                                                                     │
│     ● ESC provides forward presence of the TSC for expeditionary    │
│       operations for ASCC, JFC.                                     │
│     ● Regionally focused; globally employable and provides early    │
│       entry capability.                                            │
│     ● Uses its DMC to integrate distribution from the strategic to  │
│       the tactical in the absence of the TSC.                       │
│                                                                     │
│   Sustainment Brigade (SUST BDE)                                    │
│                                                                     │
│     ● SUST BDEs provide multifunctional logistics capability.       │
│     ● SUST BDEs are the logistics executor for the Army.            │
│     ● Conduct and direct distribution through distributions         │
│       operations section.                                          │
└─────────────────────────────────────────────────────────────────────┘
```

Figure IV-2. Theater Sustainment Command

the protection of theater distribution nodes. The TSC can employ one or more ESCs as an extension of its C2 capability; each ESC provides a rapidly deployable, regionally focused capability for executing logistic operations that are limited in scope and scale when compared to the TSC.

(b) **SUST BDEs.** SUST BDEs are subordinate commands of the TSC. All SUST BDEs plan, synchronize, monitor, and control sustainment operations within their assigned area of operations. Depending on its assigned mission, a SUST BDE will primarily focus on theater opening, theater distribution, or sustainment functions.

1. Theater opening functions set the conditions for effective support and lay the groundwork for subsequent expansion of the theater distribution system. The critical tasks for a SUST BDE in a theater opening role include: theater reception support, staging, onward movement; distribution and distribution management; life support; and initial theater sustainment.

2. Theater distribution functions enable decisive action by building and sustaining combat power at critical times and places. The critical tasks for a SUST BDE in a theater distribution role include: establishing and operating multimodal distribution hubs, synchronizing multiple node operations (inland terminals, convoy support centers),

---

IV-8   JP 4-09 maintaining visibility of the distribution system (including readiness of Army air and ground transport assets), and reallocating resources to maintain optimal system performance. The SUST BDE in a theater distribution role controls the common-user transportation assets required to complete the delivery of materiel to the point of need.

<u>3.</u> Sustainment enables the tactical commander to maintain combat power. The critical tasks for a SUST BDE in an area sustainment role include: maintaining situational awareness of the operating environment and the supported unit requirements; managing supply support activities (SSAs) IAW TSC directives; providing area maintenance support; and providing and distributing subsistence, general supplies, bulk fuel, repair parts, ammunition, and water to supported units in their assigned areas. In the distribution process, this brigade moves materiel from the point of need to the point of employment.

(c) **CSSBs.** CSSBs are the building blocks of the SUST BDEs. They are standardized modular, logistic C2 headquarters that are tailored to provide a full spectrum of support. Attached units usually consist of five to eight companies that can be task organized to support theater opening, distribution, area sustainment, or life support functions. The CSSB mission is to plan, coordinate, synchronize, and execute sustainment operations in its assigned OA. It provides C2 over subordinate logistic organizations that support all phases of operations. It oversees Army distribution requirements, sustainment, and movement control operations, and coordinates external logistic and transportation functions.

(d) **Brigade Support Battalions (BSBs).** BSBs are organic components of brigade combat teams (BCTs). They consolidate selected functions previously performed by main support battalions and forward support battalions into a single operational echelon. They provide a materiel carrying capability that enables the BCT to carry three combat loads. They plan, coordinate, synchronize, and execute logistic operations in support of BCT operations. In most instances, support brigades such as fires brigade, maneuver enhancement brigade, etc., are supported by organic BSBs with capabilities similar to those found in BCTs. BSBs typically plan and execute replenishment operations in support of maneuver force battles and engagements. They are deliberate, time sensitive operations conducted to replenish forward support companies. The intent is the rapid replenishment of essential supplies, such as fuel and ammunition, to sustain an overwhelming operational tempo. When required, a supporting SUST BDE may assist the BSB during planned replenishment operations.

(e) **United States Army Materiel Command (USAMC).** USAMC performs assigned materiel and related functions for research, development, test, and evaluation; acquisition, logistic support, and technical assistance for materiel systems; and other materiel acquisition management functions. It provides Army national level maintenance support and serves as the DOD single manager for conventional ammunition. All of the functions and capabilities below are available to the ASCC/Army forces commander through the USAMC logistic support element. USAMC missions include:

<u>1.</u> Maintaining the industrial mobilization capabilities necessary to support the Army.

2. Managing Army's worldwide pre-positioned stocks (except medical supplies).

3. Managing LOGCAP.

4. Managing operational policies, programs, objectives, and resources associated with OPROJs worldwide.

(f) **Army Sustainment Command (ASC).** ASC executes a supporting role in facilitating the predeployment process of the deploying TSC and its subordinate units. Its capabilities include: assisting US Army Forces Command in the rapid projection of Army forces to the theater of operations and return; integrating Army logistics (less medical) with joint and strategic partners in the national sustainment base; and coordinating the distribution plan with USTRANSCOM and other strategic partners.

(g) **Army Field Support Brigade (AFSB).** The AFSB provides integrated acquisition, logistics, and technology (ALT) support in the area of operations as designated by the ASCC. The Army has established AFSBs for each ASCC. Critical tasks for the AFSB that are relevant to theater distribution include: administering the Logistics Assistance Program and providing C2 for logistics support elements and brigade logistics support teams; coordinating maintenance and issue of APS and theater stay-behind packages; and managing ALT-related sustainment, redeployment, retrograde, and reset operations in theater.

(h) **The United States Army Medical Materiel Agency (USAMMA).** USAMMA serves as the Army's medical materiel life cycle manager, Class VIII materiel developer, and assembly manager and fielding agency for all medical materiel. USAMMA is the lead organization responsible for facilitating the left-behind equipment program for medical materiel; the agency also centrally manages a variety of strategic medical logistic programs including the Class VIII portion of APS and the Army Surgeon General's contingency stocks.

(i) **Medical Command (Deployment Support) (MEDCOM [DS]).** The Army's MEDCOM (DS) is the senior medical C2 element within the theater and is the medical forces provider to the ASCC. The MEDCOM (DS) is a regionally focused command that provides subordinate medical organizations that operate under the medical brigades and/or multifunctional medical battalions, including forward surgical teams. The medical logistic functions of the MEDCOM (DS) are focused on providing oversight or C2 of Class VIII supply support within subordinate units including the medical logistics management center (MLMC) support team and the medical logistics companies in the medical brigades and battalions. The US Army Medical Command is a major user of the theater distribution system and coordinates its requirements with the TSC through the MLMC support team.

(2) **Navy Component Command (NCC).** The Navy component commander is responsible for the preparation and equipping of Navy forces needed for the effective prosecution of war and other military operations IAW the integrated joint mobilization plans and the Guidance for Development of the Force. Each forward numbered fleet commander

has a logistics task force (LTF) within its organization that is responsible for naval logistics. This LTF has two main forces under its organization for Navy theater distribution.

(a) **CLF.** The CLF are those units, assigned or attached to a CCDR, that service or replenish combatant vessels forward-deployed or underway in the GCC's AOR. At-sea replenishment encompasses the coordinated movement of passengers, mail, sustainment stocks, cargo, and bulk liquids to deployed forces as large as a task force, down to individual ships and submarines conducting independent operations. The CLF includes ammunition ships, repair ships (tenders), fleet oilers, combat stores ships, and salvage vessels. Under peacetime operating scenarios, no additional shore-based infrastructure is required to enable the CLF. However, they routinely resupply through their port logistic hubs.

(b) **Naval Advanced Logistic Support Sites (NALSSs) and Naval Forward Logistic Sites (NFLSs).** These serve as the primary shore-based theater reception and distribution points for personnel, equipment, and materiel. They operate as a hub-and-spoke distribution system, with the NALSS serving as the hub and the NFLSs as the spokes. They have full capability to receive, consolidate, stow, and transfer supplies and equipment and must maintain the appropriate AIS infrastructure to support DOD ITV requirements. The NFLSs receive personnel, equipment, and materiel transshipped through the NALSS via intratheater airlift and sealift for final delivery to the supported Navy forces. The NALSS is typically located near major airports and seaports and coordinates the theater distribution with the NFLSs, which are positioned as far forward in the operating area as possible to support Navy forces. NALSSs and NFLSs also support shore-based Navy aviation units, Navy Expeditionary Medical Support Command hospitals, and naval mobile construction battalions. These forces primarily consist of two fundamental port opening capabilities:

<u>1.</u> The first is the NAVELSG, which reports to the Commander, Navy Expeditionary Combat Command. The majority of their forces are located in the Navy Reserve.

<u>2.</u> The second capability is MSC's expeditionary port units consisting of 17 reserve units. They deploy as a unit and act independently of any infrastructure to address port operations, supply contracting issues, and medical issues for arriving ships. They provide pier-side services minus cargo handling. Expeditionary port units are assigned to MSC headquarters for operational, training, and administrative purposes.

(c) When contingency operations or OPORD execution result in a high operational tempo, existing shore-based infrastructure may become inadequate to facilitate the needed level of support to increased numbers of units afloat and to Navy and Marine Corps units ashore. NALSSs and NFLSs must be expanded to provide that support. That expansion is accomplished through the Navy's ABFCs. ABFCs are preplanned modular units that provide a variety of functional capabilities to extend the logistic infrastructure supporting naval expeditionary operations. Each ABFC is comprised of a standardized grouping of active duty or reserve personnel, facilities, equipment, and materiel (or any combination thereof) designed to perform a specific function or accomplish an advanced support base mission. ABFCs augment existing advanced support of the NALSS concept.

ABFCs are modular and can be used to extend shore-based infrastructure as much or as little as needed. The primary theater distribution capabilities of the Navy are as follows:

1. Cargo handling battalions that provide personnel and equipment to offload container, breakbulk, and MPF shipping.

2. Freight terminal units that function as cargo forwarders at seaports.

3. Navy overseas air cargo terminal units that provide personnel and equipment to offload air cargo and passengers as well as operate an air terminal.

4. Supply support battalions that provide a full range of supply functions at theater distribution sites (warehousing, inventory management, AV).

5. Fixed-wing assets for cargo and passenger theater distribution.

6. Rotary-wing assets for cargo and passenger theater distribution.

7. Mobile engineering and construction units for theater physical network (support sites, bridges, and highways).

8. Health services for theater distribution support sites.

9. Service support elements to provide other logistic support for theater distribution sites (messing, berthing, finance, laundry, barber, retail outlet, and transportation).

10. Fuel operations units to provide bulk fuel storage and distribution, tank trucks, fuel service station operations, and limited pollution abatement and environmental clean-up in support of aircraft and ground vehicles.

11. Communication network support for theater distribution sites.

12. Contracting support for theater distribution sites and integrating the support at each operating node, to include the strategic operating locations.

13. Mobile mail centers to provide postal support personnel and distribution equipment for theater distribution sites.

(3) **Marine Corps Component Command**

(a) The USMC component commander is responsible to the CCDR for USMC administrative and logistic support to include the conduct of assigned missions.

(b) **Logistics Organizations.** The operational forces identify requirements, receive strategic level support from the supporting establishments, and conduct logistic support operations at the operational and tactical levels through logistic task organizations in the MAGTF. The operating forces may be supported and augmented by the reserves and supporting establishment. Theater distribution operations will be conducted under the direction of the commander, Marine Corps forces (COMMARFOR) and the task-organized MAGTF. The following information is provided to explain the Marine Corps structure that will participate in and control theater distribution operations.

    1. **Marine Corps Forces Service Component Headquarters.** The Service component headquarters is a standing organization with personnel structure and functional capabilities commensurate with the size and mission(s) of the MAGTF(s) assigned to the unified commander. The G-4 and the assistant chief of staff for aviation logistics are the component commander's principal deputies who assist and advise the commander and provide staff cognizance over planning and execution of strategic and operational logistic matters.

    2. **MAGTFs.** COMMARFOR assembles the MAGTFs to accomplish assigned missions. Each MAGTF consists of a CE, a ground combat element (GCE), an aviation combat element (ACE), and a logistics combat element (LCE). The LCE provides the theater distribution logistic support to the MAGTF to support successful combat operations and can range from a combat logistics company, combat logistics battalion (CLB), combat logistics regiment (CLR) to a Marine logistics group (MLG) based on the size of the MAGTF. Logistic considerations are as important as combat operations considerations in task-organizing MAGTFs. MAGTFs can assume any size and balance of capabilities appropriate to the mission, but there are four general types of MAGTFs: the Marine expeditionary force (MEF), MEB, Marine expeditionary unit (MEU), and the special purpose Marine air-ground task force (SPMAGTF).

    a. **MEF.** The MEF is the largest force the Marine Corps employs at the operational level and is the primary warfighter. Like every MAGTF, it is comprised of a CE, a GCE (division), an ACE (Marine air wing), and an LCE (MLG). A MEF will normally deploy in echelon and designate its lead element as the MEB. Standard accompanying sustainment for a MEF is approximately 60 days of supplies.

    b. **MEB.** The MEB is the mid-sized MAGTF. The MEB bridges the gap between the MEU, with its immediate reaction crisis response capability, and the MEF, the principal warfighter. Along with its CE, it has a reinforced infantry regiment as the GCE, a composite Marine aircraft group as the ACE, and CLR as the LCE. With 30 days of sufficient supplies for sustained operations, the MEB is capable of conducting amphibious assault operations and MPF operations. A MEB can operate independently or serve as the advanced echelon of a MEF.

    c. **MEU.** The MEU is the formation that is routinely forward-deployed aboard US Navy amphibious ships for presence and potential quick response to a developing contingency. Along with its CE, it has a GCE that is a reinforced battalion landing team, an ACE that is a composite squadron, and a CLB as the LCE. Standard accompanying sustainment for an MEU is 15 days of supplies.

    d. **SPMAGTF.** The SPMAGTF is organized to accomplish a specific mission, operation, or regionally focused exercise. The size and capabilities of its elements will vary with the mission. Normally, the LCE can be task-organized to be a combat logistics company up to MLG. Logistics functional capabilities and the level of organic sustainment will also specifically reflect the assigned mission.

3. **MLG.** The MLG is the principal and largest logistics support organization of the MAGTF and is a grouping of multifunctional units that provides tactical-level ground logistic support to all elements of the MEF. The MLG also can provide theater-level operational logistic support to the Marine component of a joint force. MLG organizations are structured to provide task-organized groups to provide support on either an as required or preplanned basis, either to independently deployed battalions, regiments, and MAGTFs or to geographically separated units in garrison. MAGTFs smaller than MEF size are supported through detachments from the MLG.

(4) **Air Force Component Command.** The primary distribution-related functions of the COMAFFOR include the following:

(a) Organize, train, equip, and provide forces for air transport, as directed.

(b) Operate air LOCs and ensure appropriate automation infrastructure is in place to support DOD ITV requirements by providing ITV data feeds to IGC.

(c) Provide weather forecasting to other Service component commands.

(d) With respect to air mobility operations, the COMAFFOR, in coordination with the director of mobility forces (DIRMOBFOR), has specific responsibility to:

1. Provide US Air Force assets for the air movement of troops, supplies, and equipment in joint airborne operations, including airland and airdrop operations.

2. Provide for intratheater airlift transportation, operating aerial ports, and MHE and CHE for air-to-land and land-to-air loading and unloading operations.

(e) Coordinate theater distribution requirements for Air Force forces (AFFOR) through the AFFOR logistics staff.

(5) **USCG.** When operating as a Service within the Department of the Navy, the USCG includes naval combat and service forces and organic aviation capability. The USCG performs its military functions in times of limited war or defense contingencies and in support of the Navy Service component commanders, without transferring from DHS to the Department of the Navy. The USCG also provides port security units and a variety of cutters to the Navy component commander for the protection of the SPODs and MSC ships. **Coast Guard forces are not self-sufficient;** they must rely on the supported GCC for logistic support, including procurement, distribution, supply, fuel and subsistence, and various levels of maintenance. One or more of the other Service component commands may be required to support USCG forces. Deployable port security units require only minimal support (fuel and water) during the first 30 days. Also, USCG high-endurance cutters are self-sufficient for 30 days, depending upon fuel consumption.

d. **Theater Distribution Nodes.** Each GCC will develop and employ its distribution capability according to the requirements outlined in the JFC's CONPLAN, OPLAN, and OPORD. The Service functional units perform the day-to-day operations of the theater distribution system to include activities referred to as distribution nodes. While the number and type of nodes are determined by the geography and the number and types of units that comprise the physical network, the primary distribution nodes are supply, maintenance, and materiel transfer. Traditionally, it is within the distribution nodes that congestion and bottlenecks occur. Therefore, nodes present the greatest challenge to the operators of the distribution process.

(1) **Supply Nodes.** These nodes undertake traditional warehousing activities (e.g., receipt, store, and issue) with the node operator normally establishing supply accountability for materiel. At these locations, the Services perform receipt operations to discharge the materiel from the delivery conveyance, in-check the shipment, and enter the appropriate information into the Service system. The efficiency and accuracy of this input is dependent upon source data and the ITV technology that accompanies the shipment. The receipt process establishes the Services' supply accountability for the materiel by placing it on the Services' asset balance file, thus making it available for redistribution. When a demand for materiel is received, the supply node performs the normal supply functions of picking, packing, and source data generation necessary to establish a record in the appropriate AIS and to perform the shipping process.

(2) **Maintenance Nodes**

(a) Maintenance nodes are maintenance as well as repair facilities. Items are repaired and returned to the owning unit or, in the case of components repaired in-theater, are placed back into the Services' supply systems. Also, if necessary, theater distribution managers can arrange for the flow of repairable items back into strategic distribution networks for movement to higher echelons of repair. While supply nodes maintain accountability for repairable items, the maintenance node establishes and maintains visibility of the materiel while it is in the repair process. This visibility includes: repair location; items awaiting maintenance; items repaired awaiting shipment; maintenance backlog; items shipped; and items to be disposed of including maintenance-generated HW.

(b) Maintenance node activities and information provide the distribution manager with an alternative source of supply to resolve critical item shortages within the theater, versus initiating requisition action from an out-of-theater source. The accountability and visibility of repair items are essential in order for the GCCs to establish the theater priority repair list and retrograde policy. Embedded health management, also known as Condition-Based Maintenance Plus, provides individual platform life cycle management information for improved maintenance management efforts, provides more accurate readiness status for commanders and logistics managers, and enables more effective global distribution processes. By providing more accurate identification and predictive notice of maintenance requirements, a reduction in priority distribution actions for components and repair parts will result. Additionally, this information provides the data source for Service and joint AISs that enables the GCC to perform redistribution of critical assets after repair.

(3) **Materiel Transfer Nodes.** These nodes perform materiel transfer or shipment reconfiguration activities. They are located between transportation segments; therefore, these node operators do not take ownership of the materiel or equipment. All these activities must have the capability to read and write to multiple devices and create and report standard materiel transactions. The functional processes involved are discussed below.

(a) **Intermodal Transfer.** At intermodal transfer nodes, transportation assets (e.g., trucks and railcars) are offloaded and intermodal platforms (e.g., containers, 463L pallets, flatracks) are in-checked and stored for follow-on movement. Service AISs provide visibility of transfer actions. Onward movement is arranged and the Service-specific documentation is prepared for the next mode of transportation.

(b) **Shipment Reconfiguration and Transfer.** This process involves breaking down and reconfiguring cargo for shipment. In the commercial industry, this is referred to as crossdock, breakbulk, or hub-and-spoke operations. Transportation is arranged, appropriate documentation prepared, and the subsequent transportation conveyance is loaded and dispatched.

(c) **Intramodal Transfer.** Intramodal transfer nodes are established along the distribution pipeline. Typically, at these nodes shipments are not deaggregated, but rather transferred between like transportation modes. These nodes report the progress of materiel and units moving in the distribution pipeline through the arrival and departure reporting process. Additionally, their functions include vehicle and cargo inspections, documentation, and dispatching of onward movement transportation assets.

3. **Supplier, Strategic, and Theater Distribution**

a. Utilizing the distribution framework discussed in the previous section, the JDDE COI must optimize organic and commercial capabilities from the point of origin/source of supply through the point of need to the point of employment or consumption. Current operational environments make these supplier-to-transporter-to-theater handoffs challenging. Furthermore, the DOD logistic support philosophy has shifted from a traditional stock-based system to a leaner, distribution-based system which reduces the traditional safety net of redundant materiel stocks and reinforces the importance of accurate planning and execution of each global distribution element. While some distribution continues to be made from producers and vendors through the military depot system, particularly for munitions and repair parts, commercial contracts for some materiel support now require CD delivery to the military customers on a global basis. Other contracts require delivery by the vendor to the DTS for movement into the overseas areas, where either the contractor takes possession to make the delivery or the shipment is moved by US military capability to the final destination.

b. The discussion above highlights that the evolution of military logistics requires an understanding of the growing complexity of global distribution execution and how it is accomplished through a variety of methods. However, while there are many variations within the DOD supply chain, the distribution process also has many common elements, regardless of commodity, destination, and mode. These elements are discussed below, from initiating action to ultimate issue/disposition. Some examples of typical distribution flow are also presented to illustrate the concept.

c. **Initiating Action.** An initiating action for distribution is a trigger that starts the need for something to be shipped to another location. These triggers include:

(1) **Requisition.** An item is requested for use. The item is sourced from a storage location (either DLA depot or other DOD installation) or through a contract order to a vendor directly. Each requisition or order has a unique identity (document) number to identify it throughout the process until receipt by the requisitioner or ultimate consignee.

(2) **Unit Move.** Unit line numbers in JOPES identify force requirements. When units are identified to deploy, in support of those force requirements, they identify specific equipment and personnel for movement. Transportation control numbers (TCNs) are then assigned to the unit cargo and accompanying sustainment.

(3) **Turn-in for Repair.** If an item requires maintenance or repair that cannot occur at its current location, the item is shipped to a maintenance depot or vendor for maintenance. Each item is provided a unique turn-in (for maintenance) document number for reference tracking and accountability purposes.

(4) **Turn-in for Reissue or Disposal.** When an item is no longer needed by the current owner, or is not serviceable or repairable, it is either disposed of locally, sent back to a supply inventory account (SSA or DLA distribution center) for restock and issue, or turned in to DLA Disposition Services for disposal or redistribution to another location. Each request for turn-in (for disposal) has a unique reference number for record keeping and accountability purposes.

(5) **Acquisition.** The item is acquired either by Service, DLA or through GSA. Each acquisition has a unique identification number to identify it through the process. The process also identifies how the item will enter into the DOD distribution process. In all cases, each initiating action contains an item unique identification number (if one exists), a national stock number (if one exists), or a commercial item number; a quantity and a unit of issue; and a unique reference number for the initiating action (such as requisition number or TCN).

d. **Prepare Shipment.** Once the need to ship is identified, the items need to be prepared for shipment. A distribution center or another inventory/storage location removes the item from storage and updates storage inventory levels in the appropriate AIS. The items are appropriately packaged and marked for the commodity, mode of transport, and destination. Each shipment unit is assigned a TCN. The TCN is derived from the guidance provided in Defense Transportation Regulation (DTR) 4500.9-R, *Defense Transportation Regulations*. Documentation is provided for the shipment unit, and electronic shipment notice information should be passed along to the original ordering activity, next interim node, carrier, and any other interested parties.

e. **Consolidate.** Depending upon the size of the single shipment unit and the destination location, the shipment unit may be consolidated with other shipments into one or more levels of consolidation. Each consolidation level is assigned a TCN. Multiple materiel release orders (MROs) may be consolidated into a multiline shipment unit or a single MRO may be divided into two or more shipment units, which, if consolidated, are then associated with a consolidated TCN. Further consolidations can occur as items are put together and higher level consolidated TCNs are assigned to the third level of consolidation. Documentation is provided for the shipment unit, and electronic shipment notice information should be passed along to the original ordering activity, next interim node, carrier, and any other interested parties. Consolidation may occur at the same location where the single shipment unit is prepared if enough single shipments occur to warrant consolidation. Otherwise, consolidation can happen at a CCP, or other supply chain nodes, such as a TCSP or an aerial port (pallets created at the aerial ports are typically for flight purposes only and are not officially consolidated—they are aggregated).

f. **Move.** Shipments can be moved from one location to another using a variety of transport methods.

(1) **Move by Truck, Rail, or Barge.** Most shipments will have one or more surface movement segments between the shipment origin and final consignee location that are made by truck, rail, barge, or a combination of these modes. The predominant mode is truck for sustainment items of supply and rail for unit movements. The truck movement may be within CONUS or OCONUS, and the shipment may be transferred from one truck to another during its in-transit movement. Most truck movements have a carrier identifier (ID), conveyance ID, and bill of lading (or similar document) that should identify all shipment pieces by TCN within the conveyance.

(2) **Move by Air.** Most air shipments are consolidated or aggregated shipments. As with truck shipment, a shipment may change aircraft multiple times between the origin and destination ports, similar to commercial air travelers who need to make connecting flights if no direct flight exists to the desired destination. Each aircraft movement has an aircraft ID and a manifest (or similar document) that identifies all consolidated shipments by TCN within the conveyance. Content detail for each consolidated or aggregated pallet is not contained within the manifest.

(3) **Move by Vessel.** Shipments may move by vessel if the required delivery time will allow this slower mode of transportation. Most sustainment shipments by sea are consolidated shipments. As with truck shipments, a consolidated shipment may change vessels multiple times between the origin and destination ports. Each vessel movement is assigned a carrier ID, vessel ID, and a manifest (or similar document) that identifies all consolidated shipments within the conveyance by TCN.

g. **Deconsolidate.** If a single shipment unit was consolidated with other shipments for transport, the shipment is deconsolidated for delivery to the consignee. Deconsolidation may happen at a POD, a theater distribution center, an SSA, or even at the final consignee activity location (if multiple shipments were sent to different organizations at the same location). Once deconsolidated, the consolidation TCN has served its purpose and is no longer used.

h. **Receive.** After the single shipment unit arrives at the final consignee location, the item is received by the supply activity. The item is noted in the supporting software system for that Service's or agency's activity. The item may be put into storage for later issue or routed directly to a consuming customer and placed in use.

i. **Initial Receipt from Vendor.** DOD orders items from vendors through a variety of contracting methods. Embedded in the purchase terms are directions concerning where and how to ship the items and what type of advanced notification the vendor should provide to DOD concerning the shipment and item details. Upon initial receipt from the vendor, the items are initiated into the defense supply chain.

DISTRIBUTION EXAMPLES

a. Outside the continental United States (OCONUS) delivery of a requisitioned item by air. A stocked item is ordered by a consuming field activity and the item manager at the inventory control point issues a materiel release order (MRO) to the distribution center that will source the requirement. This MRO triggers the item to be issued by the depot and prepared for shipment. If multiple items have been requested by the same consignee they may be combined into the same shipment. Further, if multiple shipments are destined to be handled via the same supply support activity (SSA), multiple shipments can be consolidated onto a 463L air pallet. The shipment, either loose or consolidated onto a pallet, is moved by truck to the aerial port of embarkation (APOE). At the APOE, loose shipments are aggregated onto 463L pallets for the flight. All pallets are loaded onto aircraft and flown to the aerial port of debarkation (APOD). At the APOD, the loose shipment pallets are often broken down, whereas the others remain full pallet shipments. Whether palletized or loose, the shipments are forwarded to the theater distribution center or SSA by truck. At the SSA all remaining pallets are deconsolidated, and the SSA receives the items. If the SSA ordered the item for inventory, it will be stored until issued for use by a unit. Otherwise it will be prepared for issue.

b. OCONUS delivery of a requisitioned item by surface. The item is ordered by a consuming field activity and an MRO is placed by the item manager. This MRO triggers the item to be issued by the depot and prepared for shipment. If multiple items have been requested by the same consignee they may be combined into the same shipment. Further, all shipments headed to the same SSA or other consignee that can be serviced by the same container conveyance are consolidated into an intermodal container. This consolidation may occur at a service installation shipping point, a distribution center, or at a consolidation and containerization point. The consolidated intermodal container is moved by truck to the seaport of embarkation (SPOE). All intermodal containers are loaded onto vessels and delivered to the seaport of debarkation (SPOD), either directly or via one or more transshipments. At the SPOD the containers are offloaded and cleared through customs before they are forwarded to the SSA by truck. After the SSA receives the item, it is either stored until issued for use by a unit if ordered for inventory or immediately issued.

---

c. Unit Move by Surface—Materiel and Unit Equipment. A deployment order triggers the unit to prepare materiel and equipment for movement to their deployed location. Materiel will be consolidated into intermodal containers or perhaps within trucks or other vehicles associated with the unit. Usually, but not always, the materiel and unit equipment are moved by rail to a SPOE, where they are then moved by vessel to the SPOD. Upon arrival at the SPOD, the materiel and unit equipment are offloaded, received, staged, and moved (by rail or other mode) to the unit's new location, where they are deconsolidated from the conveyance they arrived on and placed into use (employed).

d. Surface Retrograde Movements. There are many types of retrograde movements. While some items are disposed of in theater and not sent back to the US, this example illustrates the situation where the item does go back and is reissued, stored, or disposed of in the US. A retrograde decision by the inventory manager triggers disposition instructions and the item to be prepared for shipment. If the item can be containerized with other items moving to and from the same destination and origin, the item is moved to the SSA, where it will be consolidated with other retrograde materiel. The consolidated container is moved by ground transportation to the SPOE, where the container is loaded on a vessel and moved to the SPOD. At the SPOD, the container is offloaded and moved by ground transportation to the depot, or it is sent directly to a Defense Logistics Agency (DLA) Disposition Services site (if all items are headed for disposal rather than maintenance). If sent to the depot, the depot receives the shipments and stores the items until the item is reissued, sent to a DLA Disposition Services location for disposal, or sent to the maintenance unit for maintenance.

e. Maintenance Turn-In. The final example is a depot-level repairable (DLR) item that is being turned in for repair via surface movement. The owner of the item prepares the reparable component or end item for shipment. Typically, item documentation will reference a serial number and item unique identification (IUID) for accountability. The item is documented with a unique turn-in identification number for reference and accountability purposes, including the IUID (when available), and moved by truck to the SSA, a specialized contractor who manages the reverse logistics for a Service or agency, or other designated DLR materiel holding and shipping facility. From this level, the item may or may not be consolidated with other items moving to the same repair facility and then is moved by truck to a theater maintenance facility or is moved to a SPOE to be sent back to the United States (becoming a retrograde movement, as illustrated in the previous example).

Various Sources

j. **Store.** When an item is not immediately needed and does not require repair, it is placed in storage. Items may be stored in units of issue or larger groupings, such as pallets or cartons. Condition, shelf life, and security requirements should be considered for items in storage. Special monitoring requirements may also exist for sensitive, hazardous, or other special materials. Inventory/accountable records are updated to reflect the additional quantity and storage location.

    k. **Care of Supplies in Storage.** While an item is in storage, standard care for these items is performed. The type of care required depends upon the type of materiel. All materiel undergoes periodic inventory auditing to confirm quantities, locations, and shelf life. Items that require specific environmental conditions may be monitored to ensure conditions are maintained, such as the temperature for items requiring refrigeration. Other items may require periodic testing to ensure they are still serviceable.

    l. **Issue.** When an item in storage is needed for use, an order is placed and the item is issued. The item may have a minimum issue quantity based on quantity packaging. The inventory records are updated once the item is issued.

4. Retrograde, Return, Reutilization, and Disposal

    Retrograde is the process of moving nonunit equipment and materiel from a forward location to a reset (replenishment, repair, or recapitalization) program or to another directed area of operations to replenish unit stocks, or to satisfy stock requirements. Retrograde materiel consists of serviceable, unserviceable, economically repairable items and weapons systems destined to a source of repair, refurbishment program, or DLA Disposition Services. The distribution-based logistic system relies on the efficient redistribution of intratheater excesses when they are identified. The ability to capture, provide visibility of, and redistribute these assets contributes significantly to the effectiveness of the logistic effort.

    a. **Excess Usable Property: Serviceable and Repairable Property.** DLA, through its DLA Disposition Services field activity, will provide the maximum amount of excess property disposition management services possible within the AOR, and as far forward as practical through either a DDED or DST. These disposition management services include the following:

    (1) The provision of technical assistance to commanders, particularly with regard to HW management and disposal, and demilitarization requirements and procedures.

    (2) The receiving, storing, and issuing of foreign excess personal property (FEPP). FEPP is USG property physically located outside the US and its territories.

    (3) The provision of reutilization, transfer, and donation services. Redistribution of FEPP outside DOD is subject to the rules of the DOS and the Department of Commerce and will vary from country to country and operation to operation. DLA Disposition Services has a system in place to work with DOS for such redistribution and there is no need for the Services to devise ad hoc systems.

    (4) The provision of coordination for humanitarian assistance programs (HAPs).

    (5) The conduct of sales where such sales have been coordinated with the HN through DOS. Sales of FEPP constitute an export from the US and are subject to all export and import rules and restrictions.

(6) The administrative actions associated with abandonment and destruction of materiel.

(7) The overseeing of the disposal of all HAZMAT or HW.

For additional information regarding the redistribution and disposal of serviceable and repairable FEPP, see DOD 4160.21-M, Defense Materiel Disposition Manual, *and DOD 4160.21-M-1,* Defense Demilitarization Manual.

b. **Disposal of Materiel with Special Requirements.** This materiel includes radioactive items; hospital-generated infectious waste; and ammunition, explosives, and dangerous articles. Disposal of these items is a Service and national responsibility, and applicable Service and national regulations and policies apply. Disposal personnel may answer specific inquiries regarding what can and cannot be disposed of through DLA Disposition Services channels.

c. **Scrap.** The CCMD logistic and engineering staffs are responsible for providing policy on unserviceable materiel that has no value except for its basic material content. DLA Disposition Services will provide advice with regard to these issues and generally will be responsible for the sale of scrap materials. Care must be taken in the disposal of items declared to be scrap because demilitarization and trade security control requirements apply to scrap just as they do to serviceable property. Likewise, for FEPP, DOS and HN requirements must also be met. While the tenets of good recycling practices should always be followed, formal quality recycling programs as outlined in DODI 4715.4, *Pollution Prevention,* should only be established in mature, permanent theaters of operations.

d. **Munitions List Items (MLIs) and Commerce Control List Items (CCLIs).** The GCC must make provisions for proper disposal of MLIs and CCLIs. Significant quantities of DOD materiel are designated MLI and CCLI, and that designation is reflected in their demilitarization code. These items require special oversight, since it is DOD policy to identify and apply appropriate controls to areas of the world where their use would be in conflict with the interests of US foreign policy. DOD's first option for disposal of MLIs and CCLIs must be through the DLA Disposition Services since it has policies and procedures for the efficient and correct disposal of these items both inside and outside the US. When considering the disposal of MLIs and CCLIs, the CCDR should observe the following:

(1) In coordination with DLA Disposition Services, determine and implement feasible, cost-effective, and efficient options to meet DOD demilitarization requirements. (See DOD 4160.21-M-1, *Defense Demilitarization Manual.*)

(2) Ensure that Service components provide technical assistance to the disposal activity.

(3) Ensure compliance by subordinate activities with demilitarization requirements.

(4) Ensure logistic staffs are prepared to support retrograde of MLIs and CCLIs as the primary method of control if in-country disposal options are not viable.

e. **Captured or Confiscated Weapons.** Captured and confiscated conventional weapons must be handled similarly to US-owned weapons. They have an additional control requirement in that they must be entered into the DOD Small Arms Serialization Program by the Service component that captures or confiscates them prior to any demilitarization action. Consult the staff judge advocate for evacuation/disposition as a war trophy. Captured and confiscated conventional weapons are normally destroyed by the Services and/or retrograded to CONUS for destruction. Captured and confiscated CBRN weapons must be handled IAW applicable environmental, safety, and other pertinent laws and regulations, to include international and bilateral treaties. Consult the commander's guidance and the staff judge advocate for evacuation/disposition of captured and confiscated CBRN weapons. Captured or recovered improvised weapons, such as improvised explosive devices (IEDs), should be rendered safe by technical experts such as explosive ordnance disposal (EOD) teams. After the material has been rendered safe, it should be processed through a weapons technical intelligence exploitation laboratory for forensic and technical exploitation. Consult with the intelligence directorate of a joint staff within the joint force for guidance on evacuation/disposition of captured and confiscated improvised weapons. Packaging, certifying, and transporting explosives require the involvement of trained and certified personnel. EOD company and battalion representatives may facilitate the transportation of explosives by certifying that they are packaged correctly and that they are safe to ship.

For information on countering IEDs, see JP 3-15.1, Countering-Improvised Explosive Device Operations.

f. **Reutilization and Transfers.** A primary goal of disposal is to maximize reutilization of DOD property. Reutilization of DOD excess is a source of supply for combatant forces, reduces the need for retrograde transportation, and minimizes the need for abandonment and destruction of FEPP. Another effective method of dealing with FEPP in foreign countries is to use HAPs in conjunction with DLA Disposition Services and DOS to transfer excess to non-US recipients. Neither Service components nor subordinate activities should make the transfer of DOD FEPP to foreign governments or NGOs. Transfer of FEPP requires DOD and DOS concurrence. DLA Disposition Services will provide coordination with the local government, DOS, DOD HAP, and the CCDR logistic staff to expedite the selection and transfer of FEPP to authorized recipients.

g. **HAZMAT and HW**

(1) It is DOD policy to store, handle, and dispose of all regulated and/or HAZMAT and HW property IAW applicable environmental, safety, and other pertinent laws and regulations. In peacetime, the DOD components in foreign nations will comply with the final governing standards (FGSs) established for that nation related to the storage, handling, and disposition of HAZMAT and the management of HW. Where no FGSs have been established, DOD components shall comply with applicable international agreements, applicable HN standards, or the Overseas Environmental Baseline Guidance Document (OEBGD) and, in cases of conflicting requirements, shall normally comply with the standard list that is most protective of human health or the environment. In contingency operations, however, the OEBGD and FGSs do not apply. However, the USG and DOD are committed to the protection of the environment worldwide. To this end, consistent with mission

requirements, planning efforts should address a strategy for environmentally sound disposal. Early planning and coordination in contingency operations are essential. Key considerations by the CCDR's logistic staff for the disposal of HAZMAT or HW include the following:

(a) The determination of the disposal CONOPS. Historically, while not required, CONOPS has always followed the OEBGD where other guidance did not exist.

(b) Addressing pollution prevention and waste minimization requirements in OPLANs and ensuring the Services recognize the need to provide sufficient storage containers to capture hazardous property and properly store it pending disposal. Generation of HW begins immediately; disposal may take some time to arrange. Also ensure that planning supports reutilization and sales as the primary methods of disposal.

(c) Establishing country-to-country agreements with the HNs to ensure that disposal options are supportable. Options for disposal can include: retrograde either by the Services or a DLA Disposition Services contract if one can be arranged, in-theater disposal by DLA Disposition Services, and in-country disposal by a contractor. DLA Disposition Services is responsible for developing criteria and guidance for the disposal of HW for DOD per DODI 4715.6, *Environmental Compliance*.

(d) Ensuring that suitable facilities and adequate equipment and materials are available for HAZMAT or HW storage and movement.

(e) Ensuring that funds are allocated and available to satisfy HAZMAT or HW disposal requirements.

(f) Ensuring that trained personnel are assigned to perform safety and environmental tasks.

(g) Providing the same level of disposal support for captured or confiscated HAZMAT or HW.

(2) Normally, the US will not provide disposal support for non-US generated HAZMAT or HW, except as provided for above.

h. **Sales Programs.** Sale of FEPP to the private sector or to a foreign government is a primary DLA Disposition Services method of disposal. A properly executed sales program minimizes the need for in-country abandonment and destruction and realizes major cost avoidance in retrograde transportation. An in-country sales program requires a country-to-country agreement that permits internal sales of specified commodities, sales for export, and expedited tax and customs processing. The CCDR's J-4 should address these issues during the country-to-country negotiations phase. Achieving sales authority after entry into the AOR can be difficult and result in unnecessary delays or major restrictions that may impact the disposal CONOPS. Sales to governments are conducted under the authority of the Arms Export Control Act, which provides the authority for writing and implementing FMS cases with qualified foreign countries. Normally, FMS cases require months to process. However, if there are identified requirements, DLA Disposition Services can prepare FMS cases relatively quickly.

5. End-to-End Asset Visibility and In-Transit Visibility

a. AV throughout the JDDE provides the CCDR the capability to see and redirect strategic and operational commodity/force flow in support of current and projected priorities. It also provides users with timely and accurate information on the location, movement, status, and identity of units, personnel, equipment, and supplies so that they may act upon that information to improve DOD logistic practices supporting operations.

b. ITV is the ability to track the identity, status, and location of DOD units, nonunit cargo, passengers, patients, and personal property from origin to consignee or destination across the range of military operations. ITV of assets moving through the DTS or in support of DOD operations is an essential element of the DOD warfighting capability and is required by the supported CCDRs.

(1) ITV Reporting

(a) IGC. IGC is the authoritative data source (ADS) for ITV of shipments moving within the DTS and is the DOD system of record for ITV data. IGC integrates supply, cargo, passenger, and unit requirements and movements with airlift, air refueling, and sealift schedules and movements to provide ITV of personnel, materiel, and military forces. IGC integrates ITV data into a single view of the DTS.

(b) The TCN is the alphanumeric character set assigned to a shipment (unit move and sustainment) to maintain ITV. IGC links the TCN to the MILSTRIP number, if available, and to commercial express carrier tracking numbers, if applicable. This gives the user multiple ways to track an item.

(2) **ITV Is a Process.** While USTRANSCOM is the designated DOD lead proponent for the development of a comprehensive, integrated DOD ITV capability, it is not the sole process owner. The ITV process consists of numerous players who must follow designated business procedures to provide accurate source data, prompt nodal updates, shipment status information, and shipment receipt notices as well as employ various AISs and AIT in both peace and war. Those players include, but are not limited to, deploying units, node and port operators, commercial transportation service providers, installations, and depots. Each plays a critical role in ensuring seamless ITV by providing movement information to IGC within the criteria specified in JP 4-01, *The Defense Transportation System*.

(3) **Unit Cargo.** Unit cargo includes all unit equipment, accompanying supplies, Service pre-positioned forces and afloat pre-positioned equipment, and war reserve stocks. IGC receives unit movement data from various systems from point of origin, through a POE and POD, and within the CONUS and theater. Using the Service's unit move system, the unit is responsible for generating deployment data compliant with DTR 4500.9-R, *Defense Transportation Regulations.* GATES is the primary POE and POD system for sealift and air mobility. Where no GATES capability or automated ITV feeder system exists, alternative unit data capture solutions are coordinated by the lift provider and the moving organization and tailored to meet ITV requirements. AIT protocols should also be employed as

appropriate anywhere along the movement pipeline to provide timely, accurate movement updates.

(4) **Nonunit-Related Cargo.** Nonunit-related cargo includes all equipment and supplies requiring transportation to or from an OA, other than those identified as the equipment or accompanying supplies of a specific unit (e.g., resupply, military support for allies, and support for nonmilitary programs such as civil relief). IGC receives source shipment information from defense and commercial vendor shippers, nodal updates from key defense and commercial logistic activities (consolidation points, aerial ports and seaports, theater onward movement locations, etc.), and shipment status information from commercial carriers. The origin shipping activity is responsible for generating the appropriate movement documentation. IGC receives DTR 4500.9-R, *Defense Transportation Regulation*-compliant source shipment information from the Distribution Standard System (DSS) for DLA shipments. As shipments arrive and depart from USTRANSCOM seaports and aerial ports, IGC receives updates from the port/terminal management system. Finally, IGC receives shipment status information from commercial carriers and vendors using industry EDI standards. AIT protocols are also employed as appropriate to facilitate timely, accurate data capture.

(5) **Unit Personnel.** Unit personnel include all civilian and military passengers directly attached to, and moving with, a deploying unit. IGC receives unit passenger data from source systems, POE and POD systems, and CONUS and theater consignee transportation systems. It is a unit responsibility to generate deployment data compliant with DTR 4500.9-R. As passengers move through USTRANSCOM aerial ports, GATES updates the manifest information in IGC. In turn, IGC offers inbound passenger manifest data to the APOD and other receiving activities for planning and JRSOI management activities. Upon passengers' arrival at the APOD, information about their onward movement will be passed to IGC. Where there is not a GATES capability, or an automated ITV feeder system readily available, alternative unit data capture solutions are coordinated by the lift provider and the moving organizations and tailored to meet ITV requirements. The use of the common access card is directed by the Deputy Secretary of Defense and will enhance data accuracy while expediting passenger manifesting and processing procedures.

(6) **Nonunit-Related Personnel.** Nonunit passengers include all personnel requiring transportation to or from an OA, other than those assigned to a specific unit (e.g., filler personnel, replacements, temporary duty or temporary additional duty personnel, civilians, medical evacuees, and personnel). GATES serves as the primary information collection point for reservations and booking of nonunit passengers. The originating installation transportation office electronically requests airlift through GATES, which in turn provides both schedules and seat confirmation to the requester. GATES also prepares passenger manifests for departing aircraft and transmits that information to IGC. For nonunit personnel traveling from other than GATES-supported locations, passenger manifesting is accomplished and forwarded to IGC. DOD does not track passengers moving on scheduled commercial transportation (e.g., GSA City Pairs contracts), as a robust commercial capability currently exists.

(7) **Lift Assets.** An equally critical aspect of ITV is visibility over airlift, sealift, and surface lift assets (aircraft, ships, and road and rail conveyances). Visibility of lift assets in-transit or scheduled for movement is key to the C2 of those assets, port management, and scheduling the movement of both unit and nonunit cargo and personnel. USTRANSCOM port software programs feed status of shipments to IGC, Services, and DLA software programs. AMC manages validated air movement requests, plans and schedules organic and AMC chartered intertheater airlift missions, allocates lift assets, and tasks airlift providers using AMC's Consolidated Air Mobility Planning System (CAMPS). CAMPS distributes tasked airlift schedules with its associated movement requirements to the Global Decision Support System (GDSS). CAMPS also provides visibility of validated SAAM requirements directly to IGC for use during USTRANSCOM and AMC planning phases of airlift scheduling. AMC uses the GDSS for unit-level mission planning and to manage mission execution. GDSS passes airlift schedules and arrival and departure information to IGC. Similarly, MSC provides sealift schedules and updates for organic and chartered lift assets to IGC via the MSC integrated command, control, and communication system, while commercial carriers pass arrival and departure event information via EDI. There is no single DOD system for tracking all road and rail schedules; however, there are some DOD AISs and AIT that monitor portions of road and rail moves.

c. Visibility is an essential component of distribution management and provides the means to determine if the distribution pipeline is responsive to customer needs. It begins at the point where materiel is stored prior to its movement. ITV then provides the necessary means to track the identity, status, and location of DOD unit and nonunit cargo, passengers, patients, and lift assets from origin to destination, in peacetime, contingencies, and war. In order to accomplish this, information must be captured and subsequently entered into the information network where it becomes critical to have the capability to dynamically update that source data with information from logistic systems in relation to the transport, storage, maintenance, or supply status of any particular item or shipment until it is received by the ultimate consumer. This information must be accessible to all defense distribution systems users regardless of Service or echelon of command. Once materiel and units arrive in theater, visibility may become more difficult as the structure and sophistication of communications and information diminish. Joint distribution must provide current asset status to the lowest possible echelon. Each Service should endeavor to meet all visibility requirements. There are unique in-theater visibility requirements that include in-process, in-storage, intratheater excess, in-transit, and in-theater information.

6. Management and Control of Intermodal Platforms

a. **General.** Container management is the planning, organizing, directing, controlling, and executing of functions and responsibilities required to provide for positive and effective use of DOD and Military Department owned, leased, or controlled ISO containers. It includes functions and responsibilities of life cycle asset and operational management. Containers used to deploy and sustain DOD forces around the world are categorized as GO, GL, or containers furnished by an intermodal ocean carrier. Carrier furnished (CF) containers are also referred to as DOD-controlled containers. Management and control of intermodal platforms is accomplished by global, Service, and theater container and pallet managers as described below. DLA and other Service-specific entities contract for the acquisition of containers on behalf of DOD components IAW global container management policy for the efficient and effective management and use of intermodal common use containers.

Refer to DTR 4500.9-R, Defense Transportation Regulations, Part VI, Management and Control of Intermodal Containers and System 463L Equipment, *for additional information.*

   b. **Global Container and Pallet Managers.** USTRANSCOM, as DPO, has designated SDDC as DOD global container manager (GCM) and AMC as the global pallet manager (GPM). Containers and 463L pallets are intermodal platforms. GCM/GPMs provide a wide range of functions for CCMDs, Services, and DOD agencies.

      (1) **GCM**

         (a) GCM provides uninterrupted AV of all GO, GL, or CF ISO containers from entry into the DTS to exit from the DTS. This includes containers arriving, moving within, and departing AORs and those used for other purposes such as storage, force protection, office/living spaces, etc. CF containers are those containers that are provided by ocean carriers to DOD under terms of universal services contract. Exit from the DTS is defined as:

            1. Return to carriers for carrier-owned containers.

            2. Return to owners for leased containers.

            3. Change of function from transportation to nontransportation use (e.g., containers used for storage, force protection, living spaces) as directed by a CCDR or owning/leasing Service.

            4. In non-contingency environments, return of Service owned or managed containers to the Services, as coordinated between the TCM and Service container manager (SCM).

         (b) GCM provides accountability and inventory control. Accountability includes 100 percent accuracy of the assets by container identification number, location, and status (loaded, in-use, or empty) of all DOD-owned, -leased, or -controlled containers being used in DTS; standardized managerial reporting procedures for capturing data/information of containers at all transportation nodes; and the database management of DOD's system of record for global container management. Inventory control includes maintaining the DOD ISO Container Registry (owner, location, condition status, maintenance/repair, inspection/certification, etc.) for all DOD ISO containers owned by the Services, including ISO-configured equipment, such as tactical shelters, or Service-unique containers.

         (c) GCM provides financial management relating to monitoring and minimizing detention costs and equipment detention billing verification for CF containers under terms of the relevant USTRANSCOM-managed ocean transportation contracts.

(d) GCM provides contracting support as the DOD single manager, in the container arena, for intermodal equipment leasing, intermodal transportation service, and commercial shipping contracts.

(2) **GPM**

(a) GPM serves as the DOD single operational manager of 463L system equipment worldwide.

(b) GPM provides management oversight for major command and other DOD component's pallet and net monitors.

(c) GPM provides recommendations to USTRANSCOM and CCDR staffs on theater 463L asset issues.

(d) GPM manages all 463L system assets from origin to final destination to include return or allocation of assets within a theater of operations.

(e) GPM manages a global 463L system asset database to provide inventory, accountability, tracking, visibility services, and support.

c. **Service Container Management.** Services manage their inventories of intermodal containers and flatracks through either a single SCM or by decentralized management where individual major commands or units manage their own assets. An SCM is an organization designated by a Service as its single manager for management and control of that Service's owned or leased containers, flatracks, and other distribution platforms, focusing on inventory, accountability, and readiness. SCMs maintain data on inspection and maintenance of Service-owned containers or component-owned containers to allow compliance with DOD and federal standards. SCMs also maintain central repositories of International Convention for Safe Containers (CSC) inspection reports on Service-owned ISO containers and are responsible for maintaining the Service's portion of the DOD ISO container registry maintained by the GCM. SCMs also initiate, reconcile, and maintain periodic inventories of all Service-owned and -leased containers, and coordinate with the GCM on disposition of carrier-owned equipment reported through the inventory process.

d. **Theater Container Management.** Theater container management is doctrinally a function of movement control and is an overall GCC responsibility. GCCs must provide for management and control of all DOD intermodal container assets entering, moving within, and leaving their AOR. They may assign this mission to their J-4, JDDOC (if established), Service component, or designated TCM. The TCM will have overall responsibility for intermodal equipment system management and control functions within the AOR. However, the responsibility for controlling and returning intermodal equipment to the DTS or to commercial industry remains with the GCC. GCCs and their designated TCM also:

(1) Develop container requirements and policies to optimize use of the DOD intermodal container system for cargo movement between origin and destination consistent with their CONOPS. During the initial stages of an operation, DOD-owned or -leased containers are the preferred means for deployment of equipment and supplies, particularly

for forward movement to remote locations. See Appendix F, "Intermodal Container/Platform Management and Tracking Plan (Sample Template)," for an example of a GCC intermodal platform management plan.

(2) Coordinate with USTRANSCOM, Joint Staff, Service commands, DLA, and other agencies to identify and establish pure-pack pallet and/or pure-pack sealift container requirements, locations, lanes, etc., to facilitate responsiveness to DOD units operating in their AOR.

(3) Ensure nonunit-owned intermodal equipment is managed in the AOR through monitoring, tracking, and redistributing as required, all intermodal equipment moving into, within, and out of the AOR. Coordinate with SCM on nonunit, Service-owned containers, and work with the appropriate SCM on local (theater) management and disposition of Service-owned containers being employed as theater common-use assets. Topics requiring coordination with the SCM include but are not limited to the general use of Service-owned containers, theater policies and procedures that impact those containers, and specific disposition processes.

(4) Provide for effective, efficient receipt, movement, and return of DOD-owned, -leased, or -controlled intermodal equipment entering the theater of operations. DOD-controlled ISO containers are those containers furnished by carriers that are in the theater and under DOD control as part of SDDC contracts.

(5) Establish a process for identifying, controlling, and managing intermodal equipment authorized for transition to nontransportation uses (e.g., force protection, office/living space, and temporary storage).

(6) Provide container management oversight and make recommendations to GCC regarding container management.

(7) Establish container management business practices that produce actionable metrics to enable inventory reconciliation and accurate data in the Integrated Booking System-(IBS) Container Management Module.

(8) Establish and maintain procedures for return of empty containers and reallocation of empty containers for intratheater movement and retrograde support.

(9) Develop and maintain standardized reports and AOR reporting procedures for providing information and performance metrics to all units, organizations, departments, agencies, and activities.

(10) Establish and deploy container management teams to key nodes throughout the AOR to provide quality control and training to installation and unit container control officers.

(11) Coordinate with the GCC's J-4 and JDDOC and applicable country container authorities, as required, to establish transload sites at designated nodes throughout the theater.

(12) Coordinate with SDDC on container management policy and procedure implementation in theater, container usage standards, container management system use and data accuracy, reports and other areas where coordination with the GCM is applicable.

(13) Coordinate with Service level container managers on applicable policies and procedures relevant to Service owned containers. Make certain that usage of Service owned or managed containers is coordinated to ensure proper inventory, maintenance, usage, and return of Service intermodal equipment.

(14) As necessary, establish and maintain a container management element that, between the TCM staff and the container management element, will do container tracking and metrics; maintain visibility of container management processes for the theater; maintain container management system data through data corrections; provide user help support for system access issues; provide theater user general help support; perform container ownership, size/type, numbering and other research; facilitate container transfers including disposal, inventory adjustments, ownership changes, and foreign transfers; and support spreadsheet data transfer as required.

e. **Theater Pallet Manager.** IAW DTR 4500.9-R, *Defense Transportation Regulations*, Part VI, *Management and Control of Intermodal Containers and System 463L Equipment*, Air Force aerial port personnel maintain overall control of all 463L assets on their installation. At joint locations, the aerial port personnel work closely with the local movement control team and arrival/departure airfield control group to expedite the return of assets from their customers. Units should coordinate 463L requirements with the local aerial port/air terminal for redeployment and cargo movement.

(1) Air terminals must maintain aerial port tie-down equipment IAW applicable regulations. Aerial ports designate a pallet and net monitor to account for all operational assets, both serviceable and repairable, under the control of air terminals.

(2) 463L asset reporting is accomplished IAW DTR 4500.9-R, Part VI.

(3) The Air Force component of the GCC directs the reallocation of 463L pallet and net resources based on requirements in the AOR. To avoid loss and agricultural contamination fines to the DOD, it establishes and publishes pallet and net cleaning policies IAW USDA requirements.

f. **Theater Operations**

(1) **Container Operations.** SDDC in its role as GCM uses military and commercial ships, trucks, and rail to deliver containers to SPOEs and SPODs in CONUS and OCONUS. Once offloaded in a theater, containers are then moved to destination(s) via the theater distribution system. Containers delivered by commercial ocean carriers are transferred to military responsibility upon clearing customs at the SPOD or after the carrier has delivered to a specific consignee location (door-to-door delivery) within the AOR. CF containers delivered by the ocean carriers accrue detention charges after the expiration of the free time allowed to the consignee for unstuffing and returning the container to the carrier. Detention charges vary and accrue based on type of container, discharge date, and the

number of days the container is held by the government past the date the free time expires. As such, theater container management is linked to timely and accurate flow of information, the movement control process, and the reporting of container receipt (in-gate) and movement from SPOD to AOR locations (outgate), and notification of when CF containers are unstuffed and ready for pickup. During contingency operations forward-deployed units and agencies have many military requirements that containers can meet over and above use of the container as a transportation asset. These include using containers as sealable and securable dry and refrigerated storage facilities, force protection barriers, office/living spaces, bunkers, etc. Since the preponderance of sustainment moves into an AOR via commercial ocean carrier-provided door-to-door intermodal service, CF containers will enter the AOR in large quantities. In mature theater of operations, receipt, unstuffing, and timely return of CF containers is essential in order to avoid detention charges. In expeditionary environments or austere areas of operations, the ability to access dry/cold storage facilities is extremely limited or nonexistent due to lack of such facilities in the HN or limitations imposed on the GCC by DOD guidance or federal statute. As such, units and agencies operating in the AOR may have to retain CF containers past free time resulting in costly DOD container detention bills. These costs may be minimized by the GCM implementing the strategic policy of using GO/GL containers to support the GCC or by coordinating with the TCM and country container authority for reduced detention or container buy outs of CF containers once they are in the AOR. Another method for reducing detention costs is to establish transload operations whereby cargo is removed from CF containers and reloaded into GO or GL containers for movement into the AOR. Transload of containers is inherently inefficient and should be avoided unless deemed mission essential. Transload may be a cost-effective action under certain conditions such as intratheater transportation costs, operational necessity, or other determining factors. Transloading operations require GCC approval and the establishment of a pool of GO (preferred) or GL containers under the management and control of the TCM. Although fiscal discipline dictates that the payment of detention charges be minimized to the greatest extent practicable, for a host of operational situations, the payment of detention charges is a reality. Container detention charges for specified contingency operations will be billed separately from the ocean charges and shall be assessed against the lead Service component for those countries in the AOR where container detention occurs, as specified by the supported GCC.

(2) **463L Pallet Operations.** AMC and CCDR's Air Force components use 463L pallets to deliver joint cargo around the world. Due to the nature of the distribution system, once pallets arrive in the theater, they are transported back and forth among the DTS, SSAs, and end users. All units and logistic agencies will prevent abuse of these assets, and make every effort to recycle them back into the DTS for intended use. Failure to return these assets into the transportation system results in significant monetary loss to the DOD. Loss and/or misuse of 463L resources also reduces availability of these critical resources for time-sensitive cargo movement resulting in slower delivery times. The GCC through the Air Force component will establish and publicize formal policy, procedures, and timeframes for all Services/agencies to manage and return pallet and net resources to the DTS. The policy should also address abuse/misuse of these assets. Procedures will be coordinated with AMC GPM and then sent to all units and logistic agencies within the theater of operations.

g. **Postcontingency Container Management.** It may not be cost-effective to return all containers to CONUS. The TCM will work with USTRANSCOM and the GCM to determine effective and cost efficient policies for postcontingency operations. GCCs may, in consultation with applicable SCMs, retain a portion of GO containers for future contingency or theater transloading purposes. Containers remaining in theater will be stored, accounted for, tracked in the specified container management system, certified for sea movement (if required), tracked when moved, and reported on as required. In addition, containers remaining in a theater of operation become the property of the organization having possession and utilization of the item. These containers will be listed on a valid property accountability register.

Intentionally Blank

CHAPTER V
CONTROLLING DISTRIBUTION

"If words of command are not clear and distinct, if orders are not thoroughly understood, the general is to blame. But if his orders are clear, and the soldiers nevertheless disobey, then it is the fault of their officers."

Sun Tzu, *The Art of War*

1. Introduction

a. This chapter describes the authorities, organizations, and control mechanisms that enable the synchronization of joint distribution operations in support of the JFC. JP 3-0, *Joint Operations,* identifies C2 as a joint function. Command includes the authority and responsibility for effectively using available resources to plan, organize, direct, coordinate, and control military forces for the accomplishment of assigned missions. Control is inherent in command; however, end-to-end distribution rarely has unity of command making the control of distribution more challenging.

b. Throughout this publication, control of distribution is the ability to coordinate and synchronize. This construct addresses all three joint movement legs, intracontinental, intertheater, and intratheater, but does so within the context of a single, coordinated joint enterprise that possesses sufficient authority to exercise selective control across the entire joint distribution pipeline. Control over the distribution pipeline means the ability to track and shift—and potentially reconfigure (per supported commander's requirements and priorities)—forces, equipment, and supplies, even while en route, and to deliver tailored packages directly to the CCDR. Inherent in this control is the capability to expand, contract, and reconfigure the components of the distribution pipeline to meet the requirements of the supported commander. Control also includes activities such as planning, apportioning, allocating, routing, scheduling, validation of priorities, and directing—functions, for example, typically associated with movement control entities.

c. Control of movements across the entire distribution pipeline is achieved through the ability to coordinate and synchronize processes, business rules, systems/tools, and organizations. Application of centralized control and decentralized execution among the JDDE COI produces the flexibility necessary to adapt logistic structures and procedures to changing situations, missions, and concepts of operation to support fluid joint operations. Ultimately, the distribution control mechanisms outlined in this chapter provide a collaborative capability to promote end-to-end unity of effort among JDDE partners to meet joint force requirements. However, the overall success of the JDDE to effectively and efficiently support achievement of joint force objectives depends on every subordinate commander in the end-to-end process—control, lift provider, nodal, and unit levels—all leading their respective organizations to execute their assigned missions with excellence, discipline, and IAW established procedures.

2. Authorities and Responsibilities

This section describes several authorities and responsibilities that are applicable.

a. USTRANSCOM serves as the DPO, responsible for coordinating and overseeing the DOD distribution system to provide interoperability, synchronization, and alignment of DOD-wide, end-to-end distribution. In addition, the DPO serves as the DOD single coordination and synchronization element on behalf of and in coordination with the JDDE COI.

b. **Common Use.** Common use applies to services, materiel, or facilities provided by a DOD agency or a Military Department on a common basis for two or more DOD agencies, elements, or other organizations as directed.

c. **Common-User Transportation.** Common-user transportation and transportation services are those provided on a common basis for two or more DOD agencies and, as authorized, non-DOD agencies. Common-user assets within the DTS are under the COCOM of CDRUSTRANSCOM, excluding Service-organic or theater-assigned transportation assets. Theater-assigned common-user transportation assets are under the COCOM of the respective GCC.

d. **Direct Support.** Direct support is defined as a mission requiring a force to support another specific force and authorizing it to answer directly to the supported force's request for assistance.

e. **General Support.** General support is that support which is given to the supported force as a whole and not to any particular subdivision thereof.

f. **Supported Commander.** The supported commander is the commander having primary responsibility for all aspects of a task assigned by the JSCP or other joint operation planning authority. In the context of joint operation planning, this term refers to the commander who prepares OPLANs or OPORDs in response to requirements of the CJCS. In the context of a support command relationship, the supported commander receives assistance from another commander's force or capabilities, and is responsible for ensuring that the supporting commander understands the assistance required. For distribution purposes, supported organizations are JDDE customers that need something moved. JDDE customers define movement requirements—what, where, and when. They include:

(1) **JFCs.** The supported commander identifies requirements and sets priorities for all supporting commanders and organizations within the OA. These prioritized requirements drive unity of effort across the JDDE in support of the supported commander's requirements.

(2) **Joint Capability Providers.** Joint capability providers include USTRANSCOM, USSOCOM, US Strategic Command, and the Services in their roles as major customers of the JDDE.

(3) **Services.** The Services' role to organize, train, equip, and provide logistics support to their respective forces is executed through their Service components to support the

GCCs. Services, in coordination with the Joint Staff J-3 prepare their forces for deployment and follow-on execution of assigned missions.

(4) **Supporting Agencies/Organizations.** Similar to the Services, DLA and GSA function in support of the JFC by providing sustainment supplies to JFC components. Organizations within the JDDE support DLA and GSA in the movement of supplies.

(5) **Non-DOD USG Organizations, NGOs, Private IGOs, and Multinational Organizations.** When DOD approves access to JDDE movement support as required to accomplish a specified mission, these organizations are JDDE customers.

g. **Supporting Commander.** The supporting commander is the commander who provides augmentation forces or other support to a supported commander or who develops a supporting plan. This includes the designated CCMDs and DOD agencies as appropriate. In the context of a support command relationship, the supporting commander aids, protects, complements, or sustains another commander's force and is responsible for providing the assistance required by the supported commander. For distribution purposes, supporting organizations are JDDE partners with resources and responsibility to provide movement capability and are, as such, supporting. They include:

(1) **USTRANSCOM.** USTRANSCOM serves as the single coordination and synchronization element on behalf of and in coordination with the JDDE COI to establish processes to plan, apportion, allocate, route, schedule, validate priorities, track movements, and redirect forces and supplies per the supported commander's intent. This coordination and synchronization does not usurp the supported CCDR's Title 10, USC, responsibilities, but drives unity of effort throughout the JDDE to support CCDRs. In its capacity as a supporting command, USTRANSCOM leverages the DTS and commercial transportation industry to execute movement of forces and sustainment. USTRANSCOM performs another essential role in the JDDE—it integrates JDDE processes by proposing recommendations for DOD policy, directives, instructions, and decision memorandums. It sets parameters for distribution data standardization and systems configuration to provide JDDE-wide end-to-end visibility. A wide range of commercial transportation options are managed under USTRANSCOM as part of the total distribution process. Vendor support of shipments has a major role in sustaining the supported commander. The JDDE COI requires visibility of these shipments to ensure they are integrated into the overall distribution effort and that their delivery meets the supported commander's requirements.

(2) **Service Components of the Joint Force.** The Service components have organic theater movement capabilities. As such, selected Service movement capability elements are contributing members of the JDDE when directed by the JFC. The Services also have Title 10, USC, responsibilities for logistics and provide sustainment functions in conjunction with DLA and coordinate for vendor support for delivery of many commodities. They also contribute theater sustainment functions in support of the joint force.

(3) **DLA.** As an essential member of the JDDE, movement-related elements of DLA contribute to the movement of sustainment. DLA has a major role in the sourcing, packaging, and preparation of sustainment stocks and pre-positioned material to be moved

through the distribution pipeline. DLA also coordinates for vendor support for delivery of many commodities.

3. Distribution Control Functions

a. This section describes end-to-end distribution control functions required to achieve coordinated intertheater and intratheater distribution operations. A movement requirement is formally defined as a stated movement mode and time-phased need for the transport of units, personnel, and/or materiel from a specified origin to a specified destination. Movement demand, on the other hand, is typically generated in advance of the movement requirement (using some type of forecast such as a JOPES time-phased force and deployment list [TPFDL], reservation for capacity, or "advance" requisition). This demand data is often necessary to establish route structures, assess IDLs, and apportion lift assets.

b. Movement demands are normally satisfied by one of two means: on-demand (discrete) or capacity-based movements. Both types are required within a robust distribution pipeline but require different protocols to manage them.

(1) On-demand movements are identified by payload, time, and place in advance to transport specific units or materiel to a specific place and a specific time. Force movements for deployment and redeployment that are captured in a JOPES TPFDD are typical examples of on-demand movements.

(2) Capacity-based movements permit assignment of personnel and cargo to be transported against scheduled lift. Sustainment and retrograde movements rely primarily on capacity-based lift. Sustainment requirements fall into two categories: requisition and nonrequisition. Requisitions are used by customers ordering items with variable usage rates (e.g., repair parts). Nonrequisition requirements may be automatic resupply for commodities and classes of materiel with constant usage rates (e.g., subsistence) or acquisitions (e.g., new armor plating for vehicles). Sustainment movements by airlift channel mission, sealift liner service, or routine truck convoys that are scheduled on predetermined routes/times and allow booking of passengers/cargo are examples of capacity-based movements.

c. Distribution control occurs within the continuous operations cycle of planning, preparing, executing, and assessing (see Figure V-1). Planning includes collecting information about the status of the JDDE organization and activities, prospective cargo routing or LOCs, and conducting integrated planning across modes of conveyance, terminals, organizations, and LOCs. Preparing includes sharing information among JDDE elements and integrating the deployment and distribution systems (commercial, military, and interagency/multinational). Executing includes communicating with friendly forces (both JDDE and other) and coordinating and synchronizing JDDE assets. Assessing includes collecting information about JDDE performance and continuous evaluation of JDDE effectiveness and efficiency in order to update JDDE status and planning. This continuous cycle ensures that all elements of the JDDE (organizations, terminals, lift assets, and LOCs) are arranged in time, space, and purpose to deliver the supported CCDR's deployment and distribution requirements at the right time to allow the CCDR to accomplish the mission.

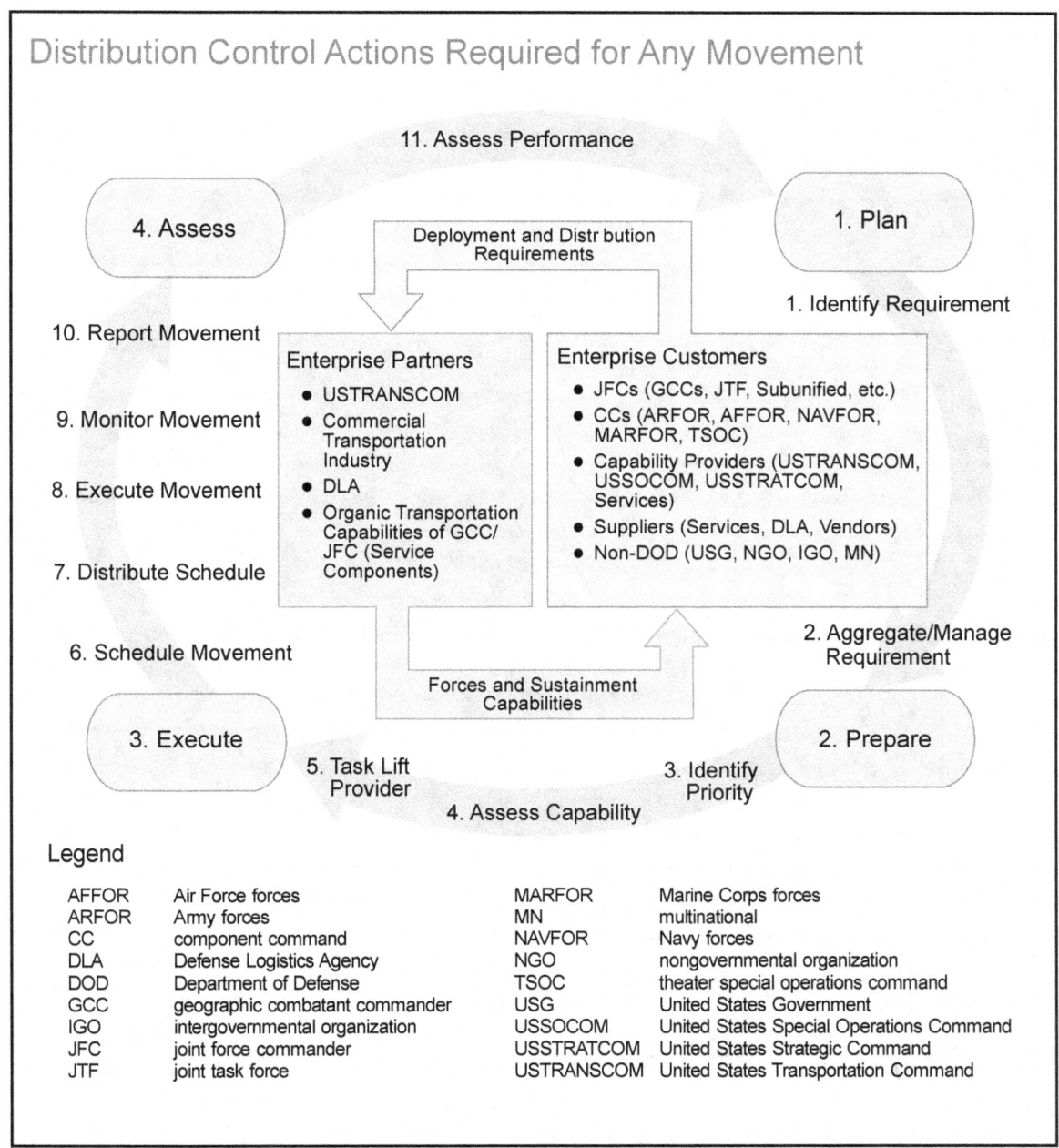

Figure V-1. Distribution Control Actions Required for Any Movement

d. The level of information required to support application of the continuous operations cycle is not needed or present at all levels and stages of the process. Information must be appropriate for the actions required at each of the various levels. Within the JDDE, there are four distinct organizational levels with differing needs in terms of timing, level of detail, and scope of information (see Figure V-2): joint control level, lift provider level, nodal level, and unit/retail level. Some examples of responsibilities at each level help to shape these distinctions. At the joint control level overall process guidance is provided, movement requirements are identified and validated, and modal determinations are made. At the lift provider level, lift assets and units are assigned and movements are scheduled. The nodal level is where physical handling of cargo, passengers, and movement assets occurs. And finally, the unit/retail level is where shipments are received and ultimately stored; enter

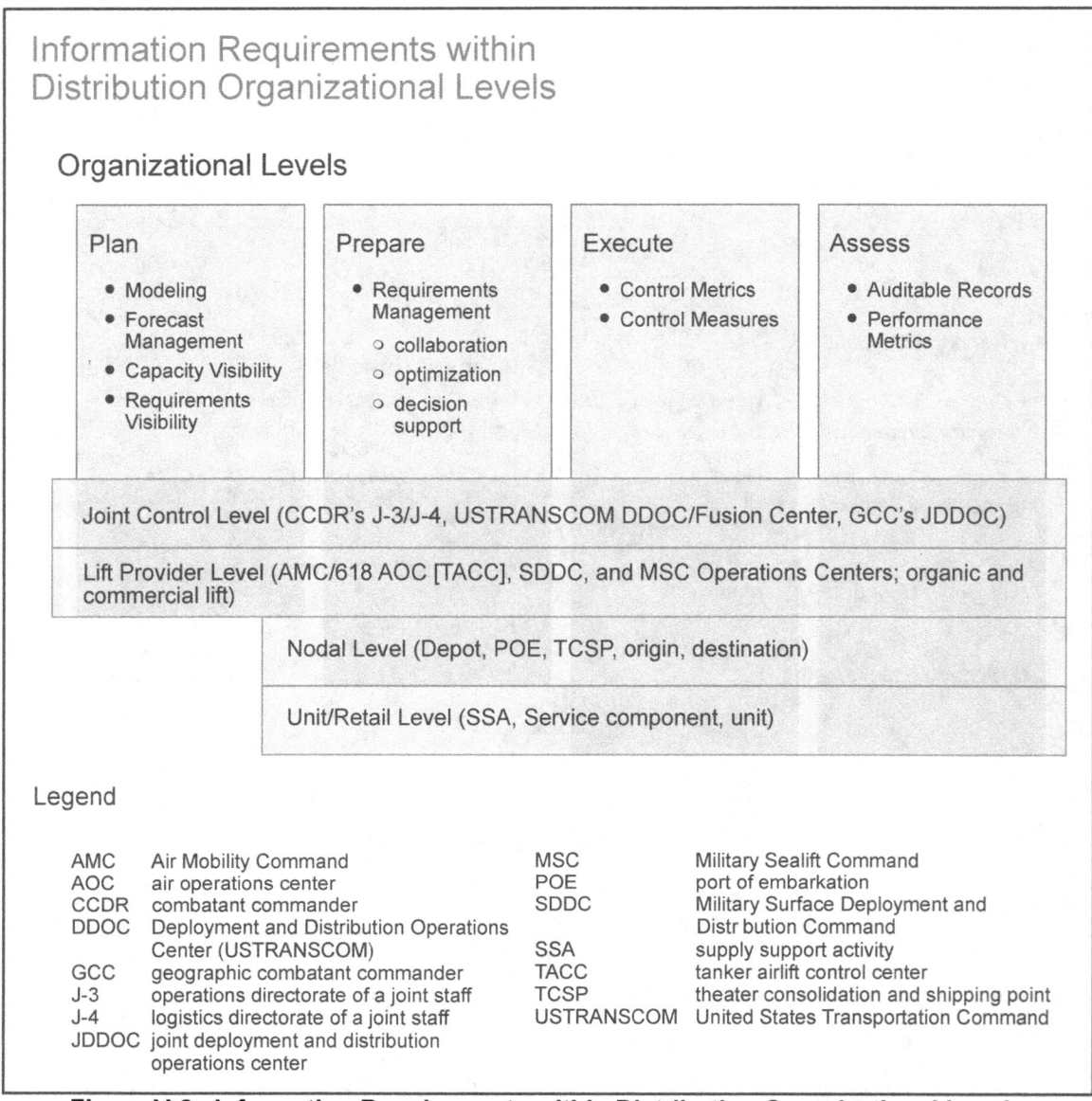

Figure V-2. Information Requirements within Distribution Organizational Levels

JRSOI; and/or are distributed, employed, or used. In general, movement planning information is shared at the joint control and lift provider levels. Preparing for distribution extends from these top two levels to the nodal level. Execution and assessment occur in various forms at all four levels. Defining the levels of activity within this organizational construct, with an understanding of movement requirements discussed above, provides the basis for process descriptions that align movement requirements with available capacity.

e. By considering the four distinct distribution organizational levels along with the continuous operations cycle outlined above, a complete set of distribution control actions or functions that must occur for any movement emerge (see Figures V-1 and V-3). All of these distribution control functions occur in all theaters and across all of the organizational levels for any lift requirement: surface/air, commercial/organic military, intertheater/intratheater, and common-use/Service-specific.

Distribution Functions

Optimize	1. Identify Requirement
	2. Aggregate/Manage Requirement
	3. Identify Priority
	4. Assess Capability
	5. Task Lift Provider
	6. Schedule Movement
Plan	7. Distribute Schedule
	8. Execute Movement
	9. Monitor Movement
	10. Report Movement
	11. Assess Movement

Figure V-3. Distribution Functions

(1) **Plan/Optimize**

(a) Identify the relationship between generic movement demand and notional lift capacity, by mode and type, as the means to identify the scope and nature of an end-to-end distribution system.

(b) Provide an integrated forecast of movement demands for the purpose of establishing distribution system capacity and nodes, and an overall operational-level movement plan that coordinates both intertheater and intratheater movements.

(c) Plan end-to-end movements in collaboration with requirement owners/sourcing organizations (CCDR, DLA, Services, GSA, etc.) and lift providers based on a shared view of the movement requirement to anticipate necessary lift capacity and shape movement requirements as necessary to achieve TDD.

(d) Optimize end-to-end movements in terms of mode, lift resources, cost, and overall risk and synchronize with theater-only movements to efficiently employ lift assets while meeting stated requirements.

(2) **Identify Requirements**

(a) Accurately identify the most current force/on-demand movement requirement that contains all the required movement information to support movement planning and execution; the intratheater leg of end-to-end movements may be predicated on previous (or subsequent for redeployment) movement legs and must contain necessary information to convey required synchronization. The ability to provide movement requirements includes the ability to pass movement information to support any subsequent Service/organic movement.

(b) Make dynamic adjustments to the force/on-demand movement requirement by appending or updating requirement information for the intratheater leg of force/on-demand movement based on dynamic changes to meet GCC requirements (JRSOI, relief in place/transfer of authority, or other operational imperatives).

(c) Develop and convey a capacity-based requirement from the validation authority to lift providers for the purpose of establishing scheduled movements in advance of sustainment, nonunit cargo/passengers, or retrograde demand to allow booking of actual cargo/passengers against scheduled lift. Capacity-based requirements include boundaries/thresholds for lift providers to independently modulate lift against actual sustainment movement requirements.

(d) Accurately identify inbound sustainment movement requirements and outbound retrograde movement requirements for the intratheater leg that contain all the required movement information to support movement planning and execution.

(e) Sense capacity-based cargo/passengers identified as awaiting movement at terminals IAW established movement priorities and generate incipient movement requirement.

(3) **Aggregate/Manage Requirements.** DDOC/JDDOC manage requirements for multiple and distinct force plan identification numbers, sustainment, on-demand, and capacity-based demands in an integrated fashion to determine overall demand, assign/adjudicate priority (based on JFC priorities, guidance, and requirements), arbitrate transportation mode, process requirement record transactions, and maintain requirement accountability.

(4) **Identify Priority**

(a) Identify echeloned priorities (multiple tiers to provide necessary specificity for precedence of movement) for force/on-demand movement records IAW JFC's dynamic movement requirements.

(b) Identify and act on an assigned sustainment/capacity-based movement precedence or end-to-end standard (TDD or CWT) and update echeloned priorities IAW JFC's dynamic movement requirements.

(c) Provide visibility of individual and aggregate sustainment/capacity-based, nonunit cargo/passengers, and retrograde movement requirements for the DDOC/JDDOC to selectively manage and redirect or change the priority of movement for items into and out of the theater based on JFC's dynamic requirements.

(5) **Assess Capacity.** Lift providers portray an assessment of overall or allocated lift capacity (to include lift assets, terminals, and LOCs) over time and/or space, to include any special lift categories/types for the purpose of movement feasibility assessments.

(6) **Task Lift Provider**

(a) Provide near real-time requirements status information to requirement owners, moving units, and Service components on movement requirements throughout the life cycle of the requirement until the movement requirement is satisfied.

(b) The Service component and the JDDOC verify/validate force/on-demand movement record attributes for the intratheater leg as accurate and IAW the latest intent of the JFC before tasking component lift providers.

(c) The controlling agency tasks a lift provider with a validated movement requirement (including boundaries and thresholds for autonomous lift provider action) and facilitates a positive handoff and accountability of the requirement.

(7) **Schedule Movement.** Provide near real-time visibility on the status of pipeline and terminal (sustainment/capacity-based) cargo/passengers, distinguish the movement status/priority, and determine current and anticipated demand for lift.

(8) **Distribute Schedule.** Provide an up-to-date movement schedule to requirement owners, terminals, Service components, supporting organizations, and the DDOC/JDDOC with adequate time to book or manifest cargo/passengers and support preliminary or supporting movement operations.

(9) **Execute Movement.** Direct lift providers to the movement of cargo/passengers and dynamically adjust while in transit to meet the JFC's movement requirements.

(10) **Monitor Movement.** Provide near real-time in-transit information on cargo/passenger movements (common-user and Service-direct movements) through commonly accessible means to requirement owners, terminals, Service components, supporting organizations, and controlling agencies such as the DDOC/JDDOC.

(11) **Report Movement**

(a) Capture closure of actual movements to reflect completion of the planned movement requirement.

(b) Transfer appropriate movement information to Service movement systems for synchronizing Service-controlled movements past the point of need.

(12) **Assess Performance**

(a) Develop a data collection plan to support performance metrics.

(b) Develop metrics for the entire joint distribution pipeline that support JDDE end-to-end performance metrics for the purpose of assessing overall pipeline performance and targeting areas for improvement.

(c) Use metrics and supporting data to provide closed-loop feedback to improve distribution system effectiveness and efficiency and to optimize movement operations.

4. Movement Control Operations

a. The employment of military forces and combat power decides the outcome of campaigns and operations. The successful employment of military forces is supported by the implementation of movement control policies, procedures, and programs guided by the supported commander's priorities. Movement control spans the strategic, operational, and tactical levels of war to ensure that the distribution pipeline is fully coordinated and operating effectively and efficiently.

b. Unity of effort ensures that all efforts are focused on a common goal regardless of command or organizational assignment and reflects the degree of coordination and alignment of JDDE movements. The foundation for integrated operations is a common understanding of optimized movement plans and a COP that promotes synchronization of key controlling organizations across all three movement legs. Synchronization is the arrangement of military actions in time, space, and purpose to produce maximum relative combat power at a decisive place and time. Synchronization produces a state where all key participants in deployment and distribution processes operate from a common strategy, concept, or plan and execute in a decentralized manner that is completely in concert with the overall plan. Collaboration in development of the strategy, concept, or plan allows shared expectations during execution. Synchronization is further enhanced through visibility of the movement requirement across all legs with clearly conveyed movement priorities to drive action toward a common outcome. Execution of joint distribution operations to satisfy movement requirements is built on the underpinning movement plans that allow active coordination, as necessary, to allow fulfillment of the movement requirement. Shared visibility on the status of movement operations also provides confidence that synchronization activities are achieving the desired outcome.

c. Active coordination is required when information is insufficient to capture all movement requirements and align them with available capacity. As an example, when movement requirements exceed lift capacity, POEs may be required to assign physical cargo/passengers to scheduled lift that differs from the planned movement. Further, the concept of "exception management," where active control at the joint control level is required for items normally handled at the lift provider or nodal level, may be required to reallocate resources to balance lift requirements with lift capacity when major imbalances occur during execution.

d. Movement control coordinates and synchronizes transportation resources to enhance combat effectiveness and meet the priorities of the CCDR. Effective and efficient transportation to and in a theater involves establishing effective collaborative control processes. Movement control is the planning, routing, scheduling, and controlling of personnel and cargo movement over LOCs. It also entails maintenance of ITV to assist commanders and operations staffs in force tracking. In addition, effective movement control enables reception, staging, and onward movement of personnel, equipment, and supplies IAW command directives and responsibilities. Movement control is a system involving the coordination of shared movement information and programs spanning the entire distribution pipeline.

e. **Intertheater Movement Control.** Control over the distribution pipeline is achieved through the ability to coordinate and synchronize force movement and sustainment across all legs of the JDDE. USTRANSCOM, as DPO, is responsible to monitor the performance of the JDDE to facilitate the flow of force movement and sustainment for the supported GCC. Control requires the ability to build and optimize executable plans through collaboration with JDDE partners and customers to allow delivery of the correct cargo and personnel to the point of need at the desired time. It also includes establishing and enforcing business rules and working protocols governing the collaborative support of contributing organizations in the JDDE. Additionally, control entails the ability to monitor and assess joint distribution operations, identify opportunities for improvement, and incorporate solutions. Effective control is reflected in the unity of effort achieved throughout the JDDE. Employment of this control capability is supported by a net-centric environment, as part of a global C2 system to facilitate an integrated approach to force movement, supply chain integration, and decision making.

(1) **USTRANSCOM.** CDRUSTRANSCOM is the CCDR responsible for coordinating and overseeing the DOD-wide end-to-end distribution. Coordination is accomplished through the USTRANSCOM Fusion Center and DDOC while execution is the responsibility of USTRANSCOM's TCCs.

(a) The USTRANSCOM Fusion Center is a matrixed organization residing within the USTRANSCOM J-3 comprised of transportation and logistics subject matter experts from across USTRANSCOM directorates, component commands, and other government agencies. The USTRANSCOM Fusion Center focuses on developing enterprise-wide, executable plans as well as monitoring, assessing, planning, and directing end-to-end movement of forces and sustainment. The USTRANSCOM DDOC resides within the Fusion Center and provides day-to-day execution oversight of USTRANSCOM missions from 24 to 72 hours prior to execution and is the primary interface to the GCCs' JDDOCs.

(b) **USTRANSCOM DDOC.** The DDOC is the single coordination and synchronization element that manages distribution operations within the JDDE. TCC planners are collocated with other joint planners as part of the USTRANSCOM Fusion Center to address requirements with a multimodal view so that supported commanders' requirements and limitations are understood.

(c) **AMC.** AMC provides air mobility for deployment, sustainment, redeployment, and special common-user missions such as AE. Military airlift may be augmented by contracted commercial air carriers. Additionally, AMC is the SPM and, where designated, operator of the common-user APOEs and APODs. The 618 AOC (TACC) is the global AOC responsible for centralized C2 of Air Force and commercial contract air mobility assets. Chapter II, "Distribution Operations Capabilities," provides additional information on AMC.

For further information, see JP 3-17, Air Mobility Operations.

(d) **SDDC.** SDDC is the CONUS transportation manager and provides worldwide common-use ocean terminal services and traffic management services to deploy, employ, sustain, and redeploy forces on a global basis. SDDC manages and employs the DOD common-user intermodal container fleet across the range of military operations. SDDC also develops transportation contracts and container-leasing agreements which support the transportation management of freight such as tanks, fuel, ammunition, combat vehicles, food, and other commodities to locations within CONUS and throughout the world. The SDDC Operations Center synchronizes deployment, sustainment, retrograde, and redeployment surface transportation and provides port management for DOD. Chapter II, "Distribution Operations Capabilities," provides additional information on SDDC.

For further information, see JP 4-01.5, Joint Terminal Operations.

(e) **MSC.** MSC is responsible for providing all strategic sealift movements using military and contracted commercial common-user and exclusive-use sealift transportation to deploy, employ, sustain, and redeploy US forces globally. The MSC Global Command Information Center provides a single point of contact to the USTRANSCOM DDOC. Chapter II, "Distribution Operations Capabilities," provides additional information on MSC.

For further information, see JP 4-01.2, Sealift Support to Joint Operations.

(2) **DLA.** DLA provides centralized materiel management and AV to the distribution pipeline. DLA supports each GCC with a DST as its focal point for coordinating DLA activities throughout a theater. The DST also provides disposal support through DLA Disposition Services, and contract administration services and support through attached elements of DCMA.

(3) **Joint Munitions Command.** Joint Munitions Command is an organization under the USAMC that provides munitions to joint fighting forces—all Services, all types of conventional munitions. Joint Munitions Command manages plants that produce conventional ammunition and the depots that store the nation's ammunition and missiles. The joint munitions transportation coordinating activity (JMTCA) was established to perform as the joint focal point for export munitions ship planning, coordination, and execution actions for those munitions moving aboard common-user sealift. The JMTCA consolidates all Services' munitions requirements into effective and efficient movement plans designed to provide ammunition community decision makers with advanced shipment planning visibility. Advanced visibility is the key to the JMTCA's comprehensive effort to provide commanders with the timely information to manage change.

(4) **Services.** The US Army, USMC, US Navy, and US Air Force (under their respective departmental secretaries) and the USCG (under DHS) are responsible for organizing, equipping, and training their Service forces. The Services provide centralized materiel management and AV to the distribution pipeline.

(5) **Vendor Support.** Intertheater POE/POD and Service movement/handling capabilities may be required to complete vendor support shipments. The JDDE, to include the agencies, USTRANSCOM, the TCCs, the JDDOC, and/or the Service components, requires shared visibility of all vendor support movements to successfully coordinate and synchronize these shipments with other movement demands. Chapter II, "Distribution Operations Capabilities," provides additional information on vendor support.

f. **Intratheater Movement Control.** The supported GCC controls intratheater movement. Theater movement control plans should provide the GCC with the highest practicable degree of influence or control over movement into, within, and out of the theater. Regardless of the option selected, the theater movement control system must allow the GCC the capability to plan, apportion, allocate, coordinate, deconflict movement requirements, and track the forces and materiel in the theater. Moreover, the theater movement control plan must coordinate incoming strategic movements with the theater distribution plan and theater JRSOI operations.

(1) **Logistics Control Options.** The need for rapid and precise response under crisis action or wartime conditions, or where critical situations make diversion of the normal logistic process necessary in the conduct of joint operations, requires flexible logistics control options. The CCDR's DAFL enables the use of logistic capabilities of assigned forces necessary for the accomplishment of the mission. As with other logistic capabilities, the CCDR may elect to control distribution through the J-4 staff tailored and augmented as appropriate, or the CCDR may also decide to control joint distribution through a subordinate organization. In the latter instance, the CCDR will delineate the authorities and command relationships that will be used by the subordinate commander to control distribution.

(2) The GCC has a wide range of movement control options available to allow a seamless intertheater-intratheater leg interface. Subordinate JFCs or Service components may be directed to carry out their own movement control. However, to facilitate a fully coordinated and responsive transportation system, the GCC may assign responsibility for theater transportation movement control to the JDDOC. The JDDOC must be equipped with sufficient communication and automation capabilities to allow adequate interface between intertheater and intratheater transportation systems and the GCC's staff. This organization must be skilled in coordinating and directing theater transportation operations in support of unit movements and logistic resupply operations. The GCC's logistic staff normally forms the nucleus of a movement control organization, but a properly executed theater movement control mission requires an additional predesignated augmentation to function as a joint organization. Ideally, such an organization would be identified as a force deployment option in an OPLAN and be established early in the theater to coordinate arrival, theater expansion, and operations movement planning and execution.

(3) **Deployment and Distribution Enablers.** During deployment, sustainment, redeployment, and retrograde operations, CCDRs state their movement requirements and RDDs with USTRANSCOM. Supported CCDRs are responsible for deployment and distribution operations executed with assigned/attached forces in their respective AORs. USTRANSCOM may also sponsor or provide other distribution process enablers, to include the DDOC-forward and JTF-PO to provide support to the GCC's JDDOC. Although all Services have organic capability to execute theater opening functions, among other logistic tasks such as port opening and distribution, JTF-PO provides a joint expeditionary capability to rapidly establish and initially operate an APOD/SPOD and conduct cargo handling and port clearance/movement control to a forward distribution node, facilitating port throughput in support of CCDR executed contingencies. JTF-PO also supports USTRANSCOM's mission of providing end-to-end synchronized cargo and passenger movement and common-user terminal management. JTF-PO is designed to be in place in advance of a deployment of forces, sustainment, or humanitarian relief supplies in order to provide AV and facilitate JRSOI and theater distribution.

(4) **DLA.** DLA provides distribution support to the JFC through the employment of the DDED. This capability provides a forward deployed TCSP and a forward deployed warehouse to manage theater wholesale inventory. This organization is a projection of supply acquisition, inventory management, and distribution systems into the theater.

(5) **JDDOC.** At time of need a supported GCC can create a JDDOC and incorporate its capabilities into their staff functions. The JDDOC develops deployment and distribution plans, integrates multinational and/or interagency deployment and distribution, and coordinates and synchronizes supply, transportation, and related distribution activities. The JDDOC synchronizes the strategic to operational movement of forces and sustainment into theater by providing advance notice to the GCC's air and surface theater movement C2 elements. In concert with the GCC's overall priorities, and on behalf of the GCC, the JDDOC coordinates common-user and theater distribution operations above the tactical level. The JDDOC enables the GCC to have the benefit of a well-coordinated and synchronized joint distribution pipeline that helps to achieve TDD. It also serves as a link between multiple organizations including coalition partners, combat support agencies, NGO liaison elements, commercial transportation providers, and other private entities. The JDDOC has organic national partner representatives assigned. Their expertise and capability to reach back to national operations and command centers create synchronization between the intertheater and intratheater legs of the distribution system. The premise behind the JDDOC capability is that theater expertise is combined with national-level, strategic knowledge and reachback authority within the GCC's command structure. The JDDOC is an organization that accomplishes theater joint movement responsibilities for any potential logistic organizational structure as directed by the GCC. Normally, the JDDOC is embedded under the direction of the GCC's J-4; however, it may be established in organizations below the GCC level at the direction of the supported commander. Although the GCC can organize this structure as appropriate for the specific theater, the JDDOC must be placed at a level where it can effectively accomplish its assigned functions. The JDDOC must also be staffed and operated in the context of a joint command structure where command authorities can be used to accomplish the joint deployment and distribution mission for the JFC.

(a) The JDDOC synchronizes the strategic to operational movement of forces and sustainment into theater by providing advance notice to the GCC's air and surface theater movement C2 elements. The JDDOC collects data and provides the GCC with ITV on lift capacity throughout both the intertheater and intratheater systems. It also coordinates all GCC common-user transportation activities and integrates commercial lift capability as far forward as appropriate to move forces and materiel as quickly as possible based on GCC requirements.

(b) In concert with GCC priorities and on behalf of the GCC, the JDDOC coordinates common-user and theater distribution operations above the tactical level. It develops deployment and distribution plans; integrates multinational and/or interagency deployment and distribution; and coordinates and synchronizes supply, transportation, and related distribution activities. The JDDOC resolves potential deployment and distribution problems through coordination of available theater logistical support capabilities and collaborates reachback to organizations critical to the GCC's operational mission.

For more information on the JDDOC, see JP 3-35, Deployment and Redeployment Operations, *or visit the DPO Web Portal https://dpo.ustranscom.mil.*

(6) **Joint Movement Center (JMC).** A JMC may be established at a subordinate unified or JTF level to coordinate the employment of all means of transportation (including that provided by allies or HNs) to support the CONOPS. This coordination is accomplished through establishment of theater and JTF transportation policies within the assigned OA, consistent with relative urgency of need, port and terminal capabilities, transportation asset availability, and priorities set by a JFC. The JTF JMC will work closely with the JDDOC.

(7) **Multinational and Interagency Arrangements.** Multinational and interagency operational arrangements regarding joint distribution operations are bound together by a web of relationships among global providers. These relationships are critical to success because capabilities, resources, and processes are vested in myriad organizations which interact throughout the operational environment (across the physical domains and the information environment) spanning the range of military operations. In today's operational environments, logisticians will likely work with multinational partners. While the US maintains the capability to act unilaterally, it is likely that the requirement and desire to operate with multinational partners will continue to increase. Coordinating and synchronizing distribution operations in a multinational environment requires developing interoperable concepts and doctrine as well as clearly identifying and integrating the appropriate distribution processes, organizations, and C2 options. Careful consideration should be given to the broad range of multinational logistic support structures.

For further guidance on multinational logistics, refer to JP 4-08, Logistics in Support of Multinational Operations.

(8) **Vendor Support.** Intertheater and intratheater and/or Service movement/handling capabilities may be required to complete vendor support shipments. The JDDE requires shared visibility of all vendor support movements to successfully coordinate

and synchronize these shipments with other movement demands. Chapter II, "Distribution Operations Capabilities," provides additional information on vendor support.

(9) **Component Movement Control.** The JFC's movement control plan is the critical element in an effective movement control system. The plan should coordinate the transportation capabilities of the component commands to produce a movement control system with centralized control and decentralized execution. The Services' component forces form the basis for theater distribution operations. The following paragraphs briefly describe the Service and SOF control and distribution management as well as movement control capabilities of each joint force component.

(a) **Army Component.** The Army component usually provides common-user land and inland waterway transportation. It also conducts water terminal operations and, when necessary, LOTS operations. The TSC commands and controls surface movement and multimodal operations in the theater. It is responsible for developing plans, policies, and programs that support the efficient use of Army transportation assets and the efficient flow of units, equipment, supplies, and materiel throughout the theater distribution system. The TSC accomplishes this, in part, through effective coordination with the JDDOC to maintain situational awareness of the strategic distribution flow and joint requirements for common-use land and air transportation assets. The TSC manages intratheater movements through its subordinate movement control battalions (MCBs), implementing priorities established by the ASCC in support of the GCC's CONOPS. Critical TSC tasks include: balancing existing transportation capabilities of the distribution system with the day-to-day and projected operational requirements; preparing estimates, plans, policies, and procedures for movement control, mode operations, and terminal operations; managing transportation velocity by maintaining visibility of resources that are being transshipped at transshipping nodes; coordinating the movement of major units; developing policies and procedures to control, regulate, and expedite the movement of intermodal assets within the theater; maintaining liaison with JDDOC, JTF-PO, HN transportation agencies, mode operators, and supported units; and protecting movement control assets.

1. In order to more efficiently control movements within the theater, the TSC may decide to divide the theater into transportation movement regions. This approach permits centralized control by the TSC and decentralized execution of movement control functions by subordinate MCBs.

2. In addition to facilitating the synchronized flow of units, supplies, equipment, and materiel along main and alternate supply routes, the MCB, through its subordinate movement control teams, performs movement control functions at APODs, SPODs, distribution hubs, and other critical nodes to expedite port clearance and provide for the uninterrupted flow of resources and capabilities in support of Army force requirements.

3. Operating IAW TSC plans and policies, the MCB is responsible for managing the use of TSC-controlled trailers, containers, 463L pallets, and flatracks located throughout the intratheater distribution system. Included in this responsibility is the requirement to coordinate with users to expedite return of these assets to the distribution system. Lessons learned demonstrate that intermodal operations are critically affected by the

manner in which container management policies are enforced and container management is subsequently executed. Therefore, it is vital to TSC distribution operations that visibility and control of containers be maintained. Adherence to GCC policies will ensure adequate numbers of containers are available to support intratheater distribution system requirements.

(b) **Air Force Component.** The Air Force component provides intratheater common-user airlift and air refueling capabilities, as required.

1. **DIRMOBFOR.** The COMAFFOR will normally appoint a DIRMOBFOR to function as coordinating authority for air mobility with all commands and agencies, both internal and external to the JTF. The DIRMOBFOR is normally a senior officer who is familiar with the AOR or JOA and possesses an extensive background in air mobility operations. When established, the DIRMOBFOR serves as the designated agent for all air mobility issues in the AOR or JOA.

DIRMOBFOR responsibilities are detailed in JP 3-17, Air Mobility Operations.

2. **Air Mobility Division (AMD).** The AMD plans, schedules, and controls air mobility missions for all theater-assigned and theater-attached air mobility assets and provides coordination of USTRANSCOM-assigned air mobility forces.

For more information on the roles and responsibilities of the AMD, see JP 3-17, Air Mobility Operations.

(c) **Navy Component.** The Navy component, through MSC, provides common-user sealift to the theater. The Navy component, through NBGs and amphibious construction battalions and in concert with Army units, can provide the GCC with over-the-shore discharge and transfer capabilities where port facilities are inadequate or unavailable. The NCHBs (which are active and reserve units) conduct limited common-user port operations. The Navy component performs its movement control operations through the NCC, NALSS, NFLS, or a designated representative. The NALSS and NFLS provide logistic support, to include movement management, to theater naval forces during contingency and wartime periods. They coordinate Navy and surface transportation requirements with Army movement control organizations or the JDDOC. The NCC submits requirements for airlift to the JDDOC.

(d) **Marine Corps Component.** The Marine air-ground task force deployment and distribution operations center (MDDOC) is a standing organization staffed by members of the MEF G-3 [Marine Corps component operations staff] or G-4 office, which includes at a minimum, strategic mobility, distribution, mobility systems and supply personnel, and will coordinate deployment and distribution operations for MAGTF forces. The MDDOC will coordinate all strategic lift to move the forces from the aerial and surface POEs to the aerial and surface PODs and will facilitate MDDOC representation at the theater JDDOC.

1. The MDDOC is responsible for ferrying operational and support aircraft from unit areas to the theater of operations. The MDDOC functions as the agency responsible for executing MEF surface movement control priorities from unit areas to the aerial and surface POEs and from the aerial and surface PODs to the unit tactical assembly

areas. Further, the MDDOC will continue to control all MEF requirements for intratheater lift, lift support, and movement control (based on the MEF commander's priorities of movement) through all operational phases and the eventual redeployment of forces. The Marine logistics command, when designated, will facilitate movement support for the MEF throughout the established communications zone (secure area).

    <u>2.</u> Each element of the MEF MAGTF will activate a unit movement control center (UMCC) to manage organic lift requirements and will funnel external requirements to the MDDOC for sourcing. Further, each UMCC will execute zonal movement control under the direction of the MDDOC.

    <u>3.</u> For smaller-scale operations, each MAGTF will activate a UMCC to coordinate and control movements and movement support.

    (e) **SOF Component System.** The TSOC J-4 or subordinate joint special operations task force J-4 normally coordinates common-user lift requirements to support SOF. The TSOC J-4 establishes a system to validate common-user lift requests from SOF units. The nature of the system depends on the composition and mission of the assigned forces. The TSOC J-4 also establishes communication links with the JDDOC and the AOC or JAOC. The special operations liaison element (SOLE) is normally located at the JAOC or AOC and assists in coordinating SOF requirements. Although the SOLE works for the SOF commander, it can assist and expedite requests for common-user lift support to SOF units.

5. Distribution Metrics

    a. Metrics are used to track trends, productivity, resources, and other key performance indicators to measure overall process performance. **Six performance measures that describe the critical characteristics required of distribution performance are velocity, responsiveness, precision, reliability, efficiency, and visibility. Collectively, these measures serve as a basis for the development of distribution metrics that are defined in collaboration with the GCC, depending on specific outcomes desired at a particular place and time.** Distribution metrics should provide a balanced perspective of tradeoffs between effectiveness and efficiency to enable leaders to evaluate the potential cost of improved performance. They should also provide the foundation to drive coordinated improvement and unity of effort throughout the JDDE by translating CCDR goals into tangible terms and presenting an objective understanding of performance and progress toward improving joint force support. See Figure V-4 for examples of how metrics may be used to support these distribution performance measures.

    (1) **Velocity.** Velocity is the speed and direction by which requirements are fulfilled by the JDDE. Rapidity is only one aspect of velocity. Requirements must be fulfilled at the right speed. This means that synchronization of the speeds of the various aspects of the distribution process is required in order to maximize effectiveness. Velocity also incorporates the ability of elements of the JDDE to forecast, anticipate, and plan distribution execution. A JDDE that has sufficient velocity meets performance expectations and satisfies mission requirements as defined by the supported commander's CONOPS.

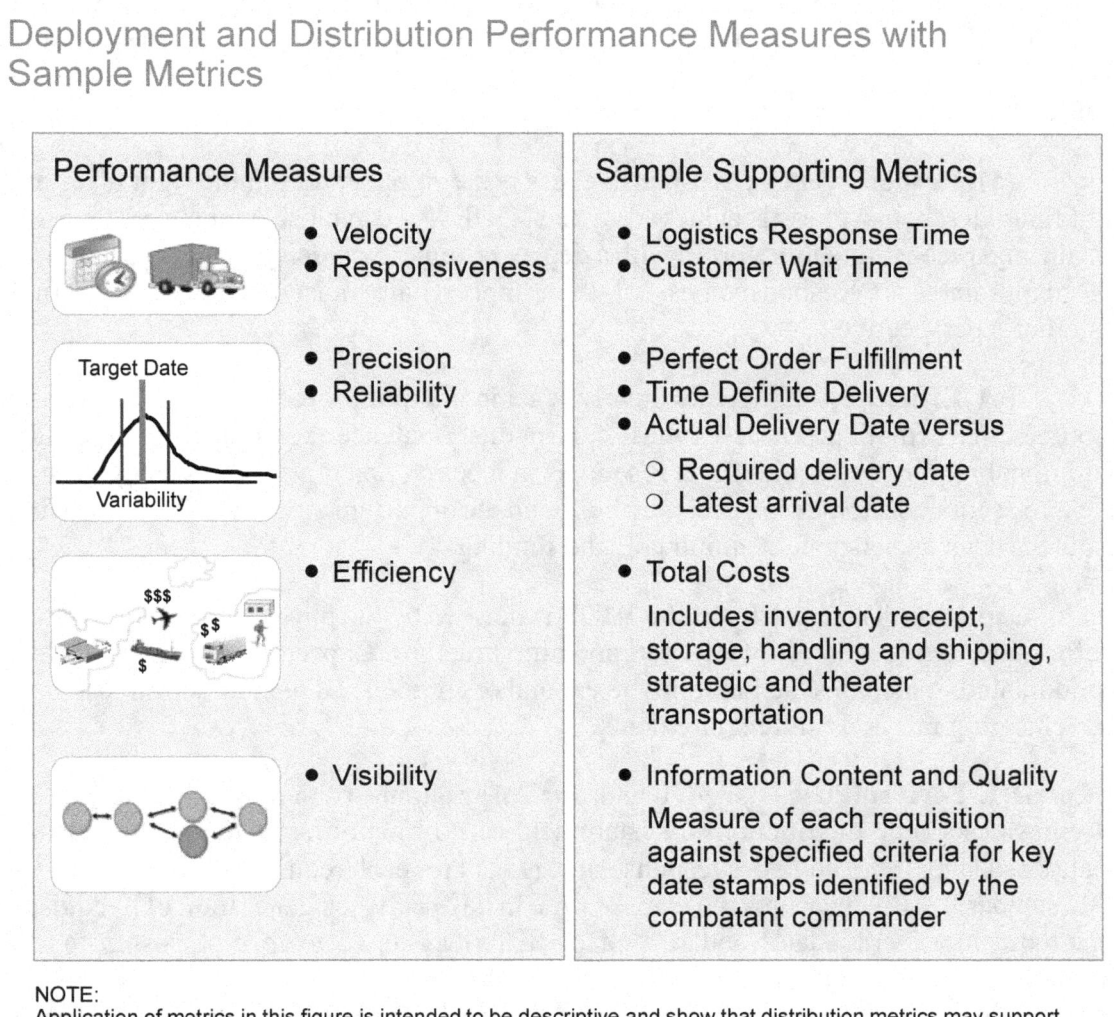

Figure V-4. Deployment and Distribution Performance Measures with Sample Metrics

(2) **Precision.** Precision within the JDDE means the accuracy with which delivery of forces, requirements, and materiel occurs at the right time, right place, right amount, and right configuration. Precision also addresses the ability of the JDDE to minimize deviation from acceptable standards as it reacts to dynamically changing conditions and requirements.

(3) **Reliability.** Reliability is the degree of assurance or dependability that the JDDE will consistently meet its support requirements to specified standards. Reliability instills trust and confidence of the customer in the certainty that the JDDE will meet joint force demands under clearly established and recognized conditions.

(4) **Visibility.** Visibility is the capability to determine the status, location, and direction of flow for all forces, requirements, and materiel in the JDDE. Joint end-to-end visibility is required over operational capabilities and capability packages, organizations, people, equipment, and sustainment. It also includes the organic military mobility forces and

commercial augmentation that move people and cargo through the pipeline, the supporting financial transactions, and the nodes and links comprising the pipeline. Visibility requires the availability of timely, accurate, and usable information essential to the maintenance of a COP within the overall distribution enterprise information network.

(5) **Responsiveness.** Responsiveness is the right support in the right place at the right time. Responsiveness is achieved by the JDDE if it can close, maneuver, reposition, sustain, and reconstitute joint forces with a degree of rapidity, precision, and control to meet JFC requirements. Responsiveness of the supply chain must be measured from the customer's perspective.

(6) **Efficiency.** Efficiency involves achieving joint force needs with wise use of resources. Distribution processes must continuously balance the competing demands of operational requirements with finite resources in meeting objectives. Efficiency must also take into account customer cost, network cost, and the opportunity cost associated with using resources such as personnel, equipment, and funding.

b. **Capacity.** The capacity of the JDDE is defined by the physical quantity, size, mix, configuration, and readiness of its assets and infrastructure. Capacity is a constraint that can be modulated; it includes the flexibility to expand or contract JDDE elements in response to ever-changing missions and requirements.

c. **IDL Performance.** An IDL is a logical grouping of supply and transportation activities describing distribution of sustainment cargo by modes, methods, and customer locations. Using IDLs, logistics response time (LRT) for each requisition is compared to its TDD standard. LRT measures the elapsed time in days between generation of a requisition (i.e., requisition serial date) and receipt of materiel (i.e., date receipt posted to stock record/property account or equivalent) not including back-order time. A graphical representation of LRT with segments is in Figure V-5. TDD standards represent the maximum amount of time, within a specified level of confidence (85 percent), in which the supply chain is capable of delivering requisitioned materiel to the customer. USTRANSCOM computes, analyzes, and presents distribution performance via distribution performance reviews.

6. **Multinational, Interagency, Intergovernmental Organization, and Nongovernmental Organization Arrangements**

a. **The purpose of multinational, interagency, IGO, and NGO coordination is to attain national objectives. This requires the efficient and effective use of the diplomatic, informational, economic, and military instruments of national power supported by and coordinated with those of our allies and various IGOs, NGOs, and regional organizations.** From a distribution perspective, the major challenges are identifying distribution capabilities and requirements across the various organizations early in the planning process and creating an architecture that provides movement visibility during execution. Observations of recent military operations highlight two key aspects, applicable both today and for the foreseeable future:

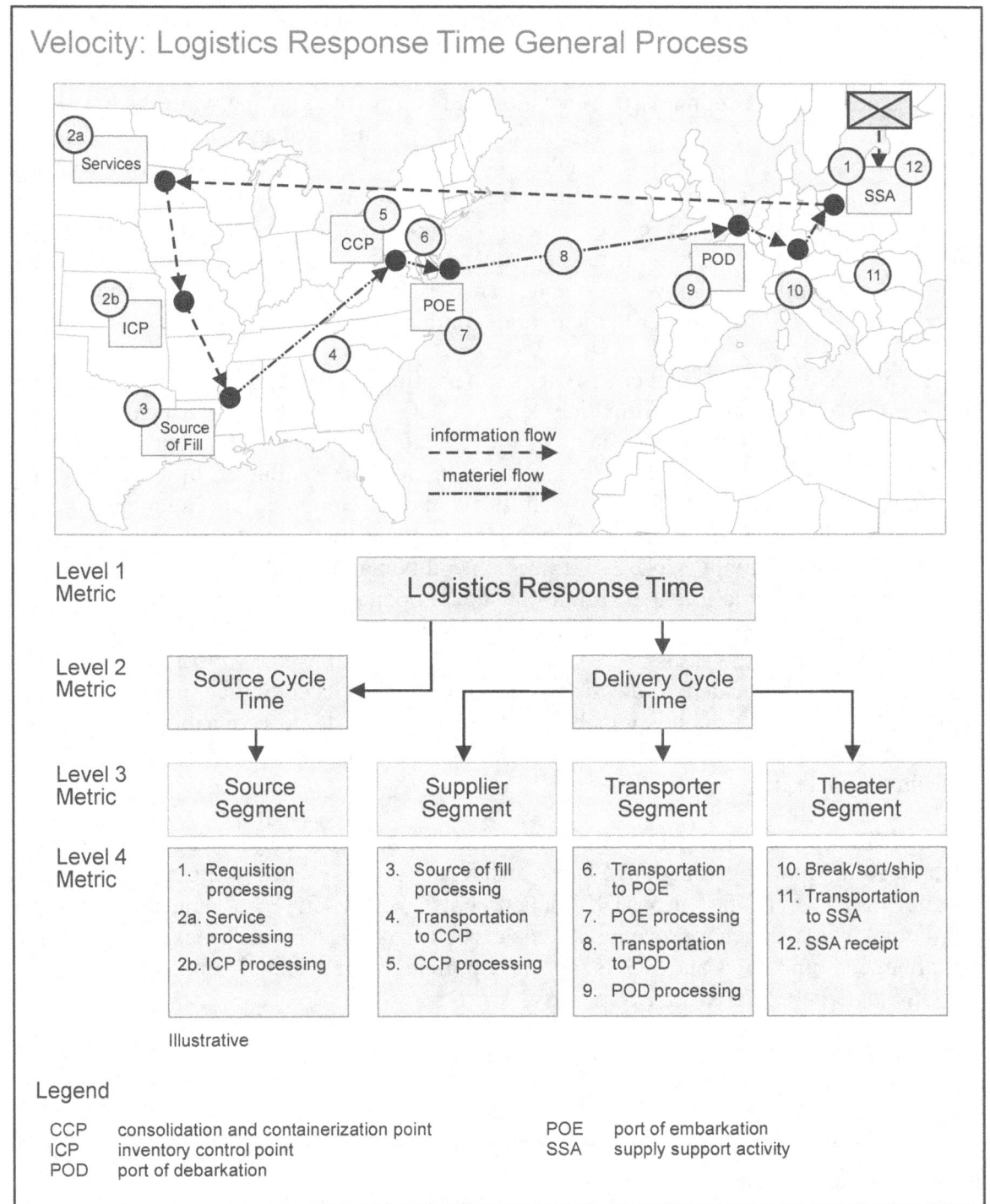

Figure V-5. Velocity: Logistics Response Time General Process

(1) The US faces a wide variety of potential situations that will require military resources.

(2) These situations require joint operations executed in a multinational environment. Given the expectation of continued, and possibly increased, operations in a multinational environment, it is important to recognize that such operations occurring with

little advance planning and involving new partnerships will usually increase the complexity of logistics.

b. The increased complexity of logistics results from the fact that while each nation is responsible for logistic support of its national forces, the sustained and synchronized logistic support to MNFs as a whole, and its resultant effect on the ability to successfully achieve mission objectives, is of vital concern to the commander, JTF. The success of future multinational operations will be determined, in large part, by the logistic interoperability of multinational partners. As with most, if not all, military operations, mobility and the resultant capability for movement and transportation of personnel, equipment, and sustainment is a critical enabler to the overall combined mission success.

c. In order to enhance movement support to multinational operations, the establishment of a combined movement coordination center (CMCC) is viewed as a critical enabler in coordinating the optimal employment of movement and transportation assets. When a CMCC is established, it must be scalable, tailorable, and flexible in order to meet the situational needs of the MNF. If in a fully functional combined environment where a multinational joint logistics component (MNJLC) has been established, the CMCC should be established as a cell in the MNJLC. If no such component is established, then the CMCC should reside alongside the lead nation logistic component. In theaters where combined movements are ongoing, this organization should be a permanent branch and not a temporary cell. For example, if the US is the lead nation, or primary contributor of lift assets, then the CMCC could be collocated, in theater, with the JDDOC as its combined movement cell or branch. Additionally, a deputy branch chief from the second largest contributor of lift assets could be assigned for the duration of operations where there is more than one lift-contributing nation.

d. Military operations depend upon a command structure that is often very different from that of civilian organizations. These differences may present significant challenges to coordination efforts. The various USG departments' and agencies' different, and sometimes conflicting, goals, policies, procedures, and decision-making techniques make unity of effort a challenge. Some IGOs and NGOs may have policies that are exactly opposite of those of the USG, and particularly the US military.

e. A variety of organizations may be established to manage, control, and coordinate strategic and operational movement for multinational operations.

(1) In US-led coalition operations, the MNFC's movement control concept is usually consistent with US joint doctrine.

(2) Normally in such operations, all air movements into, within, and out of the OA will be coordinated as a COMAFFOR responsibility through the AMD/DIRMOBFOR. Organizations such as a regional air movement coordination center (RAMCC), under the DIRMOBFOR, may be established to provide slot times for all aircraft—including multinational, IGO, and NGO aircraft—operating in the OA airspace. The RAMCC will usually be collocated with the JAOC, if established.

(3) To provide overall coordination of all movements in the OA, the US JFC may also establish a JDDOC. Depending on the composition of the MNF, the JDDOC may also function as a multinational movement center, and may be so designated, with full staff participation from multinational partners.

(4) MNF deployment will normally be executed more smoothly through use of a single integrated multinational TPFDL. In US-led coalition operations, the supported US CCDR is responsible for developing the TPFDL and incorporating forces of deploying multinational partners into the force flow.

f. **Considerations for Multinational, Interagency, Intergovernmental, and Nongovernmental Operations.** Regardless of the specific structure established to coordinate and manage movements, the following considerations will facilitate distribution control:

(1) Authority for logistic matters must be clearly defined in the OPLAN and supporting plans. Participation from many nations, agencies, and NGOs can severely complicate coordination of logistic support.

(2) A flexible C2 structure must be established early in the planning cycle to coordinate national and multinational operations and support the CONOPS.

(3) C2 activities must be organized on the basis of the operational mission and coordinated with nations to obtain support and manning for the structure. The C2 structure should be established in peacetime in order to improve planning, participate in exercises, establish manning requirements for actual operations, and serve as an integral component of the operational planning process. For coalition operations, the multinational C2 structure may not be established in advance.

(4) GCCs should establish the capability to coordinate future operations within existing US JTF planning structures/headquarters to facilitate expansion during multinational, interagency, and NGO operations to minimize the potentially adverse impact of last-minute, ad hoc support arrangements.

(5) Develop a spirit of cooperation, coordination, and communication with and among participating nations, agencies, and NGOs.

(6) The C2 structure must include coordinating mechanisms and procedures to facilitate linkages with the appropriate operational headquarters, senior coordinating agencies/organizations, component commands, and other national headquarters, as appropriate.

For more information on interagency, intergovernmental, and nongovernmental coordination, see JP 3-08, Interorganizational Coordination During Joint Operations. *For more information on multinational operations, see JP 3-16,* Multinational Operations.

Intentionally Blank

APPENDIX A
DISTRIBUTION OPERATIONS PROCESS MAPS

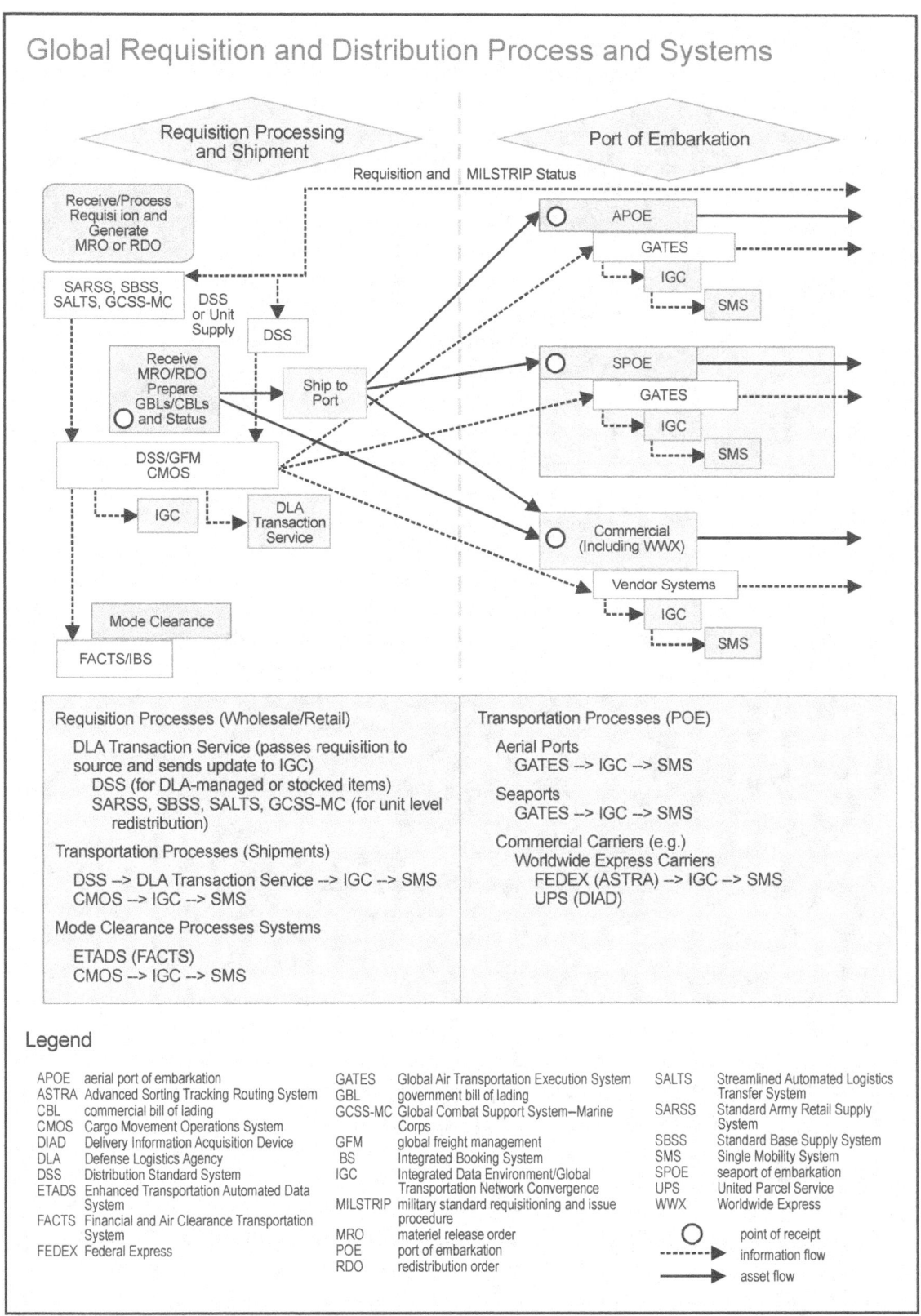

Figure A-1. Global Requisition and Distribution Process and Systems

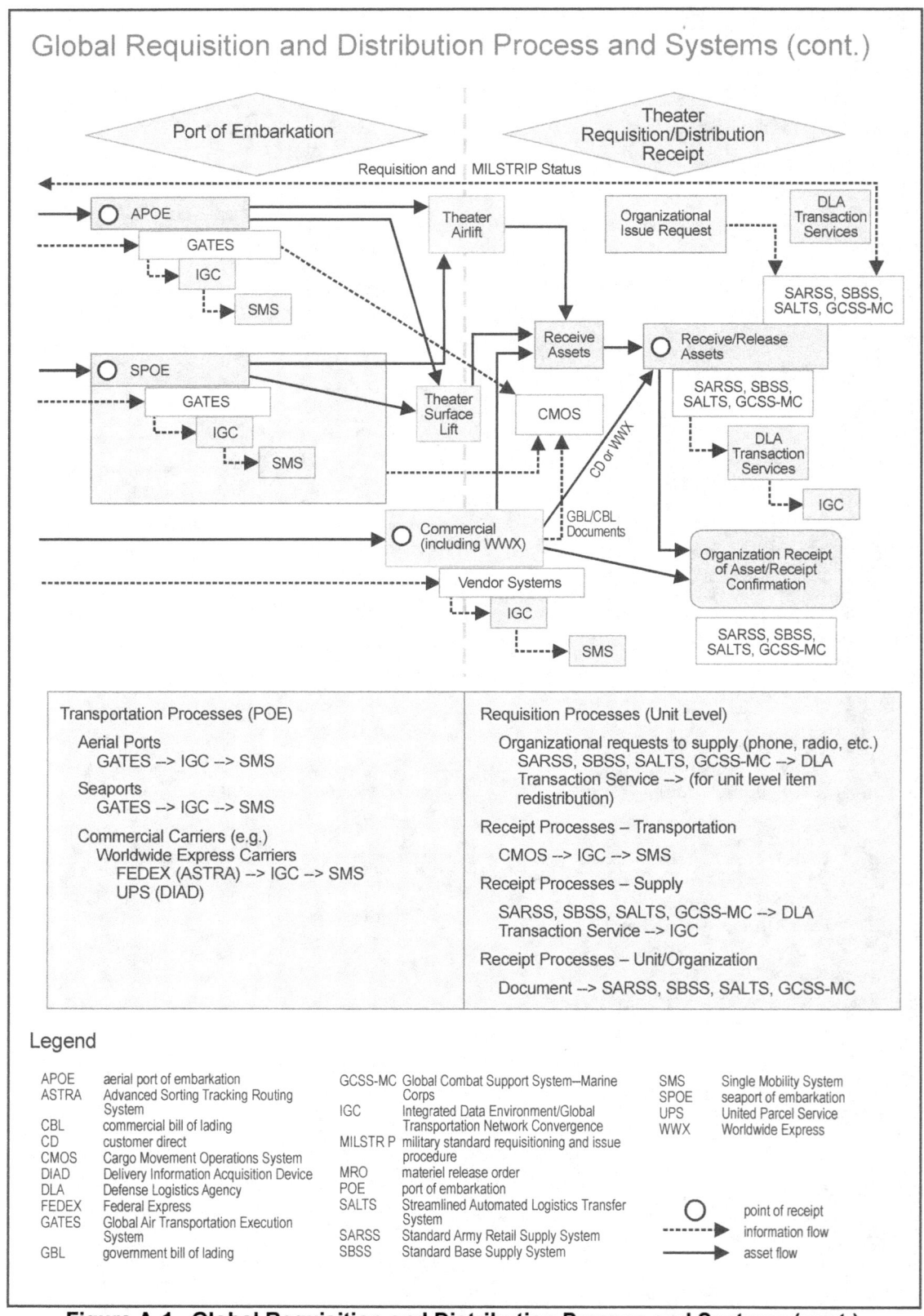

Figure A-1. Global Requisition and Distribution Process and Systems (cont.)

APPENDIX B
DEPARTMENT OF DEFENSE PRIORITY SYSTEMS APPLIED TO DEPLOYMENT/REDEPLOYMENT AND DISTRIBUTION OPERATIONS

1. General

a. The rate at which specific forces and sustainment materiel moves through the DTS is impacted by a number of priority systems which are meant to align the allocation of resources with the national strategy, as defined by the President and/or SecDef, and theater strategies, as defined by the GCCs. This appendix describes what those priority systems are and how they interact to influence the distribution of forces and materiel.

b. The foundational concept underlying all distribution movements, whether force movements, or the movement of sustainment materiel, is that they begin with the identification of a requirement. Before a deploying/redeploying unit boards a bus, aircraft, or ship, and before a spare part enters the DTS, an appropriate authority must define what must be moved, and to where and when that unit or materiel needs to be delivered.

c. Disciplined adherence to established priorities is critical to ensuring the JDDE meets the stated objectives of the President and/or SecDef and the CCDRs. Overprioritizing forces and materiel entering the distribution system can cause finite capacity to be misapplied to noncritical requirements, delaying the delivery of truly critical forces and materiel. It cannot be overstated: undisciplined, inflated definition of priorities when establishing requirements can reduce the JDDE's effectiveness in meeting national and theater strategies.

d. There are very different processes, and very different authorities involved in defining requirements for force movements and the movement of sustainment materiel. Therefore, these two broad categories will be addressed separately below.

2. Force Movements Requirements Generation and Priorities

a. CCDRs develop campaign, contingency, and posture plans, as directed through the JSCP, to support strategic guidance and defense objectives.

   (1) GCCs focus joint strategic planning on their specific AORs as defined in the *Unified Command Plan*.

   (2) **FCCs generally accomplish joint strategic planning with a global focus.** Strategic planning for possible execution of multiple operations across AOR boundaries requires prioritization of effort by SecDef or the President and coordination with all affected CCDRs.

b. Joint operation planning—activities that produce OPLANs and OPORDs for the conduct of military operations—is conducted within JOPES. It is an adaptive process, focused on developing plans that contain a variety of viable, embedded options for the President and SecDef to consider as situations develop. DOD conducts joint operation planning in two related but distinct categories—**deliberate planning** and **CAP.** These categories differ primarily in level of uncertainty, amount of available planning time, and products.

Note: JP 5-0, Joint Operation Planning, *discusses deliberate planning and CAP in greater detail.*

    c. **TPFDD.** For the JDDE, the critical output from both deliberate planning and CAP is the CCDR's CONOPS and supporting annexes to include annex A (Tasked Organization) and its associated appendix 1 (TPFDL). During the planning process, the TPFDL is substantiated and codified as the TPFDD. The TPFDD establishes the flow of forces/units, associated equipment, supplies, and sustainment materiel into the theater required to support the GCC's CONOPS. In developing the TPFDD, the supported CCDR must carefully balance the force mix and arrival sequence of combat forces and combat support/combat sustainment support units to ensure deployment support and throughput requirements can be met and that forces will remain effective once deployed. This balance and sequencing is achieved by assigning RDDs and latest arrival dates to requirements identified in the TPFDD per priorities reflected in the destination supported commander's RDD. Before the JDDE can act on the requirements, however, TPFDD requirements must be validated by the supported CCDRs.

    (1) The validation process prompts Service logistics and personnel offices to adjust and update sustainment requirements based on the latest and most accurate staff estimates. During this process, the supported CCDR also requests that the Joint Staff and supporting commands and agencies assist in resolving critical sourcing or resource shortfalls.

    (2) When the above actions are completed, the supported CCDR reviews and validates the lift requirements within the specific TPFDD window and notifies USTRANSCOM that the movement requirements are ready for lift scheduling.

    (3) USTRANSCOM develops transportation schedules to accommodate these requirements after verifying transportation feasibility. Accuracy of TPFDD movement requirements and data is critical to the lift scheduling process because it directly impacts force closure. Errors in lift scheduling or late changes to the validated TPFDD requiring a change in transportation mode (e.g., airlift to sealift) could significantly reduce the supported CCDR's operational capability or flexibility.

    (4) The supported commander issues an RFF/RFC message when it is determined that additional forces, over and above those that have been previously approved by SecDef, are required to support military operations. Once a SecDef-approved EXORD has been issued, the RFF/RFC is only necessary when additions to forces covered by the EXORD are required. Additional forces or additional individual personnel and equipment (not force augmentation or unit replacement), which require a deployment order (DEPORD), are requested by RFF/RFC.

For more information on the RFF/RFC process, see CJCSM 3122.05, Operating Procedures for Joint Operation Planning and Execution System (JOPES)–Information Systems (IS)

Governance, *and CJCS Guide 3130,* Adaptive Planning and Execution (APEX) Overview and Policy Framework.

(5) **During the initial and subsequent deployments, DOD leadership may use RFFs and DEPORDs in lieu of an EXORD and/or fragmentary order supporting OPORD execution.** Deployments under DEPORDs, as a result of RFFs and/or execution of other global operations, can significantly impact the flow of forces. Commanders and their staffs must understand the associated impact additional force flow that had not been previously planned may have.

d. **Redeployment.** Redeployment TPFDDs are normally developed with the redeployment plan and updated and refined during redeployment preparations. Redeploying forces are tailored and prioritized for redeployment based on the supported CCDR's intent expressed in the OPLAN or redeployment policy. During redeployment preparation, unit movement data is updated to reflect changes to the automated unit equipment lists caused by combat, maintenance, or supply losses. Subordinate organizations and component commands must verify unit movement data to the supported CCDR for redeployment TPFDD validation.

(1) Requirements validation for redeployment is conducted using the same process used during deployment operations. Redeploying units confirm readiness, movement available dates, passengers, and cargo details. The supported CCDR receives component redeployment data, merges this data into the redeployment TPFDD, and makes adjustments to the redeployment flow as necessary.

(2) Once adjustments are complete, the supported CCDR validates the lift requirements within the specific TPFDD movement window for USTRANSCOM movement scheduling by confirming that the TPFDD accurately reflects current movement requirements. USTRANSCOM conducts a transportation feasibility review and coordinates with the supported CCDR and supporting CCDRs who will receive the forces to resolve transportation conflicts. The end result of this process is a supported CCDR-approved redeployment TPFDD that units use to prepare for movement.

e. The deployment and redeployment TPFDDs generated through the processes above establish the priorities for force movements. Force movements will still be constrained by the availability of lift assets. The CJCS has established a priority system for blending force movement requirements with other requirements acting on DOD's IGC information.

See Paragraph 4, "Transportation Priorities for Assigning Transportation Assets," *for a description of priorities used in assigning available transportation assets.*

3. **Sustainment Requirements Generation and Associated Priority Systems**

a. Five DOD priority systems affect the rate at which sustainment materiel is distributed: (1) the force/activity designator (F/AD) assigned by SecDef, CJCS, Service Chief, or CCDR; (2) the urgency of need designator (UND) assigned by the requisitioning unit; (3) the priority designator (PD) determined by the combination of the F/AD and UND; (4) the cargo transportation priority (TP); and finally, (5) the priorities for assigning available

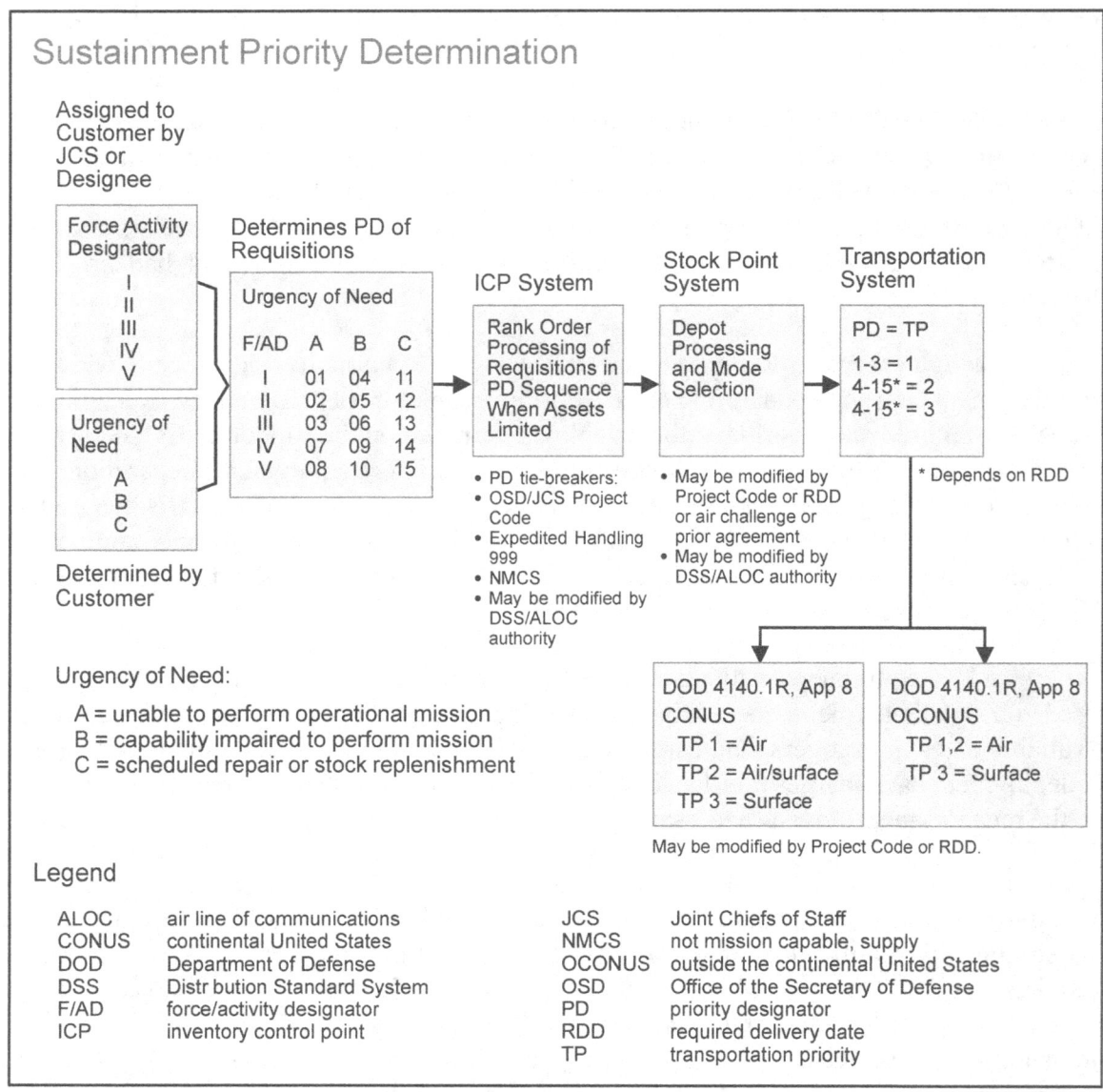

Figure B-1. Sustainment Priority Determination

lift assets, as determined by CJCS. The flow of requisitioned items through the various priority systems is shown in Figure B-1.

b. **F/AD**

(1) F/ADs are assigned to all forces, units, programs, projects, and activities within the DOD as a means to ensure resources are provided against the most critical national defense needs. Approval for F/ADs rests with SecDef, CJCS, Service Chiefs, or CCDRs, depending on which F/ADs, I through V, are being assigned. Requisitioning units do not determine their own F/AD codes. In order to allow proper distribution discipline, it is critical that proper F/AD codes be included in requisitions. Failure to do so may reduce or restrict the JDDE's ability to meet CCDRs' priorities. In addition:

(a) The lowest F/AD required of the force, activity, unit, program, or project shall be assigned.

(b) Lower F/AD assignments will be made for segments of organizations, phases, projects, or programs, where possible.

(2) F/AD assignment criteria will be IAW guidance in DOD 4140.1-R, *DOD Supply Chain Materiel Management Regulation.*

c. **UND.** The UND, an alphabetic character, is determined by the requisitioning activity. In a general sense, the highest priority, UND A, is assigned when forces, activities, units, programs, or projects are unable to perform their assigned missions, or are experiencing work stoppages. The second highest priority, UND B, is generally used when forces, activities, units, programs, or projects are impaired in their ability to perform their missions, or to preclude a work stoppage in industrial activities. The lowest priority, UND C, is generally used in requisitioning materiel to support scheduled repairs, maintenance, or manufacture, or to replenish stock to meet stock level objectives. Specific criteria for assigning UNDs can be found in Appendix 2.14 of Defense Logistics Manual (DLM) 4000.25-1, *Military Standard Requisitioning and Issue Procedures (MILSTRIP).*

d. **PDs and TPs**

(1) **PD.** The combination of the higher headquarters-directed F/AD and the unit-designated UND determine the PD as shown in Figure B-2. As an integral part of the Uniform Materiel Movement and Issue Priority System, PDs are used by materiel management systems to allocate available stocks among competing requisitions. As an example, a unit experiencing mission impairment and designated to deploy between C+31 and C+90 ("III B"—PD "06"), will have a higher priority than a unit that is unable to perform its assigned mission, but is not scheduled to deploy until C+91 or later ("IV A"—PD "07"). This example is using C-day, the unnamed day on which a deployment operation begins, with the plus number being the number of days after C-day is declared and deployment begins.

DERIVATION OF PRIORITY DESIGNATORS (Relating Force/Activity Designator to Urgency of Need Designator)			
FORCE OR ACTIVITY DESIGNATOR	URGENCY OF NEED		
	A	B	C
I	01	04	11
II	02	05	12
III	03	06	13
IV	07	09	14
V	08	10	15

Figure B-2. Derivation of Priority Designators

(2) **RDDs.** The final ingredient that determines the TP for a given requisition is the RDD. Requisitions will include unit-/activity-determined RDDs, which may influence JDDE response times. RDDs may be based on specific calendar dates or special codes listed in DOD 4140.1-R, *DOD Supply Chain Materiel Management Regulation*, and DLM 4000.25-1, *Military Standard Requisitioning and Issue Procedures (MILSTRIP)*.

(3) **Cargo TPs.** TPs (TP-1, TP-2, and TP-3) are assigned to cargo shipments IAW DTR 4500.0-R, *Defense Transportation Regulation–Part II, Cargo Movement.* TPs are derived directly from the PDs above, and RDDs identified by the requisitioning unit or activity. These TPs are directly tied to TDD standards. TDD and TP standards and their associated criteria can be found in DOD 4140.1-R.

(4) **Exceptions.** DOD has authorized additional criteria to distinguish between high priority requests. These include CJCS project codes, and not mission capable, supply (NMCS) designations to further distinguish importance of materiel within high priority PDs. Additionally, the Army direct support system/air line of communications (DSS/ALOC) system provides higher priority handling of some Army units' requisitions than would otherwise be true.

(a) **CJCS Project Codes.** CJCS project codes will be assigned only to projects and programs clearly of direct interest to the CJCS acting on behalf of SecDef. Authorization for use of a CJCS project code will be for a specified period of time, and the F/AD(s) to be used in conjunction with the CJCS project code will be designated in the authorization.

(b) **NMCS.** NMCS is a materiel condition indicating that systems and equipment are not capable of performing their assigned missions because of a supply shortage. Requisitioning activities allow expedited handling when conditions outlined in DLM 4000.25-1, *Military Standard Requisitioning and Issue Procedures (MILSTRIP),* are met.

(c) **Army's DSS/ALOC.** The DSS/ALOC is the Army's standard supply system for moving materiel through an expedited pipeline as far forward as possible. The DSS/ALOC provides scheduled air delivery of selected air-eligible repair parts (Class IX) and medical supplies (Class VIII) to overseas Army sustainment units. DSS/ALOC designation results in higher priority handling and movement of PD 09-15 requisitions than would normally be the case. To receive DSS/ALOC handling of their requisitions, Army units must be designated as ALOC units by the Department of the Army.

e. The interaction of the various supply and TP systems on identified sustainment requirements establishes how materiel will be prioritized for movement through the JDDE. Sustainment movements will be further limited by the availability of lift assets. The CJCS has established a priority system for blending these requirements with other requirements within the JDDE.

4. Transportation Priorities for Assigning Transportation Assets

a. Force movement and sustainment requirements will compete against each other for available transportation assets. The CJCS has established priorities for assigning common-user airlift and sealift resources in meeting both peacetime and wartime requirements.

b. When requirements for lift exceed capability, lift managers will apply available airlift and sealift resources to the highest priority category first. Use of lift assets will be prioritized per guidance contained in DTR 4500.9-R, *Defense Transportation Regulations*.

For more information on assigning movement and mobility priorities, see CJCSI 4120.02C, Assignment of Movement and Mobility Priority.

Intentionally Blank

APPENDIX C
COMMANDER'S CHECKLIST FOR DISTRIBUTION OF MATERIEL AND MOVEMENT OF FORCES

1. General

Distribution operations described in this publication cover the range of considerations needed to promote confidence in the joint force that global distribution operations will provide balanced, agile, and precise support to joint force missions across the range of military operations. The checklist provided below offers to the supported CCMD staff, as well as other participants in the JDDE, a planning tool for developing coordinated global distribution support.

2. Planning

a. US Forces Planning Considerations

(1) Are requirements for the movement of forces and the distribution of materiel (support personnel and equipment deployment phasing, physical distribution, and inventory decisions) included in OPLANs?

(2) Do plans specify how the physical distribution of materiel and movement of forces will be controlled and integrated between strategic, operational, and tactical levels?

(3) Is planned distribution support tailored to mission requirements and priorities?

(4) Do plans consider security and the CCDR's specific intelligence requirements, how intelligence support is to be conducted, and who will fulfill them for distribution operations? Do these plans also specify expected logistic operations support in CBRN environments?

(a) Have the levels of intelligence support and responsibilities to the CCDR and JDDE been synchronized among the intelligence directorate of a joint staff at the CCMD and appropriate subordinate commands, USTRANSCOM Joint Intelligence Operations Center, and the DOD intelligence community?

(b) Have intelligence support functions and requirements for distribution nodes been coordinated during JTF-PO planning and operations?

(c) Have intelligence tasks and responsibilities been assigned to supporting intelligence organizations and subordinate components?

(d) Has the releasability of critical information, including intelligence information, been coordinated among participating multinational and HN partners and supported/supporting flexible deterrent options?

(e) Are existing supported and supporting component commanders' critical information requirements and PIRs incorporated in global distribution operations?

(f) Are all phases of intelligence support and expectations of intelligence combat support agencies tailored to the current global distribution mission and requirements?

(5) Has the flow of sustainment materiel been integrated into the overall deployment and reflected in strategic transportation priorities?

(6) Has the impact on physical distribution, commercial or HN inventory sources due to refugees, displaced persons, MNFs, and other competing requirements for distribution capabilities been considered?

(7) Are existing and potential contracting support capabilities incorporated into distribution plans? Do they complement organic military capabilities?

(8) Has engineering intelligence been used to develop the engineer support plan?

(9) Are requirements for the DLA liaison cell and DST considered in the plan?

(10) Have considerations for conducting distribution operations in an IED environment been included in planning estimate?

(11) Have organic military capabilities for theater distribution support forces been included in plans? Are they flowed in the TPFDD when they are needed?

(12) Is use of one or more of the Services civil augmentation programs (e.g., Army's LOGCAP, Air Force's AFCAP, or Navy's global contingency construction) planned? Have coordination authorities been established? What role is envisioned for these contractors in support of theater distribution?

(13) Has contractor need for strategic and/or theater lift been assessed?

(14) Are system support contractors capable and/or willing to perform their tasks under anticipated operational conditions? Have system support contracts been reviewed to ensure that they are executable while deployed in the specified operational environment? Are system support contractors trained and equipped to continue operations under all potential operational environments?

(15) Have HN diplomatic clearances and POD access, overflight, and landing clearances for distribution operations been established? Do SOFAs and other agreements cover the movement of forces and the flow of materiel moving through commercial distribution systems to US forces or contractors supporting US forces?

(16) Is the plan sufficiently robust that no single node is a point of failure for the operation? Have planners considered the implications of the loss of overflight rights, key ports, and ground LOCs? Would the loss of one key ally or multinational partner due to changing political interests significantly impede the distribution plan?

(17) Has the flow of retrograde materiel been integrated into the overall redeployment plan and reflected in strategic transportation priorities?

b. Multinational Planning Considerations

(1) Do plans provide a summary of the requirements, taskings, and concept of multinational operations that is supported by logistic planning? Are lead nation and HN responsibilities and role specializations defined for the various logistic tasks?

(2) Have all nations participating in the operation either provided for distribution support for their forces or arranged with the MNF or bilateral arrangements for this support? Have they provided or obtained the fiscal resources to sustain distribution support of their force contributions? Are ACSAs in place between the US and MNFs?

(3) Are the multinational logistic objectives specified? Are they achievable with respect to the plans? Are national procedures for strategic movement of forces and distribution of materiel (air and sea delivery) established?

(4) Are levels of accompanying inventory or supplies with national formations addressed?

(5) Is a known or estimated CWT provided from national industrial bases to the theater?

(6) Are procedures included for support to, from, and between other multinational members and Services?

(7) Are the national theater inventory stockage objectives by class of supply or national distribution system concepts specified and complementary to the MNFC's intent?

(8) Are inventory buildup requirements specified? Are national operational packages on hand to support multinational operations until the in-country distribution and/or logistic support system is established?

(9) Are national distribution and resupply time frames consistent and reliable to support the operational concept?

(10) Have multinational critical and common items and inventory sources been identified? What provisions have been made for an integrated approach to fill critical items and items common to the MNF? Have they been quantified?

(11) What distribution support will be provided to the MNF as a national responsibility, a cooperative responsibility, solely by one nation, by HNS, and/or from contracted sources?

(12) What multinational physical distribution support must be provided to the HN or other multinational partners?

(13) Are provisions made for national emergency distribution or resupply?

(14) Are there MNF provisions for distribution support of displaced civilians, detainees, or NGOs?

(15) Are national reserve materiel inventories stored in theater or at the national industrial base? Are call forward procedures specified? Are there political constraints on the redistribution of this materiel to other parts of the same theater or to another theater?

(16) Can national reserve materiel be distributed to MNF partners?

(17) Has the use allocation of various SPODs, SPOEs, APODs, and APOEs among multinational partners been specified?

(18) Do OPLANs specify which MNF logistic elements will provide the support required?

(19) Are the national materiel distribution flow and the deployment flow of national forces from national bases balanced with the theater distribution and JRSOI capabilities? Does national distribution support complement the theater logistic plan?

(20) Is the amount of HN distribution support to be provided to various multinational partners stated in terms of workload to be performed or in MNF equivalents?

(21) Will unsourced multinational logistic force structure requirements be offset with HN, contracted, or inter-Service support?

(22) Is HN distribution support accounted for in national deployment plans to ensure that functions are covered and organic force structure is appropriately decremented or reassigned?

(23) Has commercial communications capability been allocated in sufficient quantity and quality to support national and multinational distribution operations?

(24) What types of critical distribution-related information (from planning, AV, ITV, and business operating information systems) will be shared among multinational partners? How will it be shared?

(25) Is there a multinational mechanism to coordinate the procurement of in theater inventories by all national forces? Is there a policy enforcement mechanism to ensure compliance with multinational procurement strategies?

3. Global Distribution Networks

a. Physical Network

(1) Have infrastructure assessments been conducted?

(2) Have infrastructure shortfalls been addressed either for resolution or as constraining factors in distribution plans?

b. **Information Network**

(1) Is the theater information network adequate to support distribution operations systems?

(2) Where and how will ITV information be obtained? How will it be integrated into distribution operations?

(3) Do business processes and AISs and AIT adequately support AV and ITV data capture?

(4) Is Internet access adequate to support Service component requirements for vendor and DOD requisitioning systems? Do Service components and materiel providers have alternative methods and procedures?

c. **Communications Network**

(1) Are all the AISs required to support global distribution operations identified so that the communication infrastructure can be appropriately sized during the planning process?

(2) Is there a robust communications capability available to support global distribution operations? Are communications capabilities to support distribution operations included in joint communications plans?

(3) Will the communications network support classified distribution information?

(4) Will the communications network provide adequate connectivity for logistic automated systems?

(5) Is sufficient bandwidth available to provide required voice, data, and video services?

d. **Financial Network**

(1) Are critical materiel and war reserve items adequately resourced?

(2) Are funding and accounting responsibilities for cross-service provider arrangements established?

(3) Are funding and accounting responsibilities for multinational provider arrangements established?

(4) Are there adequate financial mechanisms and resources in place to obtain access to local inventories or physical distribution capabilities?

4. **Global Distribution Elements**

a. **Requirements Determination and Stocking Policy**

(1) What is the status, quantity, and location of theater stocks and war reserve assets?

(2) Is critical materiel identified? Has the CCDR or subordinate JFC established inventory target levels for accompanying supplies and for inventory objectives for critical materiel by phase of the operation?

(3) Can adequate quantities of critical materiel be available in theater, or in the transportation pipeline, or be available and shipped from CONUS to meet velocity needs of the supported force?

(4) Has surge requirements planning been conducted with CONUS strategic level provider organizations? Have the requirements for operational surge been positioned in theater or have intertheater and/or intratheater lift resources been allocated to support timely flow from CONUS or other inventory source locations?

b. **Acquisition and Procurement**

(1) What is the level of GPC acceptability in theater?

(2) Is theater contracting support established?

(3) What single dominant user, CUL, and/or cross-servicing agreements need to be established? When and how do Service component support processes transition to these CULT processes?

(4) What existing contractor support arrangements have been established? Can these support the planned expansion of operations?

(5) Are there arrangements for the use of non-US contracts by US forces?

(6) Are there arrangements for the use of DOD contracts and forces by other federal agencies such as DOS?

(7) What HN sources for materiel and distribution support services are available in the OA or in areas adjacent to the theater? Is it acceptable and consistent with political and military objectives for US forces to use these sources? What will be the impact on indigenous populations by the use of distribution-related materiel inventories and physical distribution capabilities by US forces?

(8) Are Service component product support arrangements compatible with CCDR plans and policies?

(9) Are product support contractors included in customs and/or SOFAs and other HN agreements?

(10) What are the organic force structure alternatives needed in the event that product support contractors are unable to perform in theater? Has the flow of these capabilities been included in the TPFDD?

c. **Requisition Process**

(1) Are extant distribution velocity metrics consistent with the parameters of the operation? Do the CCDR or Service components need to adjust the F/ADs of the support elements?

(2) Are Service component requisitioning methods compatible with theater communications and/or information network constraints?

(3) Is Internet access available for requisitioning?

d. **Physical Distribution and Transportation**

(1) Have joint distribution or CULT and storage and/or warehousing requirements been established?

(2) Is the JDDOC aware of force movement and materiel distribution requirements and the variety of military and commercial transportation capabilities available to support the JFC?

(3) To what degree is materiel distribution dependent on commercial air parcel delivery? How are commercial delivery arrangements integrated into theater distribution? Are alternatives available if commercial services are unable to reach the theater or, within the theater, unable to reach the customer destination?

(4) Are HN transportation facilities and/or equipment available and included in planning? What are the implications of the HN on MNFs sharing the same facilities or capabilities?

(5) Have arrangements been made to accommodate shipping, handling, and storage of HAZMAT and HW? Has coordination with appropriate HN and transit nation authorities been completed?

(6) Are preconfigured loads included in distribution system concepts? For what commodity items? What is the theater capability to transport preconfigured loads to the end-user? What is the theater capability to reconfigure loads?

(7) Are CCDR procedures for tracking, control, and return of empty containers, 463L air pallets, and aerial delivery equipment established?

(8) How is physical distribution of US mail integrated with other materiel? Have CCDR policies and procedures for distribution of "any Service member" letter and/or parcel mail been established? Can the flow of "any Service member" mail be slowed or stopped if necessary?

e. **Cross-Leveling**

(1) What critical items are likely candidates for theater cross-leveling action?

(2) Are CCDR mechanisms for effecting cross-leveling established? Have the protocols and procedures for CCDR directive logistics authority been established for a given operation or commodity?

(3) Have adequate reimbursement procedures been established for operational cross-leveling?

(4) Have Service components established procedures and processes to cross level Service-owned materiel within the theater?

f. **Disposal**

(1) Is DLA Disposition Services support available in or near the theater? DLA Disposition Services contingency points of contact may be found by going to the DLA Disposition Services Web site: www.dispositionservices.dla.mil.

(2) Is disposal coordination or assistance available as part of the DST?

(3) Is CCDR policy on disposal of HW established?

(4) Are there HN agreements for DLA Disposition Services operations, including sales programs?

(5) What is the in-theater capability for demilitarization and disposal of MLIs and/or CCLIs?

(6) Are procedures for disposal of captured or confiscated weapons established?

(7) What is the alternative to in-theater DLA Disposition Services operations?

(8) Are contract disposal operations required and established?

g. **Environmental**

(1) Has a lead agent for environmental matters been appointed?

(2) Have operation-specific HAZMAT and HW handling and disposal standards been established?

(3) Have shipping impediments to velocity been identified and procedural solutions established?

(4) Have HN agreements to facilitate HAZMAT and HW disposal been established?

(5) Are suitable facilities, equipment, and materials available for HAZMAT/HW storage and transportation?

(6) Are adequate trained personnel assigned to perform environmental tasks?

(7) Are procedures in place to handle captured or confiscated HAZMAT and/or HW?

(8) Has a site-specific environmental plan been written for use in identifying environment, safety, and occupational health concerns?

h. **Customs**

(1) Are agreements in place to ensure that HN customs issues do not hinder movement of forces and transportation of DOD materiel?

(2) Are arrangements with other nations within the OA or theater for intratheater transit of forces and materiel established?

(3) Are administrative procedures in place for HN customs clearance?

(4) Are third country vendors/US contractors included in customs planning?

(5) Is materiel clearly marked as property of the USG to be eligible for duty free importation?

i. **Redeployment and Redistribution**

(1) What forces and materiel will remain in theater and what forces and materiel will be redeployed and/or redistributed?

(2) What methods will be used for redeployment?

(3) What are the distribution support requirements for residual forces?

(4) What is the plan to dispose of excess or unusable equipment where transportation costs exceed reprocurement costs?

(5) What are the plans for munitions download and/or removal of HAZMAT from redeploying vehicles and equipment?

(6) What arrangements have been made for agricultural inspections of large quantities of any commodity prior to shipment back to the US?

(7) Has the appropriate strategic (commercial or military) lift been allocated to support critical materiel returns?

j. **Retrograde Shipping for Repairable Assets**

(1) What methods will be used to identify, track, and expedite shipping to depots and repair facilities of reparable assets (ranging in size)?

(2) What methods will be used for retrograde shipping?

(3) What methods will be used to identify retrograde shipping needing expedited handling?

(4) What is the concept for control and movement of retrograde materiel both intertheater and intratheater?

(5) Has the appropriate tactical and strategic (commercial or military) lift been identified to support critical retrograde shipments for repairable assets?

5. Classes of Supply

a. The following generic questions apply to each of the 10 classes of supply. See Figure C-1. Specific questions pertaining to each class of supply are listed in paragraphs 5b through 5k.

(1) What is the distribution concept for materiel in theater to include off-shore? What are the theater and/or Service component critical materiel inventory objectives?

(2) What materiel is available from inventory sources in or close to the OA? What requirements can be sourced in-theater?

(3) What are the implications on the HN, indigenous populations, or MNFs using the same facilities, inventory sources, or capabilities?

(4) How will Service components requisition materiel?

(5) Is Internet-based requisitioning and/or connectivity available in-theater?

(6) Is there a requirement to designate CUL for the distribution of common items to some or all the Service components of the joint force?

b. **Class I (Subsistence)**

(1) Is subsistence vendor support already functioning in theater? Will it continue to be used during contingency operations? What expansion or modification of the vendor's distribution system will be necessary? Can the vendor's distribution network be put to use for other commodities?

(2) Are CCDR restrictions on subsistence materiel due to HN cultural constraints established?

(3) Are containerized operational ration programs planned? How far forward will they be distributed?

(4) What are the plans for redistribution, retrograde, and/or disposal of Class I materiel during redeployment?

(5) What tactical level rations will be needed, by phase, to support the operation?

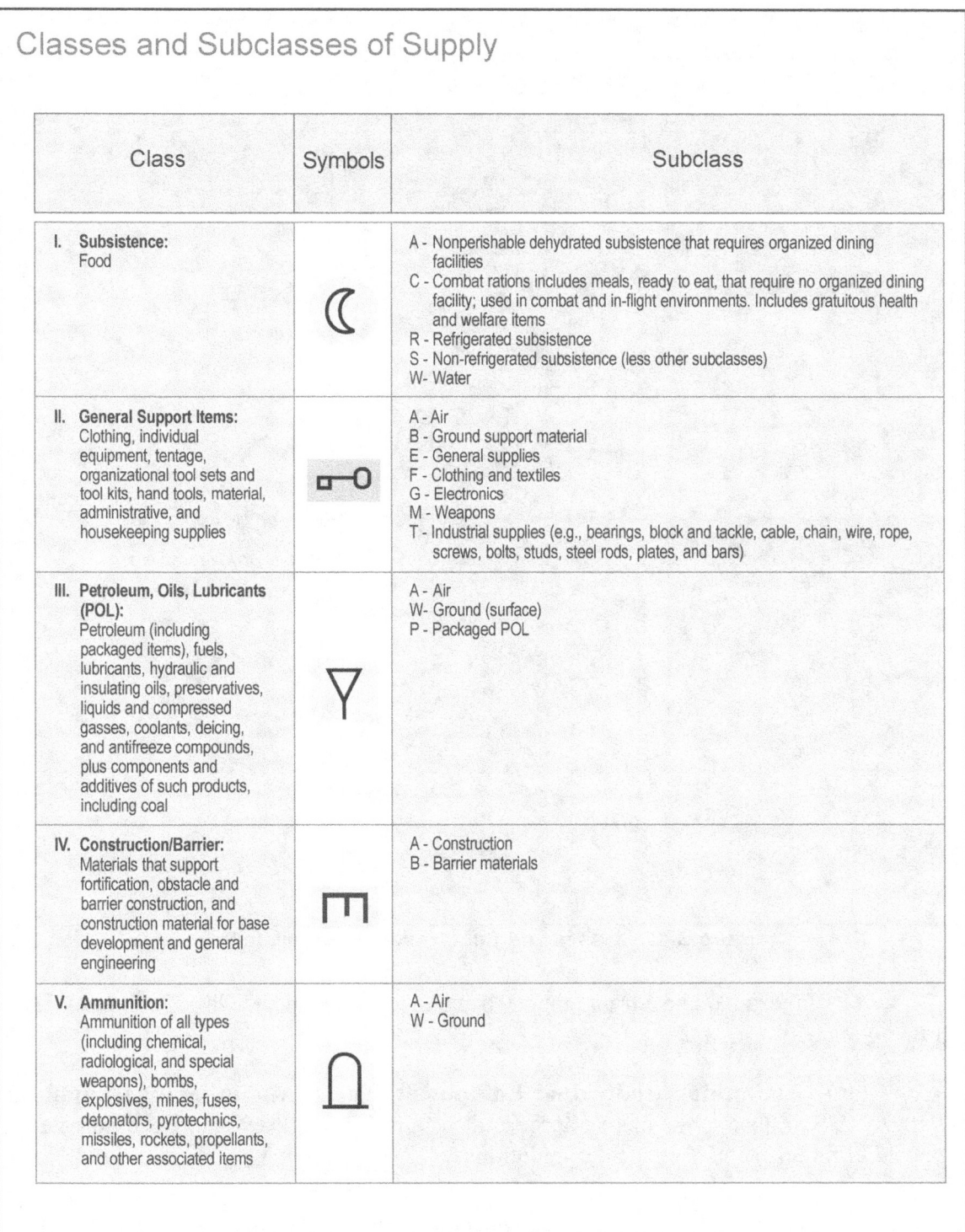

Class	Symbols	Subclass
I. **Subsistence:** Food		A - Nonperishable dehydrated subsistence that requires organized dining facilities C - Combat rations includes meals, ready to eat, that require no organized dining facility; used in combat and in-flight environments. Includes gratuitous health and welfare items R - Refrigerated subsistence S - Non-refrigerated subsistence (less other subclasses) W- Water
II. **General Support Items:** Clothing, individual equipment, tentage, organizational tool sets and tool kits, hand tools, material, administrative, and housekeeping supplies		A - Air B - Ground support material E - General supplies F - Clothing and textiles G - Electronics M - Weapons T - Industrial supplies (e.g., bearings, block and tackle, cable, chain, wire, rope, screws, bolts, studs, steel rods, plates, and bars)
III. **Petroleum, Oils, Lubricants (POL):** Petroleum (including packaged items), fuels, lubricants, hydraulic and insulating oils, preservatives, liquids and compressed gasses, coolants, deicing, and antifreeze compounds, plus components and additives of such products, including coal		A - Air W- Ground (surface) P - Packaged POL
IV. **Construction/Barrier:** Materials that support fortification, obstacle and barrier construction, and construction material for base development and general engineering		A - Construction B - Barrier materials
V. **Ammunition:** Ammunition of all types (including chemical, radiological, and special weapons), bombs, explosives, mines, fuses, detonators, pyrotechnics, missiles, rockets, propellants, and other associated items		A - Air W - Ground

Classes and Subclasses of Supply

Figure C-1. Classes and Subclasses of Supply

Classes and Subclasses of Supply (cont)

Class	Symbols	Subclass
VI. Personal Demand Items: Nonmilitary sales items	☺	A - Personal demand items not packaged as ration supplement sundry packs (RSSP) M- Personal and official letter and packaged mail. Does not include items in other classes such as spare parts P - RSSP
VII. Major End-Items: A final combination of end-products ready for intended use; e.g., launchers, tanks, racks, adapters, pylons, mobile machine shops, and administrative and tracked vehicles		A - Air B - Ground support material (includes power generators, fire-fighting, and mapping equipment) D - Administrative and general purpose vehicles (commercial vehicles used in administrative motor pools) G - Electronics J - Tanks, racks, adapters, and pylons (US Air Force only) K - Tactical and special purpose vehicles (includes trucks, truck-tractors, trailers, semi-trailers, etc.) L - Missiles M - Weapons N - Special weapons X - Aircraft engines
VIII. Medical Material/ Medical Repair	✚	A - Medical material (including repair parts special to medical items) B - Blood and fluids
IX. Repair Parts (less medical special repair parts): All repair parts and components, including kits, assemblies, material power generators sub-assemblies (repairable and nonrepairable) required for all equipment; dry batteries	☼	A - Air B - Ground support material, power generators, and bridging, fire-fighting, and mapping equipment D - Administrative vehicles (vehicles used in radio administrative motor pools) G - Electronics K - Tactical vehicles (including trucks, truck-tractors, trailers, semi-trailers, etc.) L - Missiles M- Weapons N - Special weapons T - Industrial supplies (e.g., bearings, block and tackle, cable, chain, wire, rope, screws, bolts, studs, steel rods, plates, and bars) X - Aircraft engines
X. (Code as zero '0'): Material to support military programs, not included in classes I through IX	**CA**	None

Figure C-1. Classes and Subclasses of Supply (cont)

(6) Have adequate arrangements been made to inspect Class I supplies IAW Service guidance?

c. **Class II (Clothing, Individual Equipment, Tools, Administrative Supplies).** What CONUS or outside the theater surge and sustainment requirements are anticipated to support US forces, MNFs, or local populations?

d. **Class III (POL)**

(1) Have Service component estimates of Class III bulk and packaged requirements and theater inventory levels been established?

(2) What are the Service component responsibilities for Class III distribution?

(3) What are the en route fuel support issues at ports or airfields supporting the flow of forces and follow-on sustainment?

(4) What Class III bulk fuel facilities (ports) are available for US use? What are their capabilities (depth, throughput, and storage, etc.)?

(5) What tactical and/or operational level bulk fuel units and capabilities will be needed, by phase, to support the operation? How will they be tied into DLA Energy operations?

(6) Do HNS plans exist for tanker truck, rail tanker car, pipeline, and barge support for Class III bulk fuel?

(7) Are joint petroleum office or DLA Energy region contractual arrangements for HN source Class III materiel established?

(8) Are commercial POL storage and distribution facilities available, selected, and adequate? Have these capabilities been integrated into the theater fuel distribution planning? How far forward can commercial sector distribution capabilities deliver fuel?

(9) Is force protection for POL storage and transportation established and adequate?

e. **Class IV (Construction and Barrier Materiel)**

(1) Have the Class IV material estimates contained in the engineer support plan and theater basing plans been synchronized with the staff estimates produced by theater supply chain, transportation, and distribution process planners?

(2) Does the engineer support plan specify the theater inventory level for Class IV and identify the most critical Class IV items?

(3) Does the engineer support plan specify the priority of support for Class IV materials (by operational phase)?

(4) Have the technical quality specifications for these materials (i.e., ASTM [American Society for Testing and Materials], Unified Facilities Criteria) been provided to DLA and commercial vendors? How will material quality standards be monitored?

(5) What bulk Class IV material facilities (quarry, concrete plant, saw mill) and transportation resources (large-capacity commercial dump trucks) are available for use?

(6) What tactical and/or operational level engineer units and capabilities will be needed, by phase, to support the operation?

(7) Are the joint force distribution capabilities linked to vendor delivery? How far into theater can commercial vendors deliver Class IV materials?

(8) Are Service component Class IV requirements established?

(9) Are Class IV vendor programs currently active in/near the operational theater? Can they continue to be used during contingency operations? Can the vendor distribution system be expanded or modified?

(10) Are contingency stocks of Class IV material staged in theater or available in an adjacent theater?

(11) What are the Class IV material requirements and responsibilities of civil augmentation contractors (such as LOGCAP, AFCAP, and Navy's global contingency construction)?

f. Class V (Ammunition)

(1) Does the distribution concept for Class V include the capability to distribute rapidly preconfigured ammunition packages and/or loads to operating forces?

(2) What tactical and/or operational level units and capabilities to distribute ammunition will be needed, by phase, to support the operation?

(3) Have critical munitions been identified and are sufficient levels of stocks of critical munitions available in theater, or can they be rapidly moved to theater to meet the JFC requirement?

(4) If there are shortfalls of critical munitions, can they be resolved by cross-leveling action between Service components, other CCMDs, and MNFs? Is compatibility of cross-leveling candidate items between Service components and delivery platforms known?

(5) Where do Class V stocks need to be located to support operations? Is there a capability to meet surge requirements from strategic or operational level inventories?

(6) Are Class V inventory storage sites established that meet explosive safety and security considerations?

(7) Are Class V transportation arrangements established? Are return and retrograde capabilities planned to support the repair or redistribution of low-density, high-value munitions or components of munitions?

(8) Are Class V transportation bottlenecks identified, such as limited net explosive weight capacity at essential en route airports or HN safety restrictions?

(9) Are theater organic forces or commercial sector equivalents equipped to handle and transport containerized and breakbulk munitions?

g. **Class VI (Personal Demand Items)**

(1) What is the level of Class VI support desired, by phase of the operations? Are there any types of Class VI materiel that the CCDR or Service component commanders do not want distributed to their forces?

(2) Are existing exchange services in theater? Will they continue to operate during contingency operations? Can they surge to meet planned requirements?

(3) Are deployable exchanges included in plans? When will exchanges be phased into the theater and who will determine the source, type, and location? Will multiple Service deployable exchanges be requested (Army and Air Force Exchange Service [AAFES], Marine Corps Exchange, and/or Navy Exchange)?

(4) What TP will be established for Class VI materiel?

(5) Are there GCC restrictions (based on HN considerations) on the importation of exchange merchandise such as certain types of magazines, books, or food established? Have these restrictions been communicated to the appropriate Service exchange commands?

(6) Are Class VI merchandise restrictions and/or rationing necessary due to HN black market concerns?

h. **Class VII (Major End Items)**

(1) Have joint force planners or Service components programmed in replacement systems for battle or non-battle losses? Have these estimates been coordinated with the Services? Is there a distribution plan to position replacement weapons systems or Class VII components of weapons systems in the theater or move them rapidly from outside the theater?

(2) Are there Service component or joint capabilities available to support dedicated weapons system replacement operations?

(3) What retrograde and/or return distribution capacity is available to support intratheater or intertheater movement of reparable Class VII items to repair facilities?

i. **Class VIII (Medical Materiel)**

(1) Have Class VIII sustainability and/or resupply requirements been established?

(2) Has a theater lead agent for medical materiel been designated for the AOR?

(3) Is a single integrated medical logistics manager established for Class VIII materiel?

(4) What Class VIII vendor programs are currently active in theater? Can they continue to be used during contingency operations? What expansion or modification of the vendor distribution system will be necessary?

(5) How will medical air express deliveries be integrated with theater distribution?

(6) Have arrangements been made to accommodate shipping, handling, and storage of HW? Has coordination with appropriate US, HN, transit nation, and other regulatory authorities been completed?

j. **Class IX (Repair Parts)**

(1) Are product support contractors included in Service component Class IX plans?

(2) How will vendor Class IX distribution be integrated into the theater distribution system?

(3) How will retrograde shipping of repair cycle assets be accomplished?

(4) Have critical (short supply) spares been identified and are sufficient levels of stocks of critical spares available in theater, or can they be rapidly moved to theater to meet the joint forces' requirements?

(5) Where do Class IX stocks need to be located to support operations? Is there a capability to meet surge requirements from strategic or operational level inventory?

(6) Are Class IX transportation arrangements established?

(7) Are return and retrograde capabilities planned to support the repair or redistribution of low-density, high-value spares?

(8) Are Class IX transportation/customs bottlenecks identified to ensure critical, priority, spares are not delayed en route and as retrograde?

(9) Are theater organic forces or commercial sector equivalents equipped to handle and transport oversized (engine/propeller/rotor blade) spares?

k. **Class X (Materiel for Nonmilitary Programs)**

(1) Are there existing Class X physical distribution or inventory resources in or close to the theater? How will they be integrated with the overall theater distribution system?

(2) How will NGO distribution operations be integrated with military distribution operations? How will conflicting requirements for distribution resources be resolved?

(3) Will other organizations and personnel be needed to supplement assigned and attached forces due to the unique nature of foreign humanitarian assistance or other operations?

(4) Have guidelines on acceptable and prohibited donated materiel been developed and communicated to the CONUS donated materiel coordinator?

(5) How will donated materiel shipments be integrated into existing air and/or surface lift priorities and capacity?

(6) How will donated materiel be received, controlled, and distributed in theater?

(7) How will the flow of donated materiel be reduced or ceased at the conclusion of operations?

Intentionally Blank

APPENDIX D
SAMPLE DISTRIBUTION VISIBILITY POLICY

1. General

(Combatant command), subordinate joint task forces, Service component commands, subordinate elements, and deployed forces require accurate and responsive visibility over all personnel, patient, unit equipment, and nonunit equipment (supply) movements affecting their operations. Because personnel/cargo frequently change modes and transit ports operated by different services, obtaining in-transit visibility (ITV) requires a coordinated effort between the combatant command, United States Transportation Command (USTRANSCOM), Service component commands, subordinate organizations, and commercial industry (vendors and transportation service providers) to seamlessly track personnel and cargo from origin to destination. Deploying units must provide accurate data on personnel and cargo to ensure ITV/force tracking policies, procedures, and the intent of this Distribution Visibility Policy are met.

2. Purpose

The purpose of this policy is to improve contingency responses and operational effectiveness by providing distribution visibility guidance to standing and deploying units. By standardizing ITV processes and procedures, (combatant command), its Service components, subordinate commands, and supporting combatant commanders (CCDRs) will have the ability to track and monitor unit movements and the movement of sustainment materiel. In addition, these processes will contribute to forming a common operational picture that allows key leaders to assert greater command and control of assigned forces, locate convoys and equipment, and better align forces within the area of responsibility (AOR).

3. Applicability

The provisions of this policy apply to (combatant command) headquarters, its Service components, subordinate commands, supporting commands, and combat agencies operating within the AOR unless otherwise specified in operation plans and operation orders issued by the combatant command. Subordinate units are encouraged to recommend changes through their chain of command.

4. Policy

Automated information systems (AISs) and automatic identification technology (AIT) will be used to the fullest extent possible. All units deploying to the AOR will deploy in accordance with (IAW) Defense Transportation Regulation (DTR) 4500.9-R, *Defense Transportation Regulation,* Part III Mobility, and will follow Joint Operation Planning and Execution System (JOPES) procedures as outlined in the time-phased force and deployment data (TPFDD) letter of instruction (LOI). IAW DTR 4500.9-R criteria for radio frequency identification (RFID) layer-4 shipments, write and attach RFID tags to Department of

Defense (DOD)-owned, consolidated cargo and major items of unit equipment arriving in the AOR to assist in maintaining ITV.

a. **Scope of Operations**

(1) Ground movement. This ITV policy refers to DOD assets that are transported by overland mode sources.

(2) Air movement. This ITV policy refers to passengers and cargo that are flown on DOD and/or DOD chartered aircraft.

(3) Sealift operations. This ITV policy refers to cargo that is on-loaded and off-loaded from sea vessels.

b. **Force Movement Visibility**

(1) Prior to unit movement (combatant command) will identify force movement requirements and establish supporting plan identification numbers (PIDs), to be issued by (combatant command designated agency) *(may vary by combatant command)*. Within each PID, a force module identification number will also be established. The designated force providers will source the force requirements and provide unit and command data in the working/planning PID. If requirements will move via strategic lift, (combatant command designated agency) will validate the requirements to the strategic lift provider. A force tracking number (FTN) may also be used to enhance force visibility. An FTN is an 11-character alphanumeric reference number assigned by a supported CCDR to its requested force capability requirements.

For additional information on force tracking, see Chairman of the Joint Chiefs of Staff Manual (CJCSM) 3150.16D, Joint Operation Planning and Execution System Reporting Structure (JOPESREP), *CJCSM 3122.01A,* Joint Operation Planning and Execution System (JOPES) Volume I Planning Policies and Procedures, *and Joint Publication 3-35,* Deployment and Redeployment Operations.

(2) USTRANSCOM or Air Mobility Command planners will build mission itineraries in the Global Decision Support System via the Consolidated Air Mobility Planning System or Air Mobility Command Deployment Analysis System. This information will automatically feed into the Single Mobility System and the Integrated Data Environment/Global Transportation Network Convergence (IGC), which is relayed to the Scheduling and Movement program of JOPES. For specific information, refer to the current (combatant command) TPFDD LOI.

c. **Deploying Units.** IAW DTR 4500.9-R, *Defense Transportation Regulations,* Parts I-III, deploying units must provide their higher commands, troop/chalk commanders, and load planners the following data for passenger and cargo movements.

(1) Passengers. Name, military rank/civilian designation (if applicable), Social Security number, gender, unit/organization, origin, and destination.

(2) Cargo. Consignee, required delivery date (RDD), project code (if applicable), shipment unit number (Army single item or multiple items shipped together), transportation control number (TCN), commodity code, DOD activity address code, transportation control and movement document (TCMD), national stock number (NSN), transportation account codes, special data for specific commodities (as outlined in DTR 4500.9-R, *Defense Transportation Regulation,* Part II, Chapter 203, paragraph B.19), and unit line number (ULN) (for unit move only).

(a) ULNs will correlate with TPFDD, include content level detail, and the following:

1. Pieces, weight, and cube.

2. Dimensional data.

3. Mode and shipment method.

(b) For the TCN assigned to a containerized shipment or 463L pallet and constructed IAW DTR 4500.9-R, *Defense Transportation Regulation,* Part III Mobility:

1. Identify sensitive/hazardous materials containerized/palletized shipment content and display NSN-related data on the RFID tag IAW DTR 4500.9-R, *Defense Transportation Regulations,* criteria.

2. Identify containerized major end items (e.g., vehicles, trailers) as shipment pieces and display TCN on the tag.

3. List by RDD priority. Dimensional data (expressed in length, width, and height in number of inches) of equipment in deployment sequence, by ULN.

NOTES: Army activities will enter their unit identification code in positions 2 through 7 of the TCN, and will provide their ULN in the T_9 record of the TCMD. All other Services will enter ULN in positions 2 through 8 of the TCN.

4. Coordinate with the port of embarkation manifesting station and AIS points of contact to facilitate timely and complete data exchanges to enable timely and accurate manifest generation in Cargo Movement Operations System, Transportation Coordinator's Automated Information for Movement System II, Marine air-ground task force Deployment Support System II, and Global Air Transportation Execution System (GATES).

d. **Sustainment Visibility.** Command elements must have the ability to see key sustainment distribution data elements. Effective visibility over sustainment distribution operations will be achieved when all nine elements are accurately maintained within appropriate systems. Essential data elements include:

(1) Depot or source of supply which shipped the item.

(2) Customer to whom the item was shipped.

(3) The document number on which the item was shipped.

(4) The NSN of the item shipped.

(5) The date of the requisition.

(6) The date the item was shipped.

(7) The containerization and consolidation point ship date.

(8) The POD ship date.

(9) The date the customer received the item.

e. **Patient Movement Visibility.** The following patient movement data elements must be accurately maintained within United States Transportation Regulating and Command and Control Evacuation System (TRAC2ES):

(1) Patient name and Social Security number.

(2) Originating facility.

(3) Insurance (if applicable).

(4) Gender.

(5) Diagnosis.

(6) Medical specialty required.

(7) Accepting medical doctor.

(8) Ready date.

(9) Destination facility.

f. **IGC and TRAC2ES Timelines.** As per DTR 4500.9-R, *Defense Transportation Regulation,* Parts II and III, all commands/agencies affected by this policy will ensure movement data reporting meets the following criteria:

(1) Air, truck, and rail cargo and passenger intertheater movements must be visible in IGC within one hour of departure/arrival.

(2) All intratheater cargo and passenger movements (all modes) must be visible in IGC within two hours of departure/arrival.

(3) Ocean commercial liner and charter service must be visible in IGC within 12 hours of event (goal of four hours). Ocean "gray bottom" Military Sealift Command vessels (large, medium-speed roll-on/roll-off; fast sealift ship; Ready Reserve Force) must be visible in IGC within 24 hours of event (goal of four hours) for exercise and wartime unit and sustainment moves.

(4) Patient movements on common-user aircraft must be visible in TRAC2ES within one hour of departure/arrival.

5. Responsibilities

a. (Combatant command) J-4 will:

(1) Provide theater policy and guidance on the use of AIS/AIT as they are tested, validated, and determined to be beneficial for use.

(2) Comply with DOD AIT standards.

(3) Resolve ITV issues in support of (combatant command) operations with the Army Product Director, Automated Movement and Identification Solutions, USTRANSCOM, and Joint Staff managers.

(4) Prepare, publish, revise, and update (combatant command) distribution visibility policy annually, at a minimum, or out of cycle as necessary. The (combatant command) distribution visibility policy is available on the (combatant command) J-4 home page: *(will vary by combatant command)*.

(5) Coordinate with USTRANSCOM and mandate the use of AIT as outlined in the *DOD Automatic Identification Technology Concept of Operations for Supply and Distribution Operations* (DOD AIT CONOPS), and as implemented by current implementing documents, in support of ( ) operations.

(6) Mandate use of IGC as the preferred DOD ITV system as well as appropriate functional AISs which "feed" IGC, e.g., GATES, to support ITV of unit movements and shipments of other military equipment and supplies through common-user ground, water, and aerial ports.

(7) Direct that subordinate commands develop implementation plans in support of this document.

b. USTRANSCOM will:

(1) Coordinate with participating DOD components to obtain accurate and timely end-to-end ITV of all movements in support of combatant command operations.

(2) Work with DOD components to ensure data from active RFID-instrumented nodes are fed through the radio frequency ITV server to IGC and other appropriate AISs.

(3) Support (combatant command) deployable AIT requirements, if needed, through the joint task force—port opening concept.

(4) When applicable, ensure ITV requirements are addressed when contracting for commercial transportation.

(5) Ensure USTRANSCOM transportation component commands (TCCs) and distribution partners require that transportation service contracts outline DOD timeliness criteria at commercial transportation nodes. Additionally, include the requirements for carriers to use electronic commerce or electronic data interchange to report arrival or departure at all commercial transportation nodes in the transportation service contract. This applies to all transshipment and relay operations as well.

(6) Maintain the effectiveness of ITV systems managed by USTRANSCOM.

(7) Ensure USTRANSCOM TCCs provide mission and resource updates via their approved AIS.

(8) Coordinate with medical personnel to ensure all patient status changes or clinical encounters that occur after initial reporting of patient movement requirements, during patient movement mission, or at remain overnight locations are coordinated with and reported to the supporting theater validating flight surgeon, through the patient movement requirements center. All medical personnel shall continuously and independently reassess and document patient status, update patient movement AIS, and ensure appropriate classification and treatments leading to safe patient transport outcomes.

c. **Force Provider will:**

(1) Allocate and time-phase force requirements using JOPES automated data processing tools from origin to destination, and manifest force movement using their Service unit move manifesting system. This process will ensure ITV for units moving into the (combatant command) AOR.

(2) Ensure units deploy IAW DTR 4500.9-R, *Defense Transportation Regulation,* Part III Mobility, and ensure units RFID tag cargo, equipment, and vehicles IAW this plan.

d. **Combatant Command Service Components will:**

(1) Act as their Service's lead in implementing AIT in support of (combatant command) operations. Provide guidance, as appropriate, for its use during exercises, contingencies, sustainment, and mobilization operations, and monitor the effectiveness and operational readiness of logistics AIS and supporting AIT.

(2) Ensure responsible agencies within respective commands implement and enforce the policy contained within this document.

(3) Establish, monitor, and maintain AIT/AIS training programs within respective commands.

(4) Ensure asset visibility (AV) and ITV requirements are addressed IAW this document when contracting for commercial transportation. Requests for commercial truck service moving classified and/or high priority cargo must follow transportation protective service (TPS) requirements in DTR 4500-9-R, *Defense Transportation Regulation*, Part II Cargo Movement, Chapter 205 Transportation Protective Service (TPS).

(5) Contractually require commercial standard two-dimensional (2-D) bar codes on supply and transportation documents from commercial vendors IAW the Military Standard (MIL-STD)-129, *Military Marking for Shipment and Storage;* Federal Acquisition Regulation (FAR); Department of Defense Federal Acquisition Regulation Supplement (DFARS).

(6) Comply with the policy for use of passive RFID technology in the DOD supply chain as required in the MIL-STD-129P, the DFARS, DTR 4500.9-R, *Defense Transportation Regulation*, Part II Cargo Movement, and the DOD AIT CONOPS as implemented by current implementing documents.

(7) Identify deployable AIT/AIS requirements.

(8) Identify the need for an AIT/AIS capability to support exercise and contingency requirements and submit a request for forces (RFF)/request for capabilities if necessary.

(9) Take appropriate actions to ensure complete/accurate data is provided in manifests and on RFID tags.

(10) Expand the use of premium AIT, such as commercial satellite tracking for ITV, as outlined in the DOD AIT CONOPS, when justified.

(11) Attain the DOD AIT data timeliness criteria, including the movement of information from AIS to IGC in supporting implementation plans.

(12) Incorporate data timeliness criteria for reporting arrival and departure of air/surface cargo at non-DOD nodes into commercial transportation contracts.

(13) Consider business process improvement when identifying requirements and selecting AIT.

(14) Identify deficiencies and/or problems in the logistic support of AIT through the respective Services.

(15) Identify problems obtaining frequency allocation and assignment for AIT devices to (combatant command designated agency).

(16) (Combatant command)-assigned aeromedical evacuation forces will provide patient and mission ITV updates on common-user aircraft via TRAC2ES to patient movement requirements centers.

e. **Subordinate Joint Task Force Commanders will:**

(1) Ensure responsible staff within respective commands implement and enforce the policy contained within this document.

(2) Coordinate with the appropriate Service to allow the establishment, monitoring, and maintenance of AIT/AIS training programs within respective commands.

(3) Ensure AV and ITV requirements are addressed IAW this policy when contracting for commercial transportation. Requests for commercial truck service moving classified and/or high priority cargo must follow TPS requirements in DTR 4500.9-R, *Defense Transportation Regulation*, Part II, Chapter 205.

(4) Contractually require commercial standard 2-D bar codes on supply and transportation documents from commercial vendors IAW the MIL-STD-129, FAR, and DFARS.

(5) Comply with the policy principles for use of passive RFID technology in the DOD supply chain as required in the MIL-STD-129P, the DFARS, and the DOD AIT CONOPS as implemented by current implementing documents.

(6) Comply with DOD AIT standards.

(7) Identify deployable AIT/AIS requirements.

(8) Identify problems concerning the steps to obtain frequency allocation and assignment for AIT devices to (combatant command designated agency).

(9) Identify strategic, operational, and tactical instrumentation sites for the adoption and use of AIT/AIS during all stages of a contingency.

(10) Prioritize the location and required AIT media for identified sites/nodes.

(11) Coordinate RFFs for deployable AIT capability through official message channels no later than 72 hours prior to anticipated need.

(12) Coordinate with the applicable Service and the (combatant command) for active and passive RFID capability at selected nodes during major operations.

f. **Assigned Forces.** Assigned forces will comply with the ITV requirements outlined in this policy.

APPENDIX E
SUGGESTED CHARTER FOR THE
THEATER-JOINT TRANSPORTATION BOARD

1. Mission

The GCC may convene the T-JTB during wartime or contingencies. The T-JTB will ensure that CCMD common-user transportation resources assigned or available are apportioned to achieve the maximum benefit in meeting objectives.

2. Responsibility

The command JTB represents the GCC in the performance of functions listed in paragraph 5. The chairman of the JTB has decision authority in these areas, except when a matter cannot be resolved within the JTB. In such instances, the matter is referred to the GCC for decision.

3. Membership

The command JTB normally is composed of the following:

a. **Chairman.** Normally the CCDR's director of logistics.

b. **Principal Members**

    (1) CCMD deputy director, operations directorate.

    (2) CCMD deputy director, plans and policy.

    (3) US Army component representative.

    (4) US Navy component representative.

    (5) USMC component representative.

    (6) US Air Force component representative.

    (7) Special operations component representative.

    (8) Other members as directed by the GCC.

c. **Non-Voting Member.** USTRANSCOM liaison officer to the CCMD.

d. **JTB Secretariat.** Normally a staff officer from the J-4.

4. Management Concept of a Command Joint Transportation Board

When convened, the command JTB acts for the GCC by communicating guidance to the CCMD staff and component commands and/or subunified commands. Guidance includes the establishment of priorities and allocations for the use of airlift, sealift, and surface transportation capability. The chairman of the command JTB will notify the GCC when movement requirements exceed capabilities. The JTB will then present a recommendation to either reprioritize and apportion or to request additional assets to accomplish the assigned missions.

5. Functions

The JTB will perform the following tasks:

a. Monitor transportation requirements and capabilities through JOPES and through coordination with USTRANSCOM and component commands and/or subunified commands.

b. Adjudicate competing lift requirements.

c. Recommend to the GCC COAs to resolve transportation movement problems identified by the JDDOC and/or JMC (if established).

d. Closely monitor the projected operational activities of the CCMD to anticipate developing problems or future resource requirements.

e. As needed, provide an interface among the supported CCMD, USTRANSCOM, other supporting CCMDs, and Service components on matters concerning transportation.

6. Procedures

The JTB will follow the procedures below:

a. As directed by the JTB chairman, meet in open or general sessions. These sessions may be followed by closed or executive sessions.

b. Establish standing operating procedures, including those required for relocation to an alternative command post.

c. Receive administrative support from the J-4 and the JLOC.

d. Refer matters that cannot be resolved within the command JTB to the GCC.

e. Invite, at its discretion, such representatives as may be required to attend meetings of the command JTB.

f. Honor, if appropriate, the request of other offices to attend the command JTB meetings.

7. Functions of the Joint Transportation Board Secretariat

The JTB Secretariat will be responsible for the following:

a. Provide continuity for the command JTB.

b. Attend all meetings of the command JTB.

c. Evaluate proposed COAs for the command JTB and make appropriate recommendations.

d. Monitor transportation and strategic movement requirements and capabilities.

e. Issue the decisions of the command JTB.

f. Respond to the requirements of the command JTB.

g. Provide a record of proceedings of each command JTB meeting.

Intentionally Blank

APPENDIX F
INTERMODAL CONTAINER/PLATFORM MANAGEMENT AND TRACKING PLAN (SAMPLE TEMPLATE)

1. Purpose

This appendix provides a general template for combatant commanders (CCDRs) to use in developing a plan to manage and track intermodal containers and platforms in accordance with (IAW) Defense Transportation Regulation (DTR) 4500.9-R, Part VI, *Management and Control of Intermodal Containers and System 463L Equipment*. The template includes format as well as some text examples.

2. Sample Template

BY ORDER OF THE
(Combatant command)

Intermodal Container/Platform Management and Tracking Plan
LETTER OF INSTRUCTION (LOI)

COMPLIANCE WITH THIS PUBLICATION IS MANDATORY

Office of Primary Responsibility: (Combatant command J-Staff Code)

This LOI Supplements: (List any combatant command regulation, instruction, or other document applicable)

OVERVIEW: Provide guidance on what this LOI takes precedence over with regards to existing regulations, instructions, or other orders and any documents, messages, or orders this LOI will supersede. Also identify applicability, e.g., "It is applicable to all units, organizations, departments, agencies, or activities either operating within or shipping material in containers into or out of the (combatant command) area of responsibility (AOR)."

PURPOSE: Describe what the policy and intent of LOI is, e.g., "This LOI establishes policy and directs the use of standard procedures to administer, task, and execute management of intermodal platforms …."

OBJECTIVES: State the overarching goal(s) and focus of this LOI, e.g., "The goal of (combatant command) is to improve accountability of intermodal containers and 463L pallets, minimize late fees and other charges on carrier-owned containers, and improve the overall effectiveness and efficiency of container and intermodal platform (e.g., 463L pallets) management programs and operations in the AOR. Areas of emphasis include (Identify specific areas of emphasis to achieve overarching goals/objectives, such as reducing detention and other charges on carrier-owned containers, maintaining accountability of all containers, correctly processing and dispositioning containers, and properly recording container transactions to maintain container asset visibility.)

EXECUTIVE SUMMARY

Provide concise summary of this LOI, e.g., "This LOI outlines roles and responsibilities of various entities involved in container management within the (combatant command) AOR. It also describes categories of common-use containers, as well as procedures for container handling, movement, tracking, accounting, and usage. This LOI is arranged by chapter, and contains a list of terms and definitions as well as attachments that provide further amplification in various topics."

CONTENTS

Chapter 1 Roles and Responsibilities

1.1. Enter name of CCDR and provide information on roles and responsibilities, e.g., "Will provide intermodal platform management policy, planning guidance, and direction." Identify roles, responsibilities, and authorities for the combatant command's logistics directorate (J-4), the combatant command's joint deployment and distribution operations center (JDDOC), and other subordinate component commands, joint task force commands, and units operating within the CCDR's AOR, including movement control, theater base/installation commanders, unit commanders, container control activities, and container control offices, as appropriate and designate an appropriate theater command to function as TCM. Following paragraphs are provided as examples:

1.1.1 (Combatant command) **J-4-Logistics Directorate:** Has staff responsibility and policy authority for all logistic-related issues, to include container/463L pallet management, in the AOR. (Combatant command) J-4 Staff will coordinate with logistic directorates within the Joint Staff, Service headquarters, theater Service component commands, and other combatant commands and federal agencies, as required.

1.1.2 (Combatant command) **Joint Deployment and Distribution Operations Center:** Responsible for coordinating and scheduling the movement of all commodities and personnel, via ground, sea, and air within the geographic combatant commander's (GCC's) AOR. Coordinates and interfaces with the Military Surface Deployment and Distribution Command (SDDC) to provide in-transit visibility (ITV) and asset visibility of intermodal platforms into, through, and out of the AOR.

1.2 Service component and joint task force commanders of (combatant command) will:

- Be responsible for container management operations in their respective areas.
- Assume duties as the country container authority (CCA), or designate (in writing) subordinate unit(s) as the CCA for their respective areas.
- Advise SDDC and the (combatant command) JDDOC of container requirements for support of operations.
- Provide information, coordination, and cooperation as required with regard to container management.
- In coordination with SDDC, take appropriate measures to implement the approved container management system in the area of operations to include providing infrastructure and other support for fielding and training as required.
- Take appropriate measures to allow the effective and efficient implementation of container management policies, procedures, directives, and programs promulgated by the (combatant command), SDDC, and the (combatant command) JDDOC.
- Take appropriate measures to allow the proper usage and accountability of all containers located in, and transiting through, their respective areas.
- Comply with established performance metrics.

1.2.1 **Theater Base/Installation Commanders:** Commanders of all (combatant command) AOR bases/installations (regardless of size) are responsible for accurate maintenance and reporting of container information and usage as directed in this publication and higher headquarters direction through their respective supply support activities (SSAs), or other Service specific equivalents. Base commanders will appoint, in writing, a designated container control officer (CCO).

1.2.2 **Unit Commanders:** Unit commanders at all levels are ultimately accountable for unit authorized containers on their own property books and are further responsible for any common-use government-leased (GL)/government-owned (GO) containers issued to them for their use in accomplishing their mission. Unit commanders are responsible for the timely processing and return of carrier-owned containers consigned to their unit. Unit commanders are accountable and/or responsible, as appropriate, for maintaining accurate inventory records of all containers under their control regardless of ownership. Unit commanders will appoint a designated CCO (officer or noncommissioned officer). All CCO appointments will be made during the relief-in-place/transfer of authority of a unit's initial arrival in the joint operations area (JOA).

1.2.3 **Country Container Authority (CCA):** Appointed by a Service/joint task force commander and responsible for all container management/operations for their respective operational area.

1.2.4 **Container Control Officer (CCO):** As appointed by the base commander (or appropriate authority), this individual will establish and maintain control and accountability of all containers on his/her designated area. Duties of CCO will include regular inventories (monthly) of containers and regular review/oversight of individual container custodians. CCOs are also responsible for reporting on and maintaining the established performance metrics.

1.3 **US Transportation Command (USTRANSCOM):** USTRANSCOM serves as the DOD single manager for common-user containers moving through the DTS and for providing container management services. USTRANSCOM has designated the SDDC as the global container manager (GCM) to allow effective management and efficient control of DOD-related containers across all theaters and operational environments in peace and war in support of the warfighter.

1.3.1 **Military Surface Deployment and Distribution Command (SDDC):** The designated GCM. In the (combatant command) AOR, SDDC is responsible for establishing operational capability to allow effective management and efficient control of DOD-related intermodal containers subject to directives and IAW the (combatant command) concept of operations (CONOPS). Will coordinate with, and provide support to, all (combatant command) components and joint task force commanders regarding container management issues. SDDC, through its Global Container Management Office and its Army Intermodal Distribution Platform Management Office (AIDPMO), is responsible for verifying ownership of containers. SDDC is responsible for development, implementation, utilization, and training of an automated management information system for container cost management, tracking, accounting, visibility, and reporting as required by the (combatant command) CONOPS. Additionally, SDDC is responsible for container retrograde operations, and will establish retrograde processes at joint distribution hubs at locations throughout the theater as required.

1.3.2 **Air Mobility Command (AMC):** The designated Global 463L Pallet Manager. In the (combatant command) AOR, AMC is responsible for reviewing/coordinating formal policy, procedures, and timeframes which will be established by the GCC through the Air Force component for all Services/agencies to manage and return pallet and net resources to the Defense Transportation System (DTS). Policy should also address abuse/misuse of these critical transportation assets. Once approved, this policy will be sent to all units and logistic agencies within the theater of operations.

1.4 **Defense Logistics Agency (DLA):** Responsible for ensuring that all shipments are processed through the DTS. As a primary contracting agent in the AOR, DLA also is responsible for ensuring contracts in the AOR comply with the policies outlined in this publication. As the contract holder for the Subsistence Prime Vendor contractor, DLA plays an important role in overall efficient use of containers and 463L pallets. DLA also is responsible for ensuring that all of its subordinate units/branches/support activities located in the AOR comply with this LOI.

1.5 **Service Logistics Directorates (Army G-4, Navy N-4, Air Force A-4, Marine Corps Installations and Logistics Directorate):** Have Title 10, USC, authority over all Service component-owned and -leased containers worldwide. Currently, the Army centrally procures all military specification containers for the Army and provides like services for DOD components. Additionally, the Army maintains the vast majority of the DOD-owned/leased containers supporting operations and thus has a significant role in container management support for joint operations. The Army G-4 has designated the AIDPMO with worldwide authority and responsibility for the life cycle management of all Army-owned/leased containers and has integrated AIDPMO into SDDC. AIDPMO authority does not include operational management and control that is the responsibility of SDDC GCM and theater construction manager.

1.6 **Army and Air Force Exchange Service (AAFES):** AAFES is responsible for effective and efficient use of containers in shipping its cargo. Establish memorandum of understanding with supported command for in-theater logistic operations to include container management.

Chapter 2 Container Categories and Status

2.1 **General:** This chapter provides guidance on categorizing and identifying International Organization for Standardization (ISO) containers. Purpose is to provide information to all units on the various category types of containers and the identification markings on them in order to determine ownership of the container and maintain accountability. An example of general guidance information to include on containers is the following: "The ownership of a shipping container is normally indicated by its ISO container number. All shipping containers worldwide are required to have unique 11 position alphanumeric ISO container numbers. The ISO number consists of a three-letter owner code, a one-letter equipment category identifier (the letter "U" denotes a freight container), a six-digit serial number, and a single check digit (e.g., USAU 123456-2). The ISO container number can be found on the upper right-hand section of all four container sides and at both ends on the roof of the container, as well as on the International Convention for Safe Containers' data plate. Many containers entering a theater AOR during a joint operation may have an incomplete ISO number, an invalid ISO number, or even no ISO number. SDDC GCM is responsible for resolving invalid ISO numbers and verifying ownership and making this information available to the theater container managers. Units, activities, and agencies will direct questions regarding container markings to their respective CCO, who will forward to their respective CCA."

2.2 **Container Categories:** This section provides information on the various categories of containers linked to their source or acquisition. This is an important element of container management in that each container category may or may not have certain costs associated with its use, e.g., detention, leasing per diem, leasing off hire costs, etc. Below paragraphs provide descriptions of various container categories.

2.2.1 **GO Containers:** GO containers are those purchased by the US Government. Most have ISO numbers starting with USA (Army), USF (Air Force), USM (Marine Corps), USN (Navy), or DOD (DOD common user and DLA). GO containers are typically used to support unit deployment and redeployment where a US operated/managed seaport of debarkation (SPOD) is available to support joint reception, staging, onward movement, and integration. GO containers are also used to support transload operations (when established) and are the preferred category of container for long term temporary storage during joint operations in an AOR. GO containers do not incur detention charges but can incur port storage assessments.

2.2.2 **GL Containers:** GL containers are those containers that are long term leased by the US Government. SDDC-GCM has implemented and manages a Master Leasing Agreement that provides a single vendor as the sole source for leasing containers worldwide. Units, activities, and agencies will use the designated single vendor. GL containers are typically used to fill local shortages of US GO containers in support of unit deployment and redeployment. Container leases typically last from one to two years and do not incur detention charges. GL containers might also be leased for special purposes such as ammunition shipments or other sustainment uses. Transfer of containers from one command to another will require adjustments to the terms of the lease and funding to effect the transfer. GL containers are identified by their 11 character ISO number.

2.2.3 **Contractor Acquired Government-Owned Property (CAGOP) Containers:** CAGOP containers are procured by contractors on behalf of the US Government. Contractors using or procuring CAGOP containers will follow the same procedures as outlined for other GO/GL containers to include accountability and reporting requirements. Contractors will establish accountability through appropriate means for CAGOP containers. DOD contractors are responsible for the proper use, control, inventorying, and reporting of all containers under their use or control, regardless of ownership or acquisition method. This report will include acquisition details (including the container ISO number). This report will go to SDDC-GCM and the appropriate Service container manager.

2.2.4 **Government-Furnished Equipment (GFE) Containers:** Containers provided to a contractor by the government to enable the contractor to complete contractual obligations and reduce the contracted cost to the government. GFE containers can only be GO/GL containers.

2.2.5 **Carrier-Furnished (CF) Containers:** CF containers are owned by the international shipping companies. CF containers are typically used to transport sustainment cargo but are sometimes used to support unit deployment and redeployment where a non-US operated SPOD is used. Like GO containers, CF containers are also marked with an ISO number. CF containers incur detention charges as delineated in universal service contracts or other liner agreements contracted by USTRANSCOM and administered by SDDC. Detention typically begins 10 days after the container is delivered to its contracted destination. The US Government is financially responsible for return of CF containers; empty CF containers should never be considered "abandoned." Collect and return them to the designated collection point in each country as soon as possible. Unserviceable CF containers must be turned in as soon as possible.

2.2.6 **Contractor-Owned Containers:** Contractors use containers that they own. These are not to be confused with contractor acquired government owned containers. Containers that are owned by contractors must be identified in IBS-CMM with code of "N" along with an annotation in the remarks block indicating the name of the contractor.

2.3 **Unresolved Ownership:** Containers have "Unresolved Ownership" when a container bears carrier ISO container number markings, but the carrier in question has not acknowledged that it owns the container in question. Containers that are found during inventories that have carrier markings are initially entered into the current theater container management tool as "Unresolved Owner." Until the actual ownership is resolved, it will be treated as a GO container. If an unresolved container is verified to be carrier-owned, it must immediately be treated and handled as such and returned to the carrier as soon as possible. SDDC is responsible for verifying the ownership of unresolved ownership containers. SDDC-GCM is responsible for issuing US Government ISO numbers for any new or GL/CF containers bought by the government during an operation.

2.4 **Disputed Ownership:** Disputes in ownership occur when a container that is registered in IBS-CMM, whether GO, GL, or CF, has been "lost" by a US Government entity, and found in the possession of a host nation or third country national citizen claiming they "purchased" the container. In these instances, the container's true ownership must be validated by SDDC and the appropriate Service component container representative. If an individual discovers a container in this category, they should document the container number, its location, where and when it was spotted, and report this information to the CCO. If a host nation or third country national offers some "proof" as to the legitimacy of the claim, they should be directed to SDDC for additional assistance and research of the claim.

2.5 Container Status

2.5.1 Abandoned Containers: GO/GL containers in the JOA that are not on any property books (within theater or out of theater) will become theater-owned property and will be managed by the GCC until ownership can be determined. When assigned, the theater designated container managers will assume formal accountability for all such GO/GL containers under their control. If not assigned, Service components will assume such accountability for these containers in their AORs. Commands, activities, and agencies operating at locations where abandoned containers are found will make every effort to determine the ISO number of abandoned containers and will account for such containers in their inventory (hand/custody receipts). Once under control, these containers can be used as other GO containers.

2.5.2 Unserviceable Containers: Containers that have been deemed unrepairable (or not economically repairable) by a designated container inspector will be categorized as "unserviceable" and reported to SDDC. Commands, activities, and agencies with GO/GL containers determined to be unserviceable will inform SDDC, through their respective CCO, who will provide disposition instructions upon coordination with SDDC GCM. Commands, activities, and agencies with carrier-owned containers that are unserviceable will request disposition instructions through their respective CCO, CCA to SDDC.

Chapter 3 Program Management

3.1 **General:** Successful container management requires integration and execution of common practices regarding container tracking, usage, accountability, reporting, and inventory management.

3.2. Container Tracking

3.2.1 **Use of Defense Transportation System (DTS):** All US Government agencies and departments shipping material into the (combatant command) AOR are required to use the DTS.

3.2.2 **Tracking of Carrier-Owned Containers:** SDDC, in conjunction with the respective CCA, will track all carrier-owned containers in the AOR. Carrier containers used as storage in the AOR are the responsibility of the storage SSA, unit, or contractor facility. All efforts will be made to release these containers back to the DTS. All activities using containers for storage will prepare and submit regular reports on their container usage as directed in this publication.

3.2.3 **Use of Radio Frequency Identification (RFID) Tags:** Containers of DOD-owned cargo in transit will have RFID tags (see DTR 4500.9-R, *Defense Transportation Regulations,* for tagging criteria). Container identification data will be included in the RFID tag writing process. The tag write data and tag interrogator information will be sent to the radio frequency ITV system server which will forward the information to other DOD authorized ITV systems such as IBS-CMM, Army Container Asset Management System (ACAMS), and IGC. See Chapter 4, "Information Systems and Tools," for a list of recognized systems in the (combatant command) AOR.

3.3 Container Usage

3.3.1 **General:** Containers may be used for transportation, temporary, and, in some cases, long term storage, and other uses as deemed necessary for effective execution of the operation. However, each unit will have a plan for long term storage that does not include containers. Containers used for purposes other than transportation should be either GO or GL containers. Use of carrier-owned containers for temporary storage should be avoided unless necessary for effective execution of the operation. Carrier-owned containers will not be used for office spaces, billeting, shower stalls, etc.

3.3.2 **Validation of Requirements:** Commands, activities, and agencies will minimize the use of shipping containers as storage units. All activities in the AOR that are using containers for storage of material (including all contractor activities) will validate their actual storage container requirements IAW the following guidelines:

- Document the percent filled status of all containers under their control.
- Estimate the number of filled containers needed to sustain current operations based on past receipts and issues of material and report this information to their respective CCA.

- Demonstrate that they have effectively restuffed and/or redistributed container contents as appropriate to maximize the percent filled of every container in use.
- Document that storage facilities are unavailable, and submit to CCO.

3.3.3 **Use of GO/GL Containers:** All US military units, DOD agencies, activities, and contractor facilities in the (combatant command) AOR will use their assigned containers in an efficient manner and will maintain positive control of all containers in their custody through a regular inventory program. The following accountability tracking methods may be used:

- ACAMS as a durable hand receipt.
- Unit/installation property books (only for containers assigned to a unit prior to deployment).
- Printed hand receipt or custody control card.
- Regardless of the inventory management method used, all units will maintain accurate records of the containers in their custody. Predeployment preparation will include a thorough review of all assigned containers prior to the unit departing its home or mobilization station. While in theater, units will identify containers that are considered to be excess and arrange for turn-in with their respective CCA.

3.3.4 **Use of Carrier-Owned Containers:** In countries where there is no transload facility, carrier-owned containers may be used to transport cargo to its final destination (either under the applicable universal services contract terms or by other means). Every effort must be made to unload these containers and return them to DTS within the free time period allowed under the terms of the applicable universal services contract. In countries where a transload operation is established, carrier-owned containers are only to be used to transport goods from the SPOD to the transload site. The transload facility will cross dock the supplies in the carrier-owned container to a GO or GL container and make the carrier container available for pickup by the carrier. In the event of a shortage of GO or GL transload containers, the CCA has the authority either to ship the carrier container into theater or unstuff the cargo for onward movement.

3.3.5 **Modified/Altered/Damaged/Destroyed Containers:** Local modifications to containers such as cutouts for power/lighting or air conditioning are prohibited on all categories of containers. Modified or altered carrier-owned and GL containers constitute a violation of the universal services contract or global lease agreement. Containers that have been modified, altered, damaged, or destroyed must be documented and reported by base CCOs to their respective CCAs. Initially, this will be completed no later than 30 days from the initial release of this LOI. In the future, the normal procedure will be for CCOs to report these occurrences immediately to their respective CCAs. CCAs will consolidate and forward the reports to SDDC (or other Service authority) for database adjustment, accountability relief, and financial adjustments.

3.4 **Container Accountability and Responsibility**

3.4.1 **GO/GL Containers:** GO/GL containers may, at the discretion of unit commanders, be moved to any location in the (combatant command) AOR. Unit-owned/leased containers supporting unit deployment will stay with that unit until the unit returns to its home station. If operational circumstances dictate, a unit may be authorized to transfer a unit-owned/leased container to a pre-approved receiving unit. The unit CCO will notify the CCA prior to the planned transfer. CCA will coordinate the transfer through SDDC to determine if there are any lease restrictions that need to be addressed. In addition, if GL containers are to be transferred, the gaining unit or activity will be prepared to assume any financial obligations associated with such a lease transfer or extension. In situations involving the transfer of a unit-owned container between units where the container remains in the same location (base/installation), the CCA can be notified after the transfer has taken place. Implicit in this is the maintenance of formal property book or hand/custody receipts accounting for containers by all units using GO/GL containers.

3.4.2 **Carrier-Owned Containers:** Carrier-owned containers are primarily meant for transportation of goods (primarily Class I). Once the carrier-owned container reaches its final destination, the receiving unit has a maximum of 10 days to unstuff the container and make the container ready for pick-up by the carrier before the US Government incurs penalty fees. If the receiving unit has no available storage for the container's contents the container can be used for temporary storage. This must be approved by the base CCO, who in turn must inform the CCA. Additionally, the unit must have a plan for unstuffing the container and making it available as soon as possible for return/pick-up in order to avoid detention charges.

3.4.2.1 SDDC will query IBS-CMM daily and provide CCAs with a list of carrier-owned containers that are at both the 5th day and 8th day of the 10 day free period. The CCAs will forward notice to the respective CCOs to coordinate and expedite the unstuffing of the container and return of the empty container to avoid unnecessary detention charges.

3.4.2.2 Stenciling of containers: Re-stenciling any container with a modified ISO number is not authorized by any entity unless specifically authorized to do so by SDDC. Units and activities with GO containers that need valid ISO numbers will contact the above authorities through their CCOs for valid ISO numbers and specific instructions. Under no conditions are any units authorized to re-stencil any carrier-owned or GL container.

3.5 **Inventory Management**

3.5.1 **General:** Invalid or outdated information in the computer system being used is a serious impairment to effective container management. All departments, agencies, commands, units, contractors, and any other organizations operating in the (combatant command) AOR and using any shipping containers for any purpose will maintain positive control over their containers through a regular inventory management program. Documentation of all inventories will be available for review by higher authority.

3.5.1.2 To facilitate tracking the performance of monthly inventories and provide visibility of anomalies found during the inventories, IBS-CMM will include an "inventory status" field and a "date of last inventory" field. The "inventory status" field will have four possible values which are shown below:

- "Not inventoried" – The initial value that all records will have.
- "Verified" – The container on the inventory report matched the physical check in the yard, location, etc.
- "Found" – The container was not on the report but was identified in the yard, location, etc.
- "Lost" – The container is listed on the report but was not identified during the physical check.

3.5.1.3 IBS-CMM will automatically update the "date of last inventory" field with the current date when the "inventory status" field is changed by a theater user or CCO.

3.5.2 **Inventory Procedures:** Inventories must be conducted at least once per month. Each unit (container yard) will download their respective electronic inventory from IBS-CMM (also known as an in-gated container listing) and update the spreadsheet with additions, modifications, and deletions so that the sheet reflects actual data of what is physically on the ground. CCOs will then perform one of the following actions in IBS-CMM for every container in their area:

- Verify containers that match the report by updating the "inventory status" field to "verified," (or)
- Out-gate containers to "unknown location" that are on the inventory report but not physically present. Additionally, update the "inventory status field" to "lost," (or)
- In-gate containers that are physically present but are not on the inventory report. Additionally, update the "inventory status" field to "found."
- The annotated reports will then be forwarded electronically to the senior base CCO who will forward them to the CCA and retain them for future inspection as needed. The requirements of these inventories will include the following:
  — Location/facility (for larger base camps).
  — Total count of containers (listed by size, type, owner, [if known]).
  — ISO number (container serial number).
  — The actual use of each container.
  — Fill percentage of each container.
  — Contents of each container by class of supply.
  — Serviceability condition.
  — Unit/organization/activity to which container is assigned.
  — Name of the responsible CCO.

3.5.3 **Inventory Reconciliation:** Inventory reconciliation is included in the above actions. CCOs and CCAs will monitor compliance by reviewing their respective bases and country reports and noting which locations have not performed an inventory and initiating appropriate research on containers that are "lost" or "found" during inventories. The desired monthly end-state of the reconciliation process is to ensure that every container identified on a yard or area is also reflected in IBS-CMM.

3.6 **Container Buyout and Cost Saving Methods:** Under certain circumstances, a (combatant command) Service component commander or SDDC may wish to purchase (under their Title 10, USC, authority) carrier-owned containers rather than continuing to incur late fees. (Combatant command), in conjunction with SDDC, will make recommendations to the applicable Service logistics directorate regarding containers which are candidates for purchase. (Combatant command) should provide specific instructions for identifying, validating, and purchasing carrier-owned containers; and for bringing newly-acquired containers onto government accountability records to include obtaining new ISO container number and re-stenciling/re-marking containers to reflect government ownership.

3.7 **Performance Metrics:** Theater metrics will be established by (combatant command) in conjunction with SDDC. (Examples of metrics include number and percent of CCOs assigned and trained; percent of carrier-owned containers discharged/returned within allowable free time; percent and number of carrier-owned containers incurring detention and average days of detention; number/percent of containers in-gated within 48 hours of physical receipt; number/percent of containers out-gated within 48 hours of physical departure; inventory accuracy/timeliness.)

Chapter 4 Information Systems and Tools

4.1 General: The following container management information systems are recognized by (combatant command) for tracking theater containers.

4.2 Integrated Booking System-Container Management Module (IBS-CMM): The primary tool of SDDC for tracking the location, usage, free time, and intransit data. This database management system is contracted by SDDC. This contracted system is the primary system used for the management of carrier container detention and location tracking within the (combatant command) AOR.

4.3 Pipeline Asset Tool (PAT): An SDDC developed tracking and inventory database providing users with the Web-based ability to obtain container information using multiple sources. Container data is drawn daily from the Integrated Booking System, Integrated Booking System-Commercial Sealift Solution, Global Air Transportation Execution System, and IBS-CMM. The data is integrated by key fields such as container number, carrier booking number, port call file number, lift date, arrival date, etc. Within each main search category are subcategories from which users may choose to obtain additional information on ITV history worldwide, basic booking information, vessel schedules, and container lifecycle summary.

4.4 Army Container Asset Management System (ACAMS): As the US Army's recognized global asset management system for US GO/GL containers, and all other intermodal equipment (quadruple containers, triple containers, flatracks, etc.), ACAMS provides the ability to effectively manage and track GO/GL assets. ACAMS is considered to have functionality as a durable hand receipt for accountability purposes. Additionally, ACAMS is the primary reference of ownership of US GO and GL containers.

4.5 Integrated Data Environment (IDE)/Global Transportation Network (GTN) Convergence (IGC): IGC is the reference tool for tracking shipments through the DTS. Container ID numbers associated with each shipment's transportation control number may be visible in IGC. RFID tag information may also contain associated container ID numbers that are sent to IGC.

4.6 Radio Frequency Identification (RFID): The active RFID system's function is the tracking of material in transit and the system can provide visibility of a container and its contents. However, the container management element should not use this data as a primary management tool for container tracking. The RFID system only provides tracking information for containers identified as shipments in the DTS. Therefore, the RFID tracking information cannot be relied upon for complete container location information because visibility terminates when the cargo is at its final destination.

4.7 ITV for Surface Deployment and Distribution Cargo (ISDDC) System. SDDC's source for integrated surface transportation information is available through a portal and data repository. ISDDC provides access to integrated data about ocean cargo, freight, personal property, passenger, container management, and performance metrics.

Glossary
Part I–Acronyms. Include list of acronyms and abbreviations here.
Part II–Definitions. Include glossary of definitions to key terms here.

References. Include list of all relevant publications, regulations, instructions.

APPENDIX G
INTERMODAL CONTAINERS/PLATFORMS CHARACTERISTICS

This appendix provides descriptions and characteristics for both military and commercial intermodal marine containers, flatracks, and 463L pallets.

1. Container Types

a. **End-Opening Container.** End-opening dry cargo units are the most common intermodal containers in the inventory. Containers come in various lengths, most commonly 20 feet and 40 feet. The large majority of these containers open only at one end. However, some ISO double end-opening containers do exist. These containers permit more rapid stuffing and unstuffing operations (at either origin or destination) for vehicles. All ISO end-opening containers can be readily transported by most military and commercial CHE. The commercial 20-foot end-opening container can be used to transport munitions or general cargo. The door-end corner posts are modified with angle iron to enhance blocking and bracing. As there is no permanent restraint system, wooden blocking and bracing is used to restrain munitions.

b. **Refrigerated Container.** Refrigerated containers (reefers) are owned by DOD and are available through commercial sources. They provide the capability to transport, temporarily store, and distribute temperature-sensitive cargo such as food or blood. Some military-owned reefers include a refrigeration unit with a 10-kilowatt generator. They can be plugged into an external power source or run off of their own generators. Most ships are equipped with a power source into which the containers can be plugged. Commercial reefers may not have their own generator. Several commercial reefers typically are plugged into a separate generator which fits into a container cell. Reefers have the outer dimensions of ISO containers and meet all ISO requirements for intermodal shipments.

c. **Side-Opening Container.** Twenty-foot side-opening containers are owned by the DOD and are also available through commercial sources. They are ISO containers with two double doors located on one side. These doors open to allow easy access to the container's contents. The side-opening container can be lifted and transported by commercial and military conveyances. Military versions have internal tie-down rings which can be used to secure cargo during shipment. The military often uses side-opening containers for transporting munitions.

d. **Open Top Container.** The open top container is used primarily by commercial industry to transport cargo items that are too high for a standard container. An open top container can be stuffed from the top, or one end can be opened and it can be stuffed from there. Equipped with ISO standard corner fittings at the top and bottom, it can be lifted and transported readily by commercial and military handlers and conveyances. Open top containers require tarpaulins for cover during shipping and storage. (Containers cannot be used for sensitive items requiring high security and may also have agricultural restrictions.)

e. **Tank Container.** The bulk tank container, when installed in an ISO-standard frame, is used for intermodal transport of liquids such as fuel and milk. Tank containers are only available through commercial sources. If sent by air, tank containers with cargoes must be certified for air transport to prevent dangerous changes in aircraft center of gravity.

f. **Half-Height Container.** Half-height containers are owned by the DOD and are available through commercial sources. They have the footprint of an ISO container with ISO standard structural members and corner fittings, and are approximately half the height of a standard end-opening container. With fixed sides, an open top, and one drop-end opening, material is accessible by either MHE or crane. Tarpaulins accompany the containers for cover during shipping and storage. The Navy uses the half-height containers primarily to ship drummed oils and lubricants. The Marine Corps uses the half-height container in the Maritime Pre-positioning Program and to ship ammunition.

g. **Quadruple Containers (QUADCONs).** QUADCONs are not a common-use asset. They are unit-owned military containers. They are currently part of the Marine Corps Family of Intermediate Size Containers. The Army has identified the QUADCON as the primary equipment deployment storage system container for surface movement on its common tables of allowance 50-909. The QUADCON has ISO corner fittings to allow for coupling of the QUADCONs into arrays of up to four units. An array of four QUADCONs has the same external length and width dimensions as a 20-foot ISO container and is designed to be lifted as a 20-foot unit and/or moved as a 20-foot unit in ocean shipping. The QUADCON will be certified to meet all ISO standards and CSC approval. Each has four-way forklift pockets and lockable double doors on each end that provide full access to the contents. To accommodate smaller items, a small-item storage cabinet can be installed or removable inserts may be placed as shelves inside the QUADCON.

h. **Triple Containers (TRICONs).** TRICONs are not a common-use asset. They are military containers owned by the Navy and the Army. They are a lockable, watertight container of all steel construction. TRICONs have standard ISO corner fittings and three-way forklift pockets (side and back). The TRICON's ISO corner fittings allow for coupling into arrays of up to three units. An array of three TRICONs has the same external length and width dimensions as a 20-foot ISO container (8 feet × 20 feet) and is designed to be lifted as a 20-foot unit in ocean shipping. Two styles of containers have been procured: bulk and configured. Bulk containers do not have drawers, shelves, or rifle racks. Configured containers consist of cabinets with drawers, shelves, rifle racks, or a combination thereof.

i. **Double Containers (BICONs).** BICONs are not a common-use asset. They are military containers owned by the Navy and the Marine Corps. They are a lockable, watertight container of all steel construction. BICONs have standard ISO corner fittings and three-way forklift pockets (side and back). The BICON's ISO corner fittings allow for coupling into arrays of two units. An array of two BICONs has the same external length, height, and width dimensions as a 20-foot ISO container (8 feet × 8 feet × 20 feet) and is designed to be lifted as a single 20-foot unit in ocean shipping. Two styles of containers have been procured: bulk and configured. Bulk containers do not have drawers, shelves, or rifle racks. Configured containers consist of cabinets with drawers, shelves, rifle racks, or a combination thereof.

j. **Joint Modular Intermodal Container (JMIC).** JMICs are used to effectively build and break down TEU loads or other commonly used platforms into AIT-enabled warehouse pallet-sized loads. JMICs can be transported as single units or as multiple units. Sixteen JMICs will fit into a TEU with minimal blocking and bracing. A number of these units have been procured by the USMC.

k. **Internal Airlift or Helicopter Slingable Container Unit (ISU)-60/ISU-90.** ISU has multiple configurations, depending upon the doors and internal dividers. The ISU containers provide weather-resistant storage and transport but do not meet ISO structural standards. CSC restrictions do not apply to containers specially designed for air transport; however, they are certified for internal or external helicopter transport and for all AMC transport aircraft. A number of these units have been procured by the US Army airborne and air assault units.

l. **Flatracks.** A flatrack is a structural steel frame, decked over and fitted with tie-down points, similar to a container without sides or top. Some flatracks have corner posts or end walls; others are specialized for the military and take advantage of the PLS. Many corner posts and end walls fold inward to facilitate stacking and storage. Flatracks are owned by both the DOD and commercial industry. Regular flatracks enable containerships to transport bulky items that are slightly larger than the door dimensions of a standard ISO container, and sometimes also slightly longer than the length of standard ISO containers such as lumber, steel products, or light vehicles. Other flatracks fit within a standard ISO container and allow for the expedient loading and unloading using the PLS system. Regular flatracks meeting ISO standards can readily have cargo loaded or discharged at inland sites. Regular flatracks of both 20 feet and 40 feet are also available from commercial leasing companies. Specialized military flatracks include:

(1) **M1077.** The M1077 and M1077A1 flatracks are sideless flatracks used to transport pallets of ammunition and other classes of supplies.

(2) **M1.** The M1 flatrack carries identical classes of supplies. It is ISO/CSC certified and is suitable for intermodal transport, including transport on containerships. Ammunition can be loaded on the M1 at depots, transported via containership to theater, picked up by the PLS truck, and carried forward without use of any MHE. The walls fold inward when empty to facilitate stacking for retrograde.

(3) **M3.** The M3 container roll-in/out platform is a flatrack which fits inside a 20-foot ISO container.

m. **Containerized Ammunition Distribution System (CADS).** The unique design of the CADS ammunition grade container separates it from other containers. CADS are constructed with heavier deck planking and side panels that are thicker than regular general cargo containers. They are produced specifically by the government for the transportation of ammunition. The life span of the CADS container if well maintained is more than 20 years.

2. Pallet Types

a. **Load and Roll Pallet (LRP).** The LRP is a DOD asset. It is a steel frame platform with rollers that fits inside a standard 20-foot ANSI/ISO container. The LRP allows forward units to rapidly extract a complete load of four multiple launch rocket system (MLRS) pods (each weighing 5,078 pounds) or four Army Tactical Missile System (ATACMS) pods from an end-opening container. Two 6,000-pound capacity or larger forklifts, a tactical cargo vehicle with a winch, or a wrecker lifts up one end of the fully loaded LRP just high enough to clear the floor of the container and roll the entire load into and/or out of the container. Once outside of the container, the load is fully accessible from the sides to allow rapid unloading of the cargo. The LRP unit measures 222 inches × 89 inches × 120 inches and has a tare weight of 1,970 pounds. USAMC procedural drawing 19-48-8184 depicts use of the LRP for outloading of MLRS pods, and USAMC procedural drawing 19-48-8198 depicts use of the LRP for outloading of ATACMS pods. There are approximately 500 units controlled by SDDC in the DOD inventory.

b. **463L Cargo System.** The 463L pallet is constructed of a corrosion-resistant aluminum surface with a balsa wood core. Pallet dimensions are 108 inches × 88 inches × 2.25 inches. The pallet itself weighs 290 pounds and has a maximum load capacity of 10,000 pounds when nets are used. The pallet has indent locking features at 10 inch intervals to accommodate the restraint rail locks. A lip forming the pallet perimeter provides 22 tie-down rings for securing cargo nets. The tie-down rings are capable of 240 degrees of free movement in a vertical plane that intersects the pallet edge at a right angle. The tie-down ring capacity is 7,500 pounds. The pallet permits maximum loads, including wheel loads, of 250 pounds per square inch. Loads that exceed the pounds per square inch limit must be shored to reduce the pounds per square inch to the maximum allowable. The pallet itself shall never be considered or used as shoring. Position the cargo on the pallet so the center of gravity falls within a 28-inch lateral (108-inch side) and 24-inch longitudinal (88-inch side) rectangle in the pallet center. If the center of gravity does not fall within this rectangle, mark the pallet C/G. Pallets are available to units planning or executing an air movement through their transportation office from AMC. The user is responsible for building 463L pallets and may be responsible for loading them onto aircraft.

APPENDIX H
DISTRIBUTION ENABLERS AND INFORMATION SYSTEMS

1. Communications System and Intelligence Components of the Department of Defense Information Networks

The DOD information networks provide the globally interconnected capabilities, processes, and personnel for providing information on demand to CCDRs, policy makers, and supporting organizations. Communications systems and intelligence support to the JDDE is vital to planning, initiating, conducting, sustaining, and protecting a successful joint operation. These capabilities support the communications and information networks of global distribution. Responsive communications and information systems allow CCDRs and their staffs to initiate, direct, monitor, query, and manage global distribution in support of their operations. The following major communications and information systems are essential enablers for global distribution operations.

2. Global Command and Control System–Joint

a. GCCS is DOD's computerized system of record for strategic C2 functions. GCCS enables CCDRs to plan, execute, and manage military operations. The system helps JFCs synchronize the actions of joint forces, and it has the flexibility to be used in a wide range of operations ranging from actual combat to humanitarian assistance. GCCS provides CCDRs a complete picture of the operational environment and the ability to order, respond, and coordinate communications system information. GCCS is also a comprehensive automated communications system designed to improve the JFC's ability to manage and execute joint operations. GCCS interoperates with Service and agency communications systems, providing a global network of military and commercial communications systems that the JFC uses to send and obtain critical information. GCCS supports the exchange of information from the President/SecDef to CCDRs and their components. GCCS incorporates procedures, reporting structures, automated information processing systems, and communications connectivity to provide the information necessary to effectively plan, deploy, sustain, employ, and redeploy forces.

b. **Joint Operation Planning and Execution System Editing Tool (JET).** JET provides the capability to create, add, modify, delete, and generate a TPFDD. JET processes both force and nonunit OPLAN data. Using JET, the user may view carrier-related information for selected force requirements. Reports may also be generated for JET list displays.

c. **JOPES Rapid Query Tool (RQT).** RQT is a government off-the-shelf JOPES application for GCCS. It is a query tool that includes functions to design, print, and save tailored ad hoc reports, and provides graphical and mapping displays to help visualize JOPES data.

d. **COP.** COP provides a graphical display of friendly, hostile, and neutral units, assets, overlays, and/or tracks pertinent to operations, and is a key tool for commanders in planning and conducting joint operations. The GCCS COP may include relevant information from the tactical to the strategic level of command. It is a tool to help predict force movement in combat. The purpose of COP is to provide common data and associated information to the appropriate levels of command. This includes every level, up to and including the National Security Council (NSC). The CCDR has control of the data and information overlays within the AOR. A CCMD uses the common tactical picture (CTP) as a baseline to build a COP. Information is gathered into the common tactical data set and is fed into the CTP along with filters (e.g., airlift missions) and overlays (a map, diagrams, etc.) resulting in a COP.

e. **Readiness Assessment System–Output Tool (RAS-OT).** RAS-OT is a SECRET Internet Protocol Router Network (SIPRNET) application providing query-based access to readiness data. RAS-OT provides decision type information on the status-of-force readiness. The query functionality supports retrieval, analysis, and export of current or historical information on the total force, status of each Service in the areas of personnel, equipment readiness and condition, and select JOPES data. RAS-OT provides the means to generate reports in four views: Summary, Graphic, Tabular, and Pipes.

See DODD 7730.65, Department of Defense Readiness Reporting System (DRRS), *for additional information.*

f. **Marine Air-Ground Task Force Deployment Support System II (MDSS II).** MDSS II is an automated IT system used to support force deployment planning and execution. It is the Marine Corps' single database and interface hub for unit operational plan sourcing, unit deployment planning and execution, and unit deployment ITV. Through the use of extensive reference files, the system provides data to Joint Force Requirements Generator II (JFRG II) to create an executable JOPES TPFDD. Subsequently MDSS II provides the basis for MAGTF deployment planning, rapid expeditionary support deployment, and ITV.

g. **Automated Manifesting System–Tactical (AMS-TAC).** AMC-TAC is a transportation tool that utilizes AIT to facilitate ITV for the receipt and distribution of sustainment cargo. AMS-TAC is currently the USMC's only deployable distribution AIS, with deployable Cargo Movement Operations System (CMOS) planned to assume this functionality during Fiscal Year 2017. The warehouse to warfighter tool provides ITV for the in-theater distribution of sustainment cargo and is a bridging technology system that provides a gap fill of current nodal ITV infrastructure. The tool utilizes Global Positioning System transceivers and satellite communication equipment to provide near real-time movement and location AV through a data feed to a battle C2 system.

3. Additional Distribution Management Information Systems

The global distribution network includes other key enabling planning, execution, and visibility systems. Effective distribution planning systems promote balance and responsiveness in distribution operations and promote joint force confidence in distribution support plans. Accurate distribution execution systems enhance the velocity, integration, and efficiency of distribution activities. Finally, visibility systems allow effective control and continuous improvement of distribution operations, further enhancing confidence in the

JDDE. Information systems provide the key enabler for managing global distribution velocity and precision.

a. **GCSS-J.** GCSS-J provides end-to-end information interoperability across sustainment functions, and between sustainment and C2 functions in support of CCMD and JTF sustainment requirements. GCSS-J is a query application that provides real-time, read-only information on DOD sustainment and combat service support activities. It builds on existing technology, products, procedures, and integration strategies. The primary objective for GCSS-J is to provide a fused and sustainment/combat service support picture of the operational environment to the CCDR. The GCSS-J application is focused on supporting the CCMD and JTF levels. It supplies commanders with read-only access to authoritative, comprehensive sustainment and combat service support information from various sustainment databases, and accurately portrays sustainment status. GCSS-J Portal is a Web-based application that provides a browser view of data available on COP-sustainment, and other Web-based resources. GCSS-J Portal resides on the SIPRNET, and functions as a gateway to various Web-based resources for the GCSS-J community.

(1) **JFRG II.** JFRG II is an automated, computer-based planning tool designed to support the Services in the development of both contingency OPLANs and crisis action OPORDs. It supports tactical and administrative planning by providing the following capabilities: import of Service type unit characteristics file data, rapid force list creation, lift analysis, TPFDD development and manipulation, and import and export from/to JOPES. It can be used to modify and update reference data, generate data trouble reports, and interface with JOPES, MDSS II, and Transportation Coordinator's Automated Information for Movement System II (TC-AIMS II). It is used to build force structures to meet mission requirements, source required forces, develop and assess phasing/travel mode, compute sustainment requirements, and estimate airlift and sealift requirements.

(2) **Deliberate and Crisis Action Planning and Execution Segments (DCAPES).** DCAPES provides near real-time integrated C2, planning, and execution monitoring information to Air Force functional users in operations, logistics, manpower, and personnel, providing a single integrated planning environment. With DCAPES, Air Force planners can rapidly and accurately identify and source personnel, equipment, and sustainment capabilities to meet the CCDR's operations plan requirements.

(3) **Global Status of Resources and Training System (GSORTS).** GSORTS is an internal management tool used by the CJCS, Services, CCMDs, combat support agencies, and the OSD. GSORTS indicates the level of selected resources and training status required to undertake the missions for which a unit was organized or designed. GSORTS provides the NSC and planners with accurate and timely unit identification, location, assignment, and resource information for the registered units and organizations of the Armed Forces of the United States, DOD agencies, and certain foreign and IGOs involved in military operations.

(4) **Base Resource and Capability Estimator (BRACE).** BRACE is the planning tool to model military air terminal operations. BRACE simulates airfield onloading, offloading, en route, and recovery base operations, including ground activities such as cargo handling, refueling, maintenance, and aircraft parking. The model can be used to: estimate

airfield throughput capability; estimate air, ground, and other resources required to support a given level of throughput at an airfield; and validate MOG values used in existing air transportation models such as Joint Flow and Analysis System for Transportation (JFAST).

   b. **Planning Systems.** Major distribution planning systems include the following:

   (1) **JFAST.** JFAST is an analytical tool for making detailed estimates of resources required to transport military forces (including cargo, personnel, and sustainment). JFAST is used by the CCMDs as a planning and forecasting tool for deployment planning. The system determines the transportation feasibility of the TPFDD (from origin through arrival at the POD) and generates summary data via charts, tables, maps, and other visual aids. JFAST determines closure dates, congestion points, lift utilization, and shortfalls. JFAST products include delivery profiles and lateness analysis, required lift by day versus lift available, and port workload by level of activity based on capacity. JFAST has five major capabilities: TPFDD analysis, air/land/sea movement simulation and analysis, sustainment calculation, TPFDD construction from scratch, and several useful utilities. The JFAST model contains separate air, land, and sea schedulers and operates in either a stand-alone or networked environment.

   (a) **TPFDD Analysis.** TPFDD Analysis is used to review a TPFDD to determine which records qualify for analysis, analyze records that did not qualify, and identify requirements that missed the latest arrival date.

   (b) **Notional Requirements Generator.** The notional requirements generator provides the capability to create notional movement requirements when no plan currently exists. Force selection and CONOPS can be recorded along with expected levels of activity, climate, and days of supply. This capability allows a planner to execute ad hoc queries and perform "what if" analysis.

   (c) **Sustainment Generator.** The sustainment generator module provides a joint logistics model that estimates the supplies needed to sustain deployed forces. It allows the user to create nonunit sustainment records based on Service reference planning factors and the projected population or types of units at the operational plan destination to which forces are deployed. Records are generated into logistical transportation requirements in the TPFDD format to approximate the flow of sustainment that forces would consume during an operation. The TPFDD records enable planners to see a total picture of the movement of forces and sustainment, allowing a determination of overall transportation feasibility.

   (d) **Transportation Analysis.** The transportation analysis function includes model setup, execution, and output analysis for land, air, and sea modes of transportation.

   (2) **Integrated Consumable Item Support (ICIS).** The ICIS system identifies critical items and their affected weapons systems, calculates when stock will be exhausted, guides inventory investment decisions, and identifies inventory sources for Class I, II, III, IV, VIII, and IX items. ICIS sustainment metrics are linked to the Services' readiness based models. These links allow the Services to consider DLA-managed items in determining the

operational supportability of critical weapon systems. ICIS can be used to identify critical items that have the greatest potential to adversely affect joint operations.

(3) **CAMPS.** CAMPS provides mobility planners a single integrated planning, scheduling, and analysis system for airlift and refueling assets in support of peacetime and wartime operations. CAMPS determines time-phased air refueling and airlift closure requirements based on movement priorities. Used daily, it provides flight plans, compensates for wind, and includes air refueling requirements for all DOD deployments. CAMPS interfaces with a host of C2 applications that allow realistic development of total mission support requirements. This includes large-scale mobility operations and tactical mobility operations from forward locations.

(4) **Port Simulation Model (PORTSIM).** PORTSIM is a time-stepped, discrete simulation of SPOE and SPOD events during a force deployment. PORTSIM can determine a port's reception, staging, clearance, and throughput capabilities. The model identifies systems or infrastructure constraints, and provides port-specific, time-phased force clearance profiles. PORTSIM simulates simultaneous deployment and retrograde seaport operations and assesses the impact of JLOTS.

(5) **Analysis of Mobility Platform (AMP).** AMP is an end-to-end modeling and simulation environment to support programmatic analysis, planning, execution analysis, and peacetime operations, with the primary focus being programmatic analysis. The models contained in the AMP Federation include: the Model for Intertheater Deployment by Air and Sea (MIDAS); and the Analysis of Mobility Platform Suite of Port Analysis Tools (AMP-PAT); and the Enhanced Logistics Intratheater Support Tool (ELIST).

(a) **ELIST.** ELIST is a feasibility planning and modeling system for deployment analysis. ELIST performs detailed intratheater deployment studies to analyze effects of force modernization and new force structures and changes to the DTS and to check transportation feasibility of contingency operations. ELIST enables planners to explore and model the impact of theater infrastructure limitations (through combat loss, weather, or limited HN access) and make adjustments to infrastructure and assets at any point in time in the flow. Through ELIST, planners have the ability to accurately define the infrastructure and consider the throughput capability available for a specific plan.

(b) **MIDAS.** MIDAS is a DOD strategic sealift and airlift model which can simulate multiple strategic deployment scenarios. The model is designed to measure the capability of a given set of strategic transportation assets to deploy a specified force. MIDAS projects schedules over a planning period, makes mode selection for the movement of passengers and cargo based on RDD, and adapts scenarios to expected and unexpected events.

(c) **AMP-PAT.** AMP-PAT is a suite of six integrated planning, analysis, and decision support tools designed principally for transportation and logistics analysts and planners. These tools model a full range of airport and seaport processes and resources. Transportation planners throughout the DOD use these tools for programmatic analysis,

CAP, and TPFDD development. As a component of the AMP federation, AMP-PAT adds detailed airport and seaport federates to this end-to-end transportation analysis capability.

(6) **GDSS.** GDSS is a global C2 system for managing and monitoring inter/intra-theater military and commercial airlift and air refueling missions across the range of military operations. This comprehensive system provides instant access to operational information for all users, from the headquarters down to the individual units. GDSS also feeds USTRANSCOM's IGC, the theater battle management core systems, and other joint information systems to provide visibility of air mobility missions.

(7) **TC-AIMS II.** TC-AIMS II is used for Army deployments and redeployments and for managing CULT in theater. The system is designed for commanders and their staffs, unit movement officers (UMOs), planners, movement controllers, and transportation operators to translate information into detailed movement plans. TC-AIMS II enhancements include a simplified unit movement module (wizard) that gives UMOs the ability to create organizational equipment lists, unit deployment lists, load plans, and certain transportation control movement documents faster and earlier in the movement planning process. Deployment managers use TC-AIMS II to coordinate intertheater lift via air and water; schedule unit convoy movements; schedule interrelated deployment events; prepare load plans for vehicles, rail cars, aircraft, or ships; prepare military shipping documentation; create documentation authorizations to validate services and expend funds; and account for personnel and equipment. TC-AIMS II supports the UMO in managing deployment data, creating deployment plans, and monitoring deployment status throughout all phases of the deployment. TC-AIMS II also includes capabilities for convoy planning and deconfliction, management of transportation movement requirements, tracking unit movements, and improved map graphics.

(8) **CMOS.** CMOS is a joint system that integrates computer hardware, software, and communications to effectively plan, document, and manage outbound and inbound cargo and passengers, and to plan, schedule, and monitor the execution of transportation activities in support of deployment and reception of forces. CMOS provides joint forces with an end-to-end distribution capability and real-time ITV during all passenger and cargo movements.

(9) **Integrated Computerized Deployment System (ICODES).** ICODES is an AIS designed to support multimodal load planning requirements in support of the DOD requirement for a single load planning capability. ICODES is a joint decision-support system developed to assist users with the staging and load-planning requirements for multiple military and commercial modes of transportation. The combined functionality of ship, air, rail, and the other services, provided by ICODES, gives commanders, planners, and operators at all levels a single platform capable of producing and evaluating load plans and alternative actions for units of any size, using varied modes of transportation, in support of peacetime or wartime operations. The system enables users to plan and track cargo stowage for air, ocean, rail, and truck in a single system that affords the capability of one time entry of the data. It enables the joint community to easily create, exchange, and interpret cargo movement plans through a single software application. Other features assist users by providing high quality alternative solutions to complex load planning problems. ICODES integrates multiple knowledge-based expert systems, data storage, and a graphical user

interface within a distributed and collaborative operational environment providing global services to the operating forces. ICODES currently interfaces with GATES, TC-AIMS II, and MDSS II.

(10) **United States Transportation Command Regulating and Command and Control Evacuation System (TRAC2ES).** TRAC2ES provides ITV and medical regulation of patients in both peacetime and contingencies. It provides a single overall system that ties patient accountability from the field, while in transit and at originating, destination, and en route medical treatment facilities.

c. **IGC.** IGC is the ADS for ITV of shipments moving within the DTS and is the DOD system of record for ITV data. IGC is also the automated C2 information system that enables USTRANSCOM and its components to provide global transportation management, as well as ITV to others within the joint planning and execution community. IGC integrates supply, cargo, passenger, and unit requirements and movements with airlift, air refueling, and sealift schedules and movements to provide ITV of personnel, materiel, and military forces. IGC integrates ITV data into a single view of DTS. IGC creates ITV information by consolidating and integrating data from many other automated system sources (e.g., GDSS, GATES, Joint Air Logistics Information System, CAMPS, TC-AIMS II, and Munitions Transportation Management System called "IGC data feeds."). IGC organizes and displays vital transportation asset and resource information to assist USTRANSCOM in understanding, identifying, and implementing various transportation options and COAs. The classified IGC home page is located at https://www.igc.transcom.smil.mil/igc. The unclassified IGC home page is located at https://www.igc.transcom.mil, and requires the use of a Web browser with 128-bit encryption.

(1) **Single Mobility System (SMS).** SMS visualizes ITV data used for tracking the movement of forces and materiel within the DTS. It is a Web-based application, both SIPRNET and Nonsecure Internet Protocol Router Network (NIPRNET), that provides visibility of common-user air, sea, and land transportation assets and provides aggregated reporting of cargo and passenger movements. SMS collects plane, ship, and truck movement data from other computer systems such as IGC, CAMPS, and GDSS. SMS provides requirements planners and unit schedulers visibility of planned and scheduled air missions, MSC ship schedules, commercial liner service, seaport reference data, and movement of US security risk category cargo. There are three components in SMS: Air Mobility, Sea Mobility, and Land Mobility.

(a) **Air Mobility.** The Air Mobility component of SMS is a Web-based tool that provides visibility of scheduled air mobility missions and requirements early in the planning process. All command levels of all DOD units, wings, and headquarters can use SMS as a tool to display missions.

(b) **Sea Mobility.** The Sea Mobility component provides visibility over sealift requirements through SDDC's IBS and GATES, and MSC's Integrated Command, Control, and Communications reporting system. SMS also offers a sealift assets database, a voyage finder, a port locator, and a shipping cost calculator.

(c) **Land Mobility.** The Land Mobility component provides visibility over hazardous materiel. The arms, ammunition, and explosives (AA&E) movement link in SMS allows access to the database that tracks and records positions for movement of security risk category cargo in the US, inclusive of AA&E.

d. **Execution Systems.** Major distribution execution systems include the following:

(1) **Inventory Control Point (ICP) AISs.** ICP AISs are business systems used by materiel and item managers to control on-hand wholesale and retail assets by location and condition code; manage wholesale assets due in from procurement and depot-level repair; and calculate stock levels and positioning.

(2) **DSS.** DSS is the DOD standard AIS that manages the flow and storage of stock at DLA distribution depots. DSS provides enhanced tools for improving inventory accuracy and control, improves the operating efficiency of depots, and supports AV by enabling the use of AIT to continuously update the defense automatic addressing system feeds of DLA Transaction Services to IGC.

(3) **GATES.** GATES is the single port management system servicing air, sea, and surface port functionality. It supports both peacetime and contingency operations by managing global air and surface passenger and cargo data. It supports mission-critical elements of military operations interfacing with multiple data engines, both internal and external to DOD. It provides ITV of cargo movements and mission-critical reports. The AIS also supports cargo accountability through tracking and billing functions. The automated system promotes more effective DOD resource management by providing the capability to process, track, and bill for cargo and passenger movements. It also serves as an effective C2 tool aiding unit and cargo movement scheduling, shipment forecasting, generating reports, and message routing and delivery.

(4) **Hazardous Material Information Resource System (HMIRS).** HMIRS is a DOD automated system developed and maintained by DLA. HMIRS is the central repository for material safety data sheets for the Services and civil agencies. It also contains value-added information input by the Service/agency focal points. This value-added data includes hazardous communications warning labels and transportation information. HMIRS provides this data for HAZMAT purchased by the USG through DOD and civil agencies. The system assists USG personnel who handle, store, transport, use, or dispose of HAZMAT.

(5) **IBS.** IBS is the system supporting the movement of unit and sustainment cargo by sea. The system offers continuous access to ocean shipping capabilities, and it provides booking data and ship schedule information for both unit and sustainment cargo to IGC.

(6) **Global Freight Management (GFM) System.** GFM is the system that connects military shippers to CONUS land transportation capabilities by automating the booking, rating, and routing process.

(7) **Asset Management System (AMS).** AMS is used to manage DOD freight cars, Army-owned ISO containers, and leased ISO containers for all Services. It provides

SDDC with the AIS capability to manage all aspects of the DFRIF, as well as the Army common-user container fleet.

e. **Visibility Systems.** AV systems provide the capability to collect and distribute information on the location, status, and movement of materiel in the JDDE. ITV systems provide the capability to track the identity, status, and location of DOD unit and nonunit cargo, passengers, patients, forces, and military and commercial airlift, sealift, and surface assets from origin to the destination. Process visibility systems enable the monitoring and measurement of the elements of the distribution process. The systems described below provide supported commanders and distribution process managers the ability to monitor the effectiveness of distribution processes.

(1) **AV System.** AV is the primary AIS for DOD's visibility. It is the joint logistic system that provides users with timely and accurate information on the location, movement, status, and identity of units, personnel, equipment, and supplies. It provides commanders and logisticians with the information necessary to improve overall performance of the JDDE. AV includes in-process, in-storage, and in-transit business processes.

(2) **Logistics Information Processing System (LIPS).** LIPS is the DOD central repository for information on the status of requisitions maintained by DLA Transaction Services. The data in LIPS originates with requisitions and other supply-related transactions that flow among DOD units, ICPs, and sources of supply through DLA Transaction Services. LIPS supports visibility processes through its capability to capture requisition and requisition-related data. This includes traditional military distribution transactions and new business practices such as inter-Service lateral distribution, intra-Service retail-to-retail orders, and retail-to-PV orders. LIPS supports AV by providing requisition and shipment data.

(3) **Logistics Metrics Analysis Reporting System (LMARS).** LMARS is a DOD system that captures and measures the performance of the distribution elements as material flows through the commodity supply chains. LMARS is populated with information from the MILSTRIP and military standard transaction reporting and accounting procedure transactions that flow through DLA Transaction Services. LMARS reports response time at specific points in the distribution process. It is used as an assessment tool by DOD agencies and the Services to measure logistic response time and assess distribution system performance.

(4) **Integrated Mission Support for Surface Deployment and Distribution Command (ISDDC).** The ISDDC is designated to provide SDDC with a business intelligence and decision support capability. It supports the command's goal of optimizing architecture and producing consolidated data outputs at the command level for consumption by a wide variety of audiences. ISDDC provides access to a large range of transportation-related data and metadata. ISDDC is SDDC's single source for surface transportation data.

f. **Collaboration.** GCCS supports and sustains a number of existing collaboration tools, such as newsgroups, extensible messaging and presence protocol (XMPP)-based chat for disconnected, interrupted, and limited bandwidth environments, and XMPP-based COP collaboration.

(1) **Defense Connect Online (DCO).** DCO is a personal Web communication tool that enables users to have real-time, online meetings whenever required. It also integrates the ability to share and annotate the user's screen, conduct a phone conference, and broadcast live video from the user's Web camera for efficient and productive online meetings. DCO provides multiple users with a personal online meeting room that can collaborate via the Web in real time. Meeting rooms allow users to share their computer screen, use text chat, broadcast live video, and review meeting notes.

See DCO Best Practice User Guide for Adobe Connect *for additional information.*

(2) **Distribute.mil.** Distribute.mil provides an enterprise-accessible portal that enables collaboration and situational awareness in order to realize faster execution of distribution processes. Its online workspace, on both NIPRNET and SIPRNET, organizes global distribution information in one place. The portal is operator-oriented and can be user-configured to communicate with contacts from around the world through personal pages or within a community. Applications housed on the portal provide operators the tools they need to facilitate capturing, storing, and sharing information.

APPENDIX J
REFERENCES

The development of JP 4-09 is based upon the following primary references.

1. Federal Laws

　　a. Federal Acquisition Regulation.

　　b. Title 10, USC.

2. Strategic Guidance and Policy

　　a. Global Force Management Implementation Guidance.

　　b. GEF.

　　c. JSCP.

　　d. National Defense Strategy.

　　e. National Military Strategy.

　　f. National Response Framework.

　　g. National Security Strategy.

　　h. National Strategy for Homeland Security.

　　i. Unified Command Plan.

3. Department of Defense Publications

　　a. DLM 4000.25-1, *Military Standard Requisitioning and Issue Procedures (MILSTRIP)*.

　　b. DOD 4140.1-R, *DOD Supply Chain Materiel Management Regulation*.

　　c. DOD 4160.21-M, *Defense Materiel Disposition Manual*.

　　d. DOD 4500.54E, *Foreign Clearance Program*.

　　e. DODD 2010.9, *Acquisition and Cross-Servicing Agreements*.

　　f. DODD 2310.01E, *The Department of Defense Detainee Program*.

　　g. DODD 3000.06, *Combat Support Agencies (CSAs)*.

　　h. DODD 4151.18, *Maintenance of Military Materiel*.

i. DODD 4270.5, *Military Construction.*

j. DODD 4500.09E, *Transportation and Traffic Management.*

k. DODD 4500.54E, *Foreign Clearance Program (FCP).*

l. DODD 5100.01, *Functions of the Department of Defense and Its Major Components.*

m. DODD 5101.1, *DOD Executive Agent.*

n. DODD 5101.8, *DOD Executive Agent (DOD EA) for Bulk Petroleum.*

o. DODD 5101.9, *DOD Executive Agent for Medical Materiel.*

p. DODD 5101.10, *DOD Executive Agent (DOD EA) for Subsistence.*

q. DODD 5101.11E, *DOD Executive Agent for the Military Postal Service (MPS) and Official Mail Program (OMP).*

r. DODD 5101.12, *DOD Executive Agent (DOD EA) for Construction/Barrier Materiel.*

s. DODD 5111.1, *Under Secretary of Defense for Policy (USD[P]).*

t. DODD 5134.01, *Under Secretary of Defense for Acquisition, Technology, and Logistics (USD[AT&L]).*

u. DODD 5134.12, *Assistant Secretary of Defense for Logistics and Materiel Readiness (ASD[L&MR]).*

v. DODD 5158.04, *United States Transportation Command (USTRANSCOM).*

w. DODD 6000.12E, *Health Service Support.*

x. DODD 7730.65, *Department of Defense Readiness Reporting System (DRRS).*

y. DODD 8190.1, *DOD Logistics Use of Electronic Data Interchange (EDI) Standards.*

z. DODI 1100.22, *Policy and Procedures for Determining Workforce Mix.*

aa. DODI 3110.06, *War Reserve Materiel (WRM) Policy.*

bb. DODI 4001.01, *Installation Support.*

cc. DODI 4140.01, *DOD Supply Chain Materiel Management Policy.*

dd. DODI 4500.57, *Transportation and Traffic Management.*

ee. DODI 4715.6, *Environmental Compliance.*

ff. DODI 5158.05, *Joint Deployment Process Owner.*

gg. DODI 5158.06, *Distribution Process Owner (DPO).*

hh. DTR 4500.9-R, *Defense Transportation Regulation.*

4. Chairman of the Joint Chiefs of Staff Publications

a. CJCS Guide 3130, *Adaptive Planning and Execution (APEX) Overview and Policy Framework.*

b. CJCSI 3110.01B, *Joint Strategic Planning System.*

c. CJCSI 3110.03D, *Logistics Supplement to the Joint Strategic Capabilities Plan.*

d. CJCSI 3170.01H, *Joint Capabilities Integration and Development System.*

e. CJCSI 4120.02C, *Assignment of Movement and Mobility Priority.*

f. CJCSI 5120.02C, *Joint Doctrine Development System.*

g. CJCSM 3122.01A, *Joint Operation Planning and Execution System (JOPES) Volume I Planning, Policies, and Procedures.*

h. CJCSM 3122.02D, *Joint Operation Planning and Execution System (JOPES) Volume III (Time-Phased Force and Deployment Data Development and Deployment Execution).*

i. CJCSM 3130.03, *Adaptive Planning and Execution (APEX) Planning Formats and Guidance.*

j. CJCSM 3150.14B, *Joint Reporting Structure Logistics.*

k. CJCSM 3150.16D, *Joint Operation Planning and Execution System Reporting Structure (JOPESREP).*

l. JP 1, *Doctrine for the Armed Forces of the United States.*

m. JP 1-0, *Joint Personnel Support.*

n. JP 1-02, *Department of Defense Dictionary of Military and Associated Terms.*

o. JP 1-06, *Financial Management Support in Joint Operations.*

p. JP 2-03, *Geospatial Intelligence Support to Joint Operations.*

q. JP 3-0, *Joint Operations.*

r. JP 3-08, *Interorganizational Coordination During Joint Operations.*

s. JP 3-10, *Joint Security Operations in Theater.*

t. JP 3-11, *Operations in Chemical, Biological, Radiological, and Nuclear Environments.*

u. JP 3-15, *Barriers, Obstacles, and Mine Warfare for Joint Operations.*

v. JP 3-15.1, *Counter-Improvised Explosive Device Operations.*

w. JP 3-16, *Multinational Operations.*

x. JP 3-17, *Air Mobility Operations.*

y. JP 3-29, *Foreign Humanitarian Assistance.*

z. JP 3-34, *Joint Engineer Operations.*

aa. JP 3-35, *Deployment and Redeployment Operations.*

bb. JP 3-57, *Civil-Military Operations.*

cc. JP 3-63, *Detainee Operations.*

dd. JP 4-0, *Joint Logistics.*

ee. JP 4-01, *The Defense Transportation System.*

ff. JP 4-01.2, *Sealift Support to Joint Operations.*

gg. JP 4-01.5, *Joint Terminal Operations*

hh. JP 4-01.6, *Joint Logistics Over-the-Shore*

ii. JP 4-02, *Health Services.*

jj. JP 4-03, *Joint Bulk Petroleum and Water Doctrine.*

kk. JP 4-05, *Joint Mobilization Planning.*

ll. JP 4-08, *Logistics in Support of Multinational Operations.*

mm. JP 4-10, *Operational Contract Support.*

nn. JP 5-0, *Joint Operation Planning.*

5. Service Publications

    a. Army Doctrine Publication 4-0, *Sustainment*.

    b. Army Doctrine Reference Publication 4-0, *Sustainment*.

    c. Army Tactical Publication 4-94, *Theater Sustainment Command*.

    d. Air Force Doctrine Document 3-17, *Air Mobility Operations*.

Intentionally Blank

APPENDIX K
ADMINISTRATIVE INSTRUCTIONS

1. User Comments

Users in the field are highly encouraged to submit comments on this publication to: Joint Staff J-7, Deputy Director, Joint Education and Doctrine, ATTN: Joint Doctrine Analysis Division, 116 Lake View Parkway, Suffolk, VA 23435-2697. These comments should address content (accuracy, usefulness, consistency, and organization), writing, and appearance.

2. Authorship

The lead agent for this publication is the USTRANSCOM. The Joint Staff doctrine sponsor for this publication is the J-4.

3. Supersession

This publication supersedes JP 4-09, 5 February 2010, *Distribution Operations.*

4. Change Recommendations

a. Recommendations for urgent changes to this publication should be submitted:

TO: JOINT STAFF WASHINGTON DC//J7-JE&D//

b. Routine changes should be submitted electronically to the Deputy Director, Joint Education and Doctrine, Joint Doctrine Analysis Division, 116 Lake View Parkway, Suffolk, VA 23435-2697, and info the lead agent and the Director for Joint Force Development, J-7/JE&D.

c. When a Joint Staff directorate submits a proposal to the CJCS that would change source document information reflected in this publication, that directorate will include a proposed change to this publication as an enclosure to its proposal. The Services and other organizations are requested to notify the Director, J-7, Joint Staff, when changes to source documents reflected in this publication are initiated.

5. Distribution of Printed Publications

Local reproduction is authorized and access to unclassified publications is unrestricted. However, access to and reproduction authorization for classified JPs must be IAW DOD Manual 5200.01, Volume 1, *DOD Information Security Program: Overview, Classification, and Declassification,* and DOD Manual 5200.01, Volume 3, *DOD Information Security Program: Protection of Classified Information.*

6. Distribution of Electronic Publications

a. Joint Staff J-7 will not print copies of JPs for distribution. Electronic versions are available on JDEIS at https://jdeis.js.mil (NIPRNET) and https://jdeis.js.smil.mil (SIPRNET) and on the JEL at http://www.dtic.mil/doctrine (NIPRNET).

b. Only approved JPs are releasable outside the CCMDs, Services, and Joint Staff. Release of any classified JP to foreign governments or foreign nationals must be requested through the local embassy (Defense Attaché Office) to DIA, Defense Foreign Liaison/IE-3, 200 MacDill Blvd., Joint Base Anacostia-Bolling, Washington, DC 20340-5100.

c. JEL CD-ROM. Upon request of a joint doctrine development community member, the Joint Staff J-7 will produce and deliver one CD-ROM with current JPs. This JEL CD-ROM will be updated not less than semi-annually and when received can be locally reproduced for use within the CCMDs, Services, and combat support agencies.

GLOSSARY
PART I—ABBREVIATIONS AND ACRONYMS

AA&E	arms, ammunition, and explosives
ABFC	advanced base functional component
ACE	aviation combat element (USMC)
ACSA	acquisition and cross-servicing agreement
ADS	authoritative data source
AE	aeromedical evacuation
AFCAP	Air Force contract augmentation program
AFFOR	Air Force forces
AFSB	Army field support brigade
AIS	automated information system
AIT	automatic identification technology
AJP	allied joint publication
ALT	acquisition, logistics, and technology
AMC	Air Mobility Command
AMD	air mobility division
AMP	analysis of mobility platform
AMP-PAT	analysis of mobility platform suite of port analysis tools
AMS	Asset Management System
AMS-TAC	Automated Manifesting System–Tactical
ANSI	American National Standards Institute
AOC	air operations center
AOR	area of responsibility
APEX	Adaptive Planning and Execution
APF	afloat pre-positioning force
APOD	aerial port of debarkation
APOE	aerial port of embarkation
APS	Army pre-positioned stocks
ASC	Army Sustainment Command
ASCC	Army Service component command
ATACMS	Army Tactical Missile System
AV	asset visibility
BCT	brigade combat team
BICON	double container
BRACE	Base Resource and Capability Estimator
BSB	brigade support battalion
C2	command and control
CADS	containerized ammunition distribution system
CAMPS	Consolidated Air Mobility Planning System
CAP	crisis action planning
CBRN	chemical, biological, radiological, and nuclear
CCDR	combatant commander

CCLI	commerce control list item
CCMD	combatant command
CCP	consolidation and containerization point
CD	customer direct
CDRUSTRANSCOM	Commander, United States Transportation Command
CE	command element
CF	carrier furnished
CHE	container-handling equipment
CJCS	Chairman of the Joint Chiefs of Staff
CJCSI	Chairman of the Joint Chiefs of Staff instruction
CJCSM	Chairman of the Joint Chief of Staff manual
CLB	combat logistics battalion
CLF	combat logistics force
CLR	combat logistics regiment
CMCC	combined movement coordination center
CMOS	Cargo Movement Operations System (USAF)
COA	course of action
COCOM	combatant command (command authority)
COI	community of interest
COMAFFOR	commander, Air Force forces
COMALOC	commercial air line of communications
COMMARFOR	commander, Marine Corps forces
CONOPS	concept of operations
CONPLAN	concept plan
CONUS	continental United States
COP	common operational picture
CORE	contingency response program
CRAF	Civil Reserve Air Fleet
CRE	contingency response element
CRG	contingency response group
CRW	contingency response wing
CSC	International Convention for Safe Containers
CSSB	combat sustainment support battalion
CTP	common tactical picture
CUL	common-user logistics
CULT	common-user land transportation
CWT	customer wait time
DAFL	directive authority for logistics
DCAPES	Deliberate and Crisis Action Planning and Execution Segments
DCMA	Defense Contract Management Agency
DCO	Defense Connect Online
DDED	defense distribution expeditionary depot
DDOC	Deployment and Distribution Operations Center (USTRANSCOM)

DEPORD	deployment order
DFRIF	Defense Freight Railway Interchange Fleet
DHS	Department of Homeland Security
DIRMOBFOR	director of mobility forces
DLA	Defense Logistics Agency
DLM	defense logistics manual
DOD	Department of Defense
DODD	Department of Defense directive
DODI	Department of Defense instruction
DOS	Department of State
DPO	distribution process owner
DSS	Distribution Standard System
DSS/ALOC	direct support system/air line of communications
DST	Defense Logistics Agency support team
DTC	defense transportation coordination
DTR	defense transportation regulation
DTS	Defense Transportation System
EA	executive agent
EDI	electronic data interchange
ELIST	enhanced logistics intratheater support tool
EOD	explosive ordnance disposal
ESC	expeditionary sustainment command
EUSCS	effective United States-controlled ships
EXORD	execute order
F/AD	force/activity designator
FCC	functional combatant commander
FDP	forward distribution point
FEPP	foreign excess personal property
FGS	final governing standard
FMS	foreign military sales
FSS	fast sealift ship
G-4	Army or Marine Corps component logistics staff officer (Army division or higher staff, Marine Corps brigade or higher staff)
GATES	Global Air Transportation Execution System
GCC	geographic combatant commander
GCCS	Global Command and Control System
GCE	ground combat element (MAGTF)
GCM	global container manager
GCSS-J	Global Combat Support System–Joint
GDSS	Global Decision Support System
GEF	Guidance for Employment of the Force
GFM	global freight management

GL	government-leased
GLOC	ground line of communications
GO	government-owned
GPC	government purchase card
GPM	global pallet manager
GSA	General Services Administration
GSORTS	Global Status of Resources and Training System
HAP	humanitarian assistance program
HAZMAT	hazardous materials
HMIRS	Hazardous Material Information Resource System
HN	host nation
HNS	host-nation support
HW	hazardous waste
IAW	in accordance with
IBS	Integrated Booking System
ICIS	integrated consumable item support
ICODES	integrated computerized deployment system
ICP	inventory control point
ID	identifier
IDL	integrated distribution lane
IED	improvised explosive device
IGC	Integrated Data Environment/Global Transportation Network Convergence
IGO	intergovernmental organization
ISDDC	Integrated Mission Support for Surface Deployment and Distribution Command
ISO	International Organization for Standardization
ISU	internal airlift or helicopter slingable container unit
IT	information technology
ITV	in-transit visibility
J-4	logistics directorate of a joint staff
JAOC	joint air operations center
JDDE	joint deployment and distribution enterprise
JDDOC	joint deployment and distribution operations center
JDPO	joint deployment process owner
JET	Joint Operation Planning and Execution System editing tool
JFAST	Joint Flow and Analysis System for Transportation
JFC	joint force commander
JFRG II	joint force requirements generator II
JLEnt	joint logistics enterprise
JLOC	joint logistics operations center
JLOTS	joint logistics over-the-shore
JMC	joint movement center
JMIC	joint modular intermodal container

JMRR	Joint Monthly Readiness Review
JMTCA	joint munitions transportation coordinating activity
JOA	joint operations area
JOPES	Joint Operation Planning and Execution System
JOPP	joint operation planning process
JP	joint publication
JRSOI	joint reception, staging, onward movement, and integration
JSCP	Joint Strategic Capabilities Plan
JTB	Joint Transportation Board
JTF	joint task force
JTF-PO	joint task force–port opening
k	thousand
LCE	logistics combat element (MAGTF)
LCU	landing craft, utility
LIPS	Logistics Information Processing System
LMARS	Logistics Metrics Analysis Reporting System
LMSR	large, medium-speed roll-on/roll-off
LOC	line of communications
LOGCAP	logistics civil augmentation program (Army)
LOTS	logistics over-the-shore
LRP	load and roll pallet
LRT	logistics response time
LSA	logistic support analysis
LTF	logistics task force
MAGTF	Marine air-ground task force
MARAD RRF	Maritime Administration Ready Reserve Force
MCB	movement control battalion
MDDOC	Marine air-ground task force deployment and distribution operations center
MDSS II	Marine air-ground task force Deployment Support System II
MEB	Marine expeditionary brigade
MEDCOM (DS)	medical command (deployment support) (Army)
MEF	Marine expeditionary force
MEU	Marine expeditionary unit
MHE	materials handling equipment
MIDAS	model for intertheater deployment by air and sea
MILALOC	military air line of communications
MILSTRIP	military standard requisitioning and issue procedure
MLG	Marine logistics group
MLI	munitions list item
MLMC	medical logistics management center
MLRS	multiple launch rocket system
MNF	multinational force

MNFC	multinational force commander
MNJLC	multinational joint logistics component
MOG	maximum (aircraft) on ground
MPF	maritime pre-positioning force
MPS	maritime pre-positioning ship
MPSRON	maritime pre-positioning ships squadron
MRO	materiel release order
MSC	Military Sealift Command
NALSS	naval advanced logistic support site
NAVELSG	Navy expeditionary logistic support group
NBG	naval beach group
NCC	Navy component command
NCHB	Navy cargo-handling battalion
NFLS	naval forward logistic site
NGO	nongovernmental organization
NIPRNET	Nonsecure Internet Protocol Router Network
NMCS	not mission capable, supply
NSC	National Security Council
NSE	Navy support element
NUFEA	Navy-unique fleet essential aircraft
OA	operational area
OCONUS	outside the continental United States
OEBGD	Overseas Environmental Baseline Guidance Document
OPCON	operational control
OPDS	offshore petroleum discharge system (Navy)
OPLAN	operation plan
OPORD	operation order
OPROJ	operational project
OSA	operational support airlift
OSD	Office of the Secretary of Defense
PD	priority designator
PIR	priority intelligence requirement
PLS	palletized load system
POD	port of debarkation
POE	port of embarkation
POL	petroleum, oils, and lubricants
PORTSIM	port simulation model
PPTO	petroleum pipeline and terminal operating
PREPO	pre-positioned force, equipment, or supplies
PV	prime vendor
QUADCON	quadruple container
RAD	routine aerial distribution

RAMCC	regional air movement control center
RAS-OT	readiness assessment system–output tool
RDD	required delivery date
RFC	request for capabilities
RFF	request for forces
RO/RO	roll-on/roll-off
ROS	reduced operating status
RPOE	rapid port opening element
RQT	rapid query tool
SAAM	special assignment airlift mission
SCM	Service container manager
SDDC	Surface Deployment and Distribution Command
SDP	strategic distribution platform
SecDef	Secretary of Defense
SIPRNET	SECRET Internet Protocol Router Network
618 AOC (TACC)	618 Air Operations Center (Tanker Airlift Control Center)
SMCA	single manager for conventional ammunition
SMS	single mobility system
SOF	special operations forces
SOFA	status-of-forces agreement
SOLE	special operations liaison element
SPM	single port manager
SPMAGTF	special purpose Marine air-ground task force
SPOD	seaport of debarkation
SPOE	seaport of embarkation
SSA	supply support activity
STON	short ton
SUST BDE	sustainment brigade
TC-AIMS II	Transportation Coordinator's Automated Information for Movement System II
TCC	transportation component command
TCM	theater container manager
TCN	transportation control number
TCSP	theater consolidation and shipping point
TDD	time-definite delivery
TEU	twenty-foot equivalent unit
T-JTB	theater-joint transportation board
TP	transportation priority
TPFDD	time-phased force and deployment data
TPFDL	time-phased force and deployment list
TRAC2ES	United States Transportation Command Regulating and Command and Control Evacuation System
TRICON	triple container
TSC	theater sustainment command (Army)

TSOC	theater special operations command
UMCC	unit movement control center
UMO	unit movement officer
UND	urgency of need designator
USAMC	United States Army Materiel Command
USAMMA	United States Army Medical Materiel Agency
USC	United States Code
USCG	United States Coast Guard
USDA	United States Department of Agriculture
USG	United States Government
USMC	United States Marine Corps
USSOCOM	United States Special Operations Command
USTRANSCOM	United States Transportation Command
VISA	Voluntary Intermodal Sealift Agreement
VPV	virtual prime vendor
WRSA	war reserve stocks for allies
WWX	worldwide express
XMPP	extensible messaging and presence protocol

PART II—TERMS AND DEFINITIONS

assembly area. None. (Approved for removal from JP 1-02.)

automatic identification technology. A suite of technologies enabling the automatic capture of data, thereby enhancing the ability to identify, track, document, and control assets (e.g., materiel), deploying and redeploying forces, equipment, personnel, and sustainment cargo. Also called **AIT.** (Approved for replacement of "automated identification technology" and its definition in JP 1-02.)

basic load. The quantity of supplies required to be on hand within, and which can be moved by, a unit or formation, expressed according to the wartime organization of the unit or formation and maintained at the prescribed levels. (Approved for incorporation into JP 1-02.)

battle damage repair. Essential repair, which may be improvised, carried out rapidly in a battle environment in order to return damaged or disabled equipment to temporary service. Also called **BDR.** (JP 1-02. SOURCE: JP 4-09)

breakbulk cargo. None. (Approved for removal from JP 1-02.)

breakbulk ship. A ship with conventional holds for stowage of breakbulk cargo and a limited number of containers, below or above deck, and equipped with cargo-handling gear. (Approved for incorporation into JP 1-02.)

classes of supply. The ten categories into which supplies are grouped in order to facilitate supply management and planning. I. Rations and gratuitous issue of health, morale, and welfare items. II. Clothing, individual equipment, tentage, tool sets, and administrative and housekeeping supplies and equipment. III. Petroleum, oils, and lubricants. IV. Construction materials. V. Ammunition. VI. Personal demand items. VII. Major end items, including tanks, helicopters, and radios. VIII. Medical. IX. Repair parts and components for equipment maintenance. X. Nonstandard items to support nonmilitary programs such as agriculture and economic development. (JP 1-02. SOURCE: JP 4-09)

commodity manager. None. (Approved for removal from JP 1-02.)

common-use container. Any Department of Defense-owned, -leased, or -controlled 20- or 40-foot International Organization for Standardization container managed by United States Transportation Command as an element of the Department of Defense common-use container system. (Approved for incorporation into JP 1-02.)

common-user logistics. Materiel or service support shared with or provided by two or more Services, Department of Defense agencies, or multinational partners to another Service, Department of Defense agency, non-Department of Defense agency, and/or multinational partner in an operation. Also called **CUL.** (Approved for incorporation into JP 1-02.)

component-owned container. A 20- or 40-foot International Organization for Standardization container procured and owned by a single Department of Defense component. (Approved for incorporation into JP 1-02.)

container control officer. A designated official (E6 or above or civilian equivalent) within a command, installation, or activity who is responsible for control, reporting, use, and maintenance of all Department of Defense-owned and controlled intermodal containers and equipment from the time received until dispatched. Also called **CCO.** (Approved for incorporation into JP 1-02.)

container-handling equipment. Items of materials-handling equipment required to specifically receive, maneuver, and dispatch International Organization for Standardization containers. Also called **CHE.** (JP 1-02. SOURCE: JP 4-09)

container management. Planning, organizing, directing, and executing functions and responsibilities required to provide effective use of Department of Defense and Military Department owned, leased, or controlled International Organization for Standardization containers. (Approved for inclusion in JP 1-02.)

containership. A ship, usually non-self-sustaining, specially constructed and equipped to carry only containers without associated equipment, in all available cargo spaces, either below or above deck. (Approved for incorporation into JP 1-02.)

customer direct. A materiel acquisition and distribution method that requires vendor delivery directly to the customer. Also called **CD.** (JP 1-02. SOURCE: JP 4-09)

customer wait time. The total elapsed time between issuance of a customer order and satisfaction of that order. Also called **CWT.** (JP 1-02. SOURCE: JP 4-09)

Department of Defense container system. All Department of Defense owned, leased, and controlled 20- or 40-foot intermodal International Organization for Standardization containers and flatracks, supporting equipment such as generator sets and chassis, container handling equipment, information systems, the 463L system, and other infrastructure that supports Department of Defense transportation and logistic operations, including commercially provided transportation services. (Approved for incorporation into JP 1-02.)

distribution manager. The executive agent for managing distribution within the combatant commander's area of responsibility. (JP 1-02. SOURCE: JP 4-09)

distribution pipeline. Continuum or channel through which the Department of Defense conducts distribution operations, representing the end-to-end flow of resources from supplier to consumer and, in some cases, back to the supplier in retrograde activities. (Approved for incorporation into JP 1-02.)

distribution plan. A reporting system comprising reports, updates, and information systems feeds that articulate the requirements of the theater distribution system to the strategic and operational resources assigned responsibility for support to the theater. (Approved for incorporation into JP 1-02.)

distribution point. A point at which supplies and/or ammunition, obtained from supporting supply points by a division or other unit, are broken down for distribution to subordinate units. (Approved for incorporation into JP 1-02.)

distribution system. That complex of facilities, installations, methods, and procedures designed to receive, store, maintain, distribute, and control the flow of military materiel between the point of receipt into the military system and the point of issue to using activities and units. (JP 1-02. SOURCE: JP 4-09)

double container. A 9.8125 feet by 8 feet by 8 feet (2991 millimeters by 2438 millimeters by 2438 millimeters) reusable International Standards Organization compliant double container, with double doors at both ends, used for the storage, transportation, and distribution of dry cargo. Also called **BICON.** (Approved for inclusion in JP 1-02.)

end-to-end. A term that describes joint distribution operations boundaries, which begin at the point of origin and terminate at the geographic combatant commander's designated point of need within a desired operational area, including the return of forces and materiel. (Approved for incorporation into JP 1-02.)

evacuation. 1. Removal of a patient by any of a variety of transport means from a theater of military operation, or between health services capabilities, for the purpose of preventing further illness or injury, providing additional care, or providing disposition of patients from the military health care system. (JP 4-02) 2. The clearance of personnel, animals, or materiel from a given locality. (JP 3-68) 3. The controlled process of collecting, classifying, and shipping unserviceable or abandoned materiel, United States or foreign, to appropriate reclamation, maintenance, technical intelligence, or disposal facilities. (JP 4-09) 4. The ordered or authorized departure of noncombatants from a specific area by Department of State, Department of Defense, or appropriate military commander. This refers to the movement from one area to another in the same or different countries. The evacuation is caused by unusual or emergency circumstances and applies equally to command or non-command sponsored family members. (JP 3-68) (Approved for incorporation into JP 1-02.)

flatrack. Portable, open-topped, open-sided units that fit into existing below-deck container cell guides and provide a capability for container ships to carry oversized cargo and wheeled and tracked vehicles. (JP 1-02. SOURCE: JP 4-09)

flatted cargo. None. (Approved for removal from JP 1-02.)

force/activity designator. Number used in conjunction with urgency of need designators to establish a matrix of priorities used for supply requisitions. Also called **F/AD.** (Approved for incorporation into JP 1-02.)

463L system. A material handling system that consists of military and civilian aircraft cargo restraint rail systems, aircraft pallets, nets, tie down, coupling devices, facilities, handling equipment, procedures, and other components designed to efficiently accomplish the air logistics and aerial delivery mission. (Approved for incorporation into JP 1-02.)

general cargo. Cargo that is suitable for loading in general, nonspecialized stowage areas or standard shipping containers; e.g., boxes, barrels, bales, crates, packages, bundles, and pallets. (Approved for incorporation into JP 1-02.)

global distribution. The process that coordinates and synchronizes fulfillment of joint force requirements from point of origin to point of employment. (JP 1-02. SOURCE: JP 4-09)

global distribution of materiel. The process of providing materiel from the source of supply to its point of consumption or use on a worldwide basis. (JP 1-02. SOURCE: JP 4-09)

hub. An organization that sorts and distributes inbound cargo from wholesale supply sources (airlifted, sealifted, and ground transportable) and/or from within the theater. (JP 1-02. SOURCE: JP 4-09)

hub and spoke distribution. A physical distribution system, in which a major port serves as a central point from which cargo is moved to and from several radiating points to increase transportation efficiencies and in-transit visibility. (Approved for incorporation into JP 1-02.)

Integrated Data Environment/Global Transportation Network Convergence. The in-transit visibility system of record providing expanded common integrated data and application services enabling a common logistics picture, distribution visibility, and materiel asset/in-transit visibility for distribution solutions. Also called **IGC.** (Approved for inclusion in JP 1-02.)

integrated materiel management. The exercise of total Department of Defense-level management responsibility for a federal supply group or class, commodity, or item for a single agency, which normally includes computation of requirements, funding, budgeting, storing, issuing, cataloging, standardizing, and procuring functions. Also called **IMM.** (Approved for inclusion in JP 1-02.)

intermodal. Type of international freight system that permits transshipping among sea, highway, rail, and air modes of transportation through use of American National Standards Institute and International Organization for Standardization containers, line-haul assets, and handling equipment. (JP 1-02. SOURCE: JP 4-09)

International Convention for Safe Containers. A convention held in Geneva, Switzerland, on 2 Dec 1972, which resulted in setting standard safety requirements for containers moving in international transport. These requirements were ratified by the United States on 3 January 1978. Also called **CSC.** (JP 1-02. SOURCE: JP 4-09)

International Organization for Standardization. None. (Approved for removal from JP 1-02.)

inventory control. That phase of military logistics that includes managing, cataloging, requirements determinations, procurement, distribution, overhaul, and disposal of materiel. Also called **inventory management; materiel control; materiel management; supply management.** (JP 1-02. SOURCE: JP 4-09)

inventory control point. An organizational unit or activity within a Department of Defense supply system that is assigned the primary responsibility for the materiel inventory management of a group of items either for a particular Service or for the Defense Department as a whole. Also called **ICP.** (Approved for incorporation into JP 1-02.)

inventory management. None. (Approved for removal from JP 1-02.)

inventory managers. None. (Approved for removal from JP 1-02.)

item manager. An individual within the organization of an inventory control point or other such organization assigned management responsibility for one or more specific items of materiel. (JP 1-02. SOURCE: JP 4-09)

joint deployment and distribution operations center. A combatant command movement control organization designed to synchronize and optimize national and theater multimodal resources for deployment, distribution, and sustainment. Also called **JDDOC.** (JP 1-02. SOURCE: JP 4-09)

joint distribution. The operational process of synchronizing all elements of the joint logistic system using the Joint Deployment and Distribution Enterprise for end-to-end movement of forces and materiel from point of origin to the designated point of need. (JP 1-02. SOURCE: JP 4-09)

materiel control. None. (Approved for removal from JP 1-02.)

materiel inventory objective. The quantity of an item required to be on hand and on order on M-day in order to equip, provide a materiel pipeline, and sustain the approved United States force structure and those Allied forces designated for United States materiel support, through the period prescribed for war materiel planning purposes. (Approved for incorporation into JP 1-02.)

materiel management. None. (Approved for removal from JP 1-02.)

materiel planning. A subset of logistic planning consisting of the four-step process of: a. **requirements definition.** Requirements for significant items are calculated at item-level detail to support sustainability planning and analysis. b. **apportionment.** Items are apportioned to the combatant commanders based on a global scenario to avoid sourcing of items to multiple theaters. c. **sourcing.** Sourcing is the matching of available capabilities on a given date against item requirements to support sustainability analysis and the identification of locations to support transportation planning. d.

documentation. Sourced item requirements are translated into movement requirements and documented in the Joint Operation Planning and Execution System database for transportation feasibility analysis. (Approved for incorporation into JP 1-02.)

materiel release order. An order issued by an accountable supply system manager directing a non-accountable activity within the same supply distribution complex to release and ship materiel. Also called **MRO.** (Approved for incorporation into JP 1-02.)

materiel requirements. Those quantities of items of equipment and supplies necessary to equip, provide a materiel pipeline, and sustain a Service, formation, organization, or unit in the fulfillment of its purposes or tasks during a specified period. (JP 1-02. SOURCE: JP 4-09)

means of transport. None. (Approved for removal from JP 1-02.)

military specification container. A container that meets specific written standards. Also called **MILSPEC container.** (JP 1-02. SOURCE: JP 4-09)

MILSPEC container. None. (Approved for removal from JP 1-02.)

mode of transport. One of, or a combination of, the following modes used for a movement: a. inland surface transportation (rail, road, and inland waterway); b. sea transport (coastal and ocean); c. air transportation; and d. pipelines. (Approved for incorporation into JP 1-02.)

movement control team. An Army team used to decentralize the execution of movement responsibilities on an area basis or at key transportation nodes. Also called **MCT.** (JP 1-02. SOURCE: JP 4-09)

movement data. Those essential elements of information to schedule lift, obtain transportation assets, manage movement of forces, and report in-transit visibility of movements and associated forces (people, equipment, and supplies). (JP 1-02. SOURCE: JP 4-09)

movement requirement. A stated movement mode and time-phased need for the transport of units, personnel, and/or materiel from a specified origin to a specified destination. (JP 1-02. SOURCE: JP 4-09)

movement schedule. A timetable developed to monitor or track the movement of a separate entity, whether it is a force requirement, cargo or personnel increment, or lift asset, that reflects the assignment of specific lift resources, shows a flow and workload at each location, and supports plan implementation. (Approved for incorporation into JP 1-02.)

movement table. A table giving detailed instructions or data for a move. (Approved for incorporation into JP 1-02.)

national stock number. The 13-digit number that identifies a stock item consisting of the 4-digit federal supply classification code plus the 9-digit national item identification number and arranged as follows: 9999-00-999-9999. Also called **NSN.** (Approved for incorporation into JP 1-02.)

net explosive weight. The actual weight in pounds of explosive mixtures or compounds, including the trinitrotoluene equivalent of energetic material, that is used in determination of explosive limits and explosive quantity data arcs. Also called **NEW.** (JP 1-02. SOURCE: JP 4-09)

not mission capable, maintenance. None. (Approved for removal from JP 1-02.)

not mission capable, supply. Material condition indicating that systems and equipment are not capable of performing any of their assigned missions because of maintenance work stoppage due to a supply shortage. Also called **NMCS.** (Approved for incorporation into JP 1-02 with JP 4-09 as the source JP.)

on hand. The quantity of an item that is physically available in a storage location and contained in the accountable property book records of an issuing activity. (JP 1-02. SOURCE: JP 4-09)

point of employment. In distribution operations, a physical location designated by the commander at the tactical level where force employment, emplacement, or commodity consumption occurs. (JP 1-02. SOURCE: JP 4-09)

point of need. In distribution operations, a physical location within a desired operational area designated by the geographic combatant commander or subordinate commander as a receiving point for forces or materiel, for subsequent use or consumption. (JP 1-02. SOURCE: JP 4-09)

point of origin. In distribution operations, the beginning point of a deployment, redeployment, or movement where forces or materiel are located. (JP 1-02. SOURCE: JP 4-09)

prime vendor. A contracting process that provides commercial products to regionally grouped military and federal customers from commercial distributors using electronic commerce. Also called **PV.** (Approved for incorporation into JP 1-02.)

quadruple container. A 57.5 inches by 96 inches by 96 inches container box with a metal frame, pallet base, and International Organization for Standardization corner fittings; four of these boxes can be lashed together to form a 20-foot American National Standards Institute or International Organization for Standardization intermodal container. Also called **QUADCON.** (Approved for incorporation into JP 1-02.)

railhead. A point on a railway where loads are transferred between trains and other means of transport. (JP 1-02. SOURCE: JP 4-09)

reorder point. None. (Approved for removal from JP 1-02.)

repairable item. An item that can be reconditioned or economically repaired for reuse when it becomes unserviceable. (JP 1-02. SOURCE: JP 4-09)

repair cycle. The stages through which a repairable item passes from the time of its removal or replacement until it is reinstalled or placed in stock in a serviceable condition. (JP 1-02. SOURCE: JP 4-09)

requisitioning objective. None. (Approved for removal from JP 1-02.)

residual forces. Undeployed United States forces that have an immediate combat potential for continued military operations, and that have been deliberately withheld from utilization. (Approved for incorporation into JP 1-02.)

resupply. The act of replenishing stocks in order to maintain required levels of supply. (JP 1-02. SOURCE: JP 4-09)

retrograde. The process for the movement of non-unit equipment and materiel from a forward location to a reset (replenishment, repair, or recapitalization) program or to another directed area of operations to replenish unit stocks, or to satisfy stock requirements. (JP 1-02. SOURCE: JP 4-09)

Service-unique container. Any 20- or 40-foot International Organization for Standardization container procured or leased by a Service to meet Service-unique requirements. (Approved for incorporation into JP 1-02.)

shelter. An International Organization for Standardization container outfitted with live- or work-in capability. (JP 1-02. SOURCE: JP 4-09)

spoke. The portion of the hub and spoke distribution system that refers to transportation mode operators responsible for scheduled delivery to a customer of the "hub." (JP 1-02. SOURCE: JP 4-09)

stuffing. Packing of cargo into a container. (JP 1-02. SOURCE: JP 4-09)

supply chain. The linked activities associated with providing materiel from a raw materiel stage to an end user as a finished product. (JP 1-02. SOURCE: JP 4-09)

supply chain management. A cross-functional approach to procuring, producing, and delivering products and services to customers. (Approved for incorporation into JP 1-02.)

supply management. None. (Approved for removal from JP 1-02.)

supply support activity. Activities assigned a Department of Defense activity address code and that have a supply support mission. Also called **SSA.** (Approved for incorporation into JP 1-02.)

Surface Deployment and Distribution Command. None. (Approved for removal from JP 1-02.)

table of allowance. An equipment allowance document that prescribes basic allowances of organizational equipment, and provides the control to develop, revise, or change equipment authorization inventory data. Also called **TOA.** (JP 1-02. SOURCE: JP 4-09)

tare weight. None. (Approved for removal from JP 1-02.)

theater distribution. The flow of personnel, equipment, and materiel within theater to meet the geographic combatant commander's missions. (JP 1-02. SOURCE: JP 4-09)

time-definite delivery. The consistent delivery of requested logistics support at a time and destination specified by the receiving activity. Also called **TDD.** (JP 1-02. SOURCE: JP 4-09)

total materiel requirement. None. (Approved for removal from JP 1-02.)

traffic management. The direction, control, and supervision of all functions incident to the procurement and use of freight and passenger transportation services. (JP 1-02. SOURCE: JP 4-09)

transportation feasibility. A determination that the capability exists to move forces, equipment, and supplies from the point of origin to the final destination within the time required. (JP 1-02. SOURCE: JP 4-09)

transportation priorities. Indicators assigned to eligible traffic that establish its movement precedence. (Approved for incorporation into JP 1-02.)

unitized load. None. (Approved for removal from JP 1-02.)

unstuffing. The removal of cargo from a container. Also called **stripping.** (JP 1-02. SOURCE: JP 4-09)

Intentionally Blank

JOINT DOCTRINE PUBLICATIONS HIERARCHY

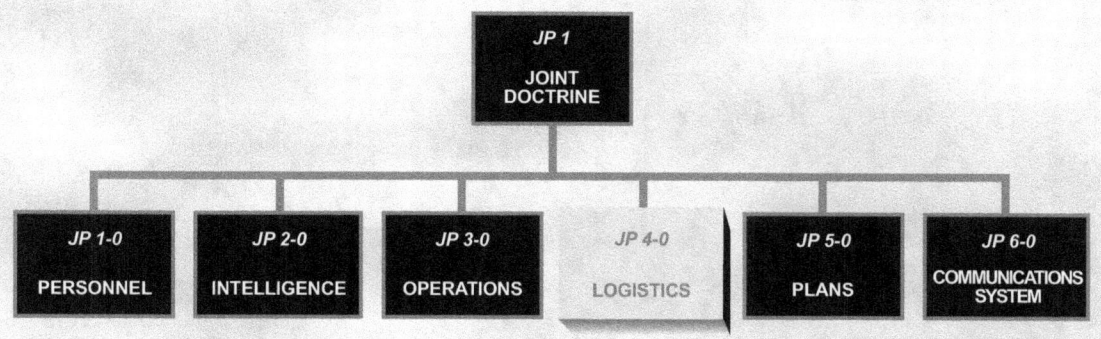

JP 1
JOINT DOCTRINE

JP 1-0	JP 2-0	JP 3-0	JP 4-0	JP 5-0	JP 6-0
PERSONNEL	INTELLIGENCE	OPERATIONS	LOGISTICS	PLANS	COMMUNICATIONS SYSTEM

All joint publications are organized into a comprehensive hierarchy as shown in the chart above. **Joint Publication (JP) 4-09** is in the **Logistics** series of joint doctrine publications. The diagram below illustrates an overview of the development process:

STEP #4 - Maintenance

- JP published and continuously assessed by users
- Formal assessment begins 24 27 months following publication
- Revision begins 3.5 years after publication
- Each JP revision is completed no later than 5 years after signature

STEP #1 - Initiation

- Joint doctrine development community (JDDC) submission to fill extant operational void
- Joint Staff (JS) J 7 conducts front end analysis
- Joint Doctrine Planning Conference validation
- Program directive (PD) development and staffing/joint working group
- PD includes scope, references, outline, milestones, and draft authorship
- JS J 7 approves and releases PD to lead agent (LA) (Service, combatant command, JS directorate)

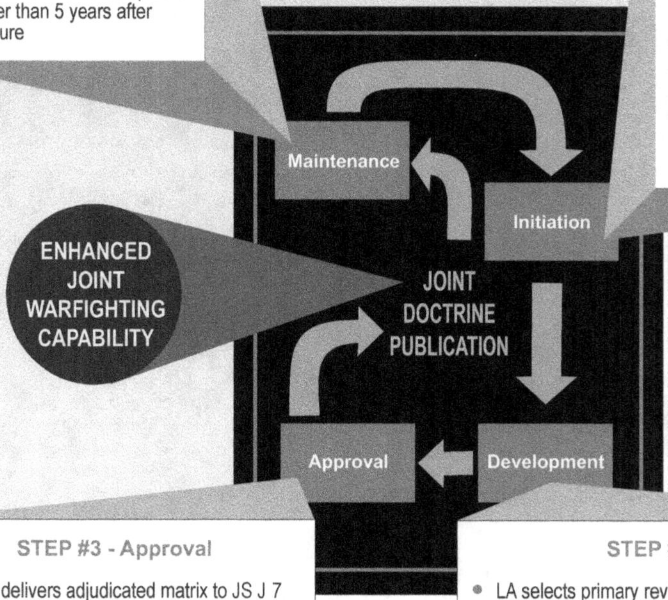

ENHANCED JOINT WARFIGHTING CAPABILITY

Maintenance

Initiation

JOINT DOCTRINE PUBLICATION

Approval

Development

STEP #3 - Approval

- JSDS delivers adjudicated matrix to JS J 7
- JS J 7 prepares publication for signature
- JSDS prepares JS staffing package
- JSDS staffs the publication via JSAP for signature

STEP #2 - Development

- LA selects primary review authority (PRA) to develop the first draft (FD)
- PRA develops FD for staffing with JDDC
- FD comment matrix adjudication
- JS J 7 produces the final coordination (FC) draft, staffs to JDDC and JS via Joint Staff Action Processing (JSAP) system
- Joint Staff doctrine sponsor (JSDS) adjudicates FC comment matrix
- FC joint working group